WITHDRAWN

MEDIEVALIA ET HUMANISTICA

MEDIEVALIA ET HUMANISTICA

Editor
Paul Maurice Clogan
University of North Texas

BOOK REVIEW EDITORS

Robert E. Boenig
Texas A&M University

Eric Rasmussen
University of Nevada, Reno

Walther Ludwig
Universität Hamburg

Miri Rubin
University of London

EDITORIAL BOARD

David Bevington
University of Chicago

Stephen Jaeger
University of Illinois

Marvin L. Colker
University of Virginia

Claudio Leonardi
*Società Internazionale
per lo Studio
del Medioevo Latino*

Michael Curschmann
Princeton University

Peter Dembowski
University of Chicago

Jill Mann
University of Notre Dame

Peter Dronke
University of Cambridge

Eugene Vance
University of Washington

Barbara Hanawalt
Ohio State University

Charles Witke
University of Michigan, Ann Arbor

Jan M. Ziolkowski
Harvard University

MEDIEVALIA ET HUMANISTICA

STUDIES IN MEDIEVAL AND
RENAISSANCE CULTURE
NEW SERIES: NUMBER 31

Reengaging History

EDITED BY
PAUL MAURICE CLOGAN

ROWMAN & LITTLEFIELD PUBLISHERS, INC.
Lanham • Boulder • New York • Toronto • Oxford

ROWMAN & LITTLEFIELD PUBLISHERS, INC.

Published in the United States of America
by Rowman & Littlefield Publishers, Inc.
A wholly owned subsidiary of The Rowman & Littlefield Publishing Group, Inc.
4501 Forbes Boulevard, Suite 200, Lanham, Maryland 20706
www.rowmanlittlefield.com

PO Box 317
Oxford
OX2 9RU, UK

Copyright © 2005 by Rowman & Littlefield Publishers, Inc.

All rights reserved. No part of this publication may be reproduced, stored in a retrieval system, or transmitted in any form or by any means, electronic, mechanical, photocopying, recording, or otherwise, without the prior permission of the publisher.

British Library Cataloguing in Publication Information Available

The Library of Congress has catalogued this serial publication as follows:

Medievalia et humanistica, fasc. 1–jan. 1943–;
New ser. No 1– 1970–
Totowa, N.J. [etc.] Rowman & Littlefield [etc.]
no. 31 cm.
Annual, 1943–
"Studies in medieval and renaissance culture."
Vols. for 1970–1972 issued by the Medieval and neo-Latin Society;
1973– by the Medieval and Renaissance Society.
Key title: Medievalia et humanistica, ISSN 0076-6127.

ISBN 0-7425-4949-6 (alk. paper)
Library of Congress (8101)

Printed in the United States of America

∞ ™ The paper used in this publication meets the minimum requirements of American National Standard for Information Sciences—Permanence of Paper for Printed Library Materials, ANSI/NISO Z39.48-1992.

Contents

Editorial Note	ix
Articles for Future Volumes	xi
Preface	xiii
Andreas Capellanus and Reception Theory: The Third Dialogue Don A. Monson, *College of William and Mary*	1
Virgilian Hauntings in Boccaccio's *De casibus virorum illustrium* Karen Elizabeth Gross, *Lewis and Clark College*	15
Reinventing the Ideal Sovereign in Christine de Pizan's *Livre des fais et bonnes meurs du sage roy Charles V* Daisy Delogu, *University of Chicago*	41
Cupid's Wheel: Love and Fortune in *The Knight's Tale* Robert Stretter, *Yeshiva College*	59
Clément Marot, the *Roman de la Rose*, and Poetic Identity Jennifer Monahan, *Berkeley, California*	83
Atrocities and the Executions of Peasant Rebel Leaders in Late Medieval and Early Modern Europe Paul Freedman, *Yale University*	101

REVIEW ARTICLE

Two New Dictionaries of Old French Suzanne Kocher, *University of Louisiana at Lafayette*	115

REVIEW NOTICES

John Aberth, *A Knight at the Movies: Medieval History on Film* (Robert Bartlett)	119
Peter Hunter Blair, *An Introduction to Anglo-Saxon England* (Robert Boenig)	122
Paul Brand, *Kings, Barons and Justices: The Making and Enforcement of Legislation in Thirteenth-Century England* (David Carpenter)	123
Julia Boffey and A. S. G. Edwards, editors, *Medieval Manuscripts in the Norlin Library and the Department of Fine Arts at the University of Colorado at Boulder: A Summary Catalogue* (Marvin L. Colker)	128

Joanna Cannon and André Vauchez, *Margherita of Cortona and the Lorenzetti: Sienese Art and the Cult of a Holy Woman in Medieval Tuscany* 132
   (Daniel Bornstein)

Jane Chance, editor, *Tolkien and the Invention of Myth: A Reader* 137
   (Robert Barrett)

Philomena Connolly, *Medieval Record Sources* 140
   (Virginia Davis)

Philomena Connolly, *Statute Rolls of the Irish Parliament: Richard III–Henry VIII* 141
   (Virginia Davis)

Olivia Remie Constable, *Housing the Stranger in the Mediterranean World: Lodging, Trade, and Travel in Late Antiquity and the Middle Age* 143
   (Charles Witke)

Carolyn Dinshaw and David Wallace, editors, *The Cambridge Companion to Medieval Women's Writing* 145
   (Julia Boffey)

Albert Derolez, *The Palaeography of Gothic Manuscript Books from the Twelfth to the Early Sixteenth Century* 147
   (Marvin L. Colker)

Eamon Duffy, *The Voices of Morebath: Reformation and Rebellion in an English Village* 149
   (Daniel Bornstein)

Karl A. E. Enenkel and Arnoud S. Q. Visser, editors, *Mundus Emblematicus: Studies in Neo-Latin Emblem Books* 151
   (Walther Ludwig)

Mary C. Erler and Maryanne Kowaleski, editors, *Gendering the Master Narrative: Women and Power in the Middle Ages* 154
   (Z. J. Kosztolnyik)

Jussi Hanska, *Strategies of Sanity and Survival: Religious Responses to Natural Disasters in the Middle Ages* 155
   (Daniel Bornstein)

Yitzhak Hen and Rob Meens, editors, *The Bobbio Missal: Liturgy and Religious Culture in Merovingian Gaul* 157
   (Charles Witke)

Isaac Ibn Sahula, *Meshal Haqadmoni: Fables of the Distant Past* 160
   (Marvin L. Colker)

Walter E. Kaegi, *Heraclius: Emperor of Byzantium* 164
   (Stephen H. Rapp, Jr.)

Shannon McSheffrey and Norman Tanner, editors, *Lollards of Coventry, 1486–1522* 165
   (Ian Forrest)

Miri Rubin, *Gentile Tales: The Narrative Assault on Late Medieval Jews*   167
   (Anthony Bale)

Emily Steiner, *Documentary Culture and the Making of Middle English Literature*   168
   (Julia Boffey)

Benjamin C. Withers and Jonathan Wilcox, editors, *Naked Before God: Uncovering the Body in Anglo-Saxon England*   170
   (Robert Boenig)

Books Received   173

Editorial Note

Since 1970, this new series has sought to promote significant scholarship, criticism, and reviews within the fields of medieval and Renaissance studies. It has published articles drawn from a variety of disciplines, and it has given attention to new directions in humanistic scholarship and to significant topics of general interest. This series has been particularly concerned with the exchange between specializations, and scholars of diverse approaches have complemented each other's efforts on questions of common interest.

Medievalia et Humanistica is sponsored by the Modern Language Association of America. Publication in the series is open to contributions from all sources, and the editorial board welcomes scholarly, critical, or interdisciplinary articles of significant interest on relevant material. Contributors are urged to communicate in a clear and concise style the larger implications and the material of their research, with documentation held to a minimum. Text, maps, illustrations, diagrams, and musical examples are published when they are essential to the argument of the article. In preparing and submitting manuscripts for consideration, potential contributors are advised to follow carefully the instructions given on page xi. Articles in English may be submitted to any of the editors. Books for review and inquiries concerning *Fasciculi* I–XVII in the original series should be addressed to the Editor, *Medievalia et Humanistica*, P.O. Box 28428, Austin, Texas 78755–8428. Inquiries concerning subscriptions should be addressed to the publisher:

> Rowman & Littlefield Publishers, Inc.
> 4501 Forbes Boulevard, Suite 200
> Lanham, Maryland 20706

Articles for Future Volumes

Articles may be submitted to any of the editors, but it would be advisable to submit them to the nearest or most appropriate editor for consideration. A prospective author is encouraged to contact his or her editor at the earliest opportunity to receive any necessary advice. The length of the article depends on the material, but brief articles or notes normally are not considered. The entire manuscript should be typed, double-spaced, on standard 8½-by-11 bond paper, with ample margins; documentation should be held to a minimum. The submission must also include a final copy of the manuscript in Microsoft Word, WordPerfect, or RTF format, on an IBM-PC compatible, 3½-inch formatted diskette. Endnotes, prepared according to *The Chicago Manual of Style*, fifteenth edition (University of Chicago Press), should be double-spaced and numbered consecutively, and they should appear at the end of the article. All quotations and references should be in finished form. Submissions should be in triplicate and accompanied by a stamped, self-addressed envelope. Authors' names should not appear on manuscripts, but a cover letter with the author's name and address should be included with each manuscript.

The addresses of the American editors can be determined by their academic affiliations. The addresses of the editors outside the United States and their respective area of interest are as follows:

Professor Peter Dronke, Faculty of Modern and Medieval Languages, University of Cambridge, Sidgwick Avenue, Cambridge CB3 9DA, U.K. (Medieval Latin Poetry and Thought)

Professor Claudio Leonardi, Certosa del Galluzzo, I-50124, Florence, Italy (Medieval Philosophy)

Professor Walther Ludwig, Institut fur Griechische und Lateinische Philologie, Universität Hamburg, Von-Melle-Park 6, 20146 Hamburg, Germany (Neo-Latin Language and Literature)

Professor Miri Rubin, Department of History, Queen Mary, University of London, Mile End Road, London E1 4NS, U.K. (History, Church History)

Preface

Volume thirty-one in the new series contains six original and refereed articles that represent a reengagement with history. They focus on a variety of topics, ranging from reception theory in Andreas Capellanus and the ideal sovereign in Christine de Pizan to peasant rebel leaders in late-medieval and early-modern Europe. Don Monson's article makes good usage of Jauss's reception theory and analyzes the third Dialogue of Book I, Chapter 6 of *De Amore* in a thorough and intelligent way. Important aspects of the relationship between "scientific" Latin treaties and Provençal courtly poetry are neatly demonstrated.

Karen Gross examines structural and thematic resemblances between the *Aeneid* and *De casibus*, arguing that Anchises' "pageant of future Roman worthies" (*Aen*. VI) is connected to the frame structure of *De casibus*. The author is interested in "global similarities, not local verbal echoes," and believes that the "structure resonances" have implications for "how Boccaccio understood the interaction between history and poetry, between the living and the dead." Especially thought provoking and original are the discussion of the motif of father/son piety and commemoration and the contrast of Virgil's *fortuna* in Roman history and Boccaccio's in world history.

Daisy Delogu's article on Christine de Pizan is a timely one, and also represents reengagement with history that is very healthy for students of medieval literature. The essay is forthright and it provides interesting perspective on a work of Christine's that is less commonly read. It serves as a breather from the bright (yet very appropriate) feminist nimbus that hangs over Christine's image in time.

Robert Stretter discusses the connection between love and fortune, as manifested through "amatory fatalism." Both love and fortune reduce human beings to an essentially passive role; both produce a characteristic response in the form of complaint. Although these ideas are in their separate forms familiar to Chaucer scholars, they have not been brought together in quite this way before, and some interesting perceptions result. The essay is clearly structured, with appropriate scholarly presentation.

Jennifer Monahan's article on poetic identity is a clear, intelligent contribution to specific textual history. The critical stances on Clément Marot, and, in particular, the attribution question of the edition of the *Roman de la Rose*, are undeniably useful to those who specifically discuss these questions. The article appeals to more general medieval and Renaissance scholars.

Paul Freedman's well-researched article, "Atrocities and Executions of

Peasant Rebel Leaders in Late-Medieval and Early-Modern Europe," shows excellent command of sources. The publication, with permissions, of three illustrations, including that of the martyrdom of Saint Christopher from the Museum of Catalan Art in Barcelona, are of particular interest to scholars in general.

In addition to these six articles, one review article and seventeen review notices examine recent publications in medieval and early modern studies. I am grateful to the editorial board for their advice and to the staff of Rowman and Littlefield for their assistance in the production of the annual volume.

P. M. C.

Andreas Capellanus and Reception Theory: The Third Dialogue

DON A. MONSON

The development of reception theory in Germany over the last three decades has given students of medieval literature important new tools for approaching works whose temporal remoteness and cultural "otherness" make them difficult of access. The fruitfulness of this method for medieval studies was illustrated, even as it was being formulated, by one of its major theoreticians, Hans Robert Jauss, who was also a practicing medievalist.[1] Jauss's theories were applied by Alfred Karnein to one of the most intractable and problematic texts of the medieval corpus, Andreas Capellanus's *De amore*.[2] In his De Amore *in volkssprachlicher Literatur*, Karnein traced the reception of Andreas's treatise from the thirteenth to the early sixteenth century, examining the manuscript tradition of the work, its vernacular translations, and allusions to it found in Latin and vernacular authors. In the process he attempted to show a major "change in paradigm" in the *De amore*'s reception, taking place toward the end of the thirteenth century, thus transforming subsequent understanding of the work, including our own, in a way that separates it radically from the meaning that it had for Andreas's own contemporaries.[3]

Karnein's analysis concentrates primarily on the reception of the *De amore* by later writers. There is another way, however, in which Jauss's theories can be brought to bear on this text: through the examination of Andreas's reception in the *De amore* of the works and genres that preceded his own. This is the subject addressed in the present study. But first a few words about Jauss's approach to reception theory.

Jauss's influential article, "Literary History as a Challenge to Literary Theory," proposes an ambitious program intended to mediate between aesthetics and history, between formalist and Marxist criticism, between the diachronic and synchronic study of literature, and between literary history and literary theory.[4] This program is articulated in seven theses, of which the most salient features are as follows.

According to Jauss, "a renewal of literary history demands the removal of the prejudices of historical objectivism and the grounding of the traditional aesthetics of production and representation in an aesthetics of re-

Medievalia et Humanistica, New Series, Number 31 (Paul Maurice Clogan, ed.), Rowman & Littlefield Publishers, Inc., 2005.

ception and influence" (20). To avoid the "pitfalls of psychology" the reception and influence of a work must be described within what Jauss, borrowing a concept from Husserl, calls its "horizon of expectation," that is, "the objectifiable system of expectations that arises for each work in the historical moment of its appearance," and which includes three main factors: "a pre-understanding of the genre," "the form and themes of already familiar works," and "the opposition between poetic and practical language" (22). The reconstruction of the horizon of expectation of a work "allows one to determine its artistic character by the kind and degree of its influence on a presupposed audience"; this is measured in terms of "aesthetic distance," that is, "the disparity between the given horizon of expectation and the appearance of the new work, whose reception can give rise to a 'change of horizons'" (25).

The reconstruction of the horizon of expectation also allows us, in the terms of the hermeneutics of Gadamer, to ask the questions to which the work gave answers, thus overcoming the dichotomy between past and present without recourse to an atemporal model such as classicism or modernity (28). To go from the history of the reception of a work to a new conception of literary history requires the insertion of the work into its "literary series"; thus the passive reception of readers and critics gives way to the active reception of authors, and each work answers the aesthetic and moral questions left open by previous works, while presenting new problems to be solved by subsequent works (32). To overcome the distortions of the historical method, one can, as in linguistics, distinguish between the diachronic and the synchronic study of literature, effecting synchronic cross-sections at various points in the historical continuum, "to discover an overarching system of relationships in the literature of a historical moment" (36). Finally, the "special history" of literary evolution must be placed in relation to "general history," not only as a reflection of social practice but also as a formative influence upon it (39).

Coming back to Andreas's *De amore*, we can see that it provides an excellent object for the application of the methods of Jauss. A protoscholastic treatise in Latin employing the standard philosophic discourse used in the twelfth century to describe the world,[5] it also makes significant use of poetic material drawn not only from the didactico-erotic poetry of Ovid, which provides its general structure, but also from medieval vernacular love literature, which furnishes much of its substance.[6] It thus embodies a manifest transgression of genre[7] resulting in a corresponding creation of aesthetic distance and change in the horizon of expectation.[8]

The third dialogue of book 1, chapter 6, provides a particularly interesting example of this phenomenon. It is one of eight dialogues, constituting more than one-half of the treatise, that serve to illustrate the acquiring of love through eloquence. We may wonder why this extraordinarily extended development of a subject that Ovid merely mentions in passing, usually in connection with letter-writing.[9] The explanation lies, I believe, in the existence of a genre of vernacular poetry devoted to the winning of love through eloquence: the *canso* or *chanson*, that is, the love song. Despite Andreas's famous definition, "Amor est passio. . . ." (*DA* 1.1.1: 32), love was viewed in contemporary literature, as in Ovid, not so much as a state of suffering but rather as an activity of acquisition, and thanks to the influence of the courtly lyric, this activity was seen primarily as a discourse.

The dialogues constitute rhetorical models for the would-be lover, according to the standard rhetorical principle of imitation of models.[10] They are also organized according to another rhetorical principle, the distinction of three levels of style, which medieval rhetoricians associated with differences in social class.[11] They thus present all but one of the possible combinations of male and female interlocutors from each of three classes: the middle class (*plebeius/plebeia*), the simple nobility (*nobilis*), and the higher nobility (*nobilior*).[12]

The third dialogue presents the maximum social distance between the participants, with a man from the middle class addressing a woman from the higher nobility. This corresponds roughly to the stereotypical situation of the troubadour lyric, illustrated most clearly by the *vida* of Bernart de Ventadorn, that of a lover of humble origin who addresses a high-born lady.[13] The common lyric themes of ennoblement through love and nobility of heart or of merit will thus become prominent subjects of discussion in the dialogue.[14]

The interaction between Latin and vernacular rhetorical models is evident in the first speech of the man (*DA* 1.6.124–27: 74, 76). Like the vernacular love song, this speech is loosely modeled on the medieval art of letter-writing (*ars dictaminis*), which distinguishes the following five parts of a letter: the "salutation" (*salutatio*), the "securing of good will" (*captatio benevolentiae*), the "narration" (*narratio*), the "petition" (*petitio*), and the "conclusion" (*conclusio*).[15]

The passage begins with praise of the lady, a common topic of the *captatio benevolentiae*, introducing it, however, through the figure of *praeteritio*, which claims to pass over something in the very process of enunciating it.[16] It does not seem at all appropriate to emphasize the praise of her person, he declares, because her character and beauty resound throughout the world, and praise uttered in the presence of the person praised appears to be flattery (124: 74). This opening represents an example of the subtle type of exordium which Cicero calls *insinuatio*.[17]

Contrary to standard rhetorical practice, the petition follows almost immediately. The man has come to the lady, as he explains, to offer her his services and beg her to accept them (125: 74). It will be echoed at the very end of the speech, in the somewhat veiled request for the granting of hope, for only hope, the man contends, can preserve him from the perils of death (127: 76). The rest of the speech constitutes the *narratio*, or recounting of the circumstances that support the request.

If the form of this first speech reflects the model of medieval Latin epistolary rhetoric, much of its content is attributable to the vernacular love song. Thus the praise of the lady includes both her physical beauty (*venustas*) and her moral qualities (*probitas*), as in the troubadour *canso*, and the mention of flattery (*blandimenti*) introduces the important lyric theme of sincerity that will reemerge later in the dialogue. The attenuation of the petition also reflects the practice of the vernacular lyric: although the man's goal, throughout the dialogues, is the acquiring of love, here he only asks for permission to serve and to hope.

The influence of vernacular poetry is most apparent in the use of figurative language from the lyric tradition. If his agitation should remain fruitless, the man argues, after many stormy seas he will have to suffer the shipwreck of death (127: 74, 76), thus combining two standard lyric images, the nautical metaphor and the hyperbolic image of dying of love.[18] Even more important is the language of "service" and "reward" that provides the major argument for the *narratio*. The man's firm intention, he claims, is to serve the lady humbly and cheerfully, confident that his labors cannot fail to bear sweet fruit (126: 74). This is a reflection of the "feudal metaphor," a standard lyric device that compares the relationship of lover and lady to the feudal bond of reciprocal obligation linking vassal and lord.[19]

Insofar as the vernacular love song furnished the primary model for the lover's discourse in the dialogue, it also presumably provided the "horizon of expectation" that Andreas's public brought to this passage. But Andreas modifies this horizon of expectation through two major structural changes: the introduction of an authorial commentary at the beginning of the dialogue and the subsequent response of the lady addressed. These structural modifications have important repercussions for the tone and content of the passage, some of which are already anticipated in the man's first speech.

The introductory authorial commentary (*DA* 116–23: 72, 74) serves structurally to insert the dialogue into the overall framework of the *De amore*, the didactic discourse addressed to "Walter." The longest introduction of any of the dialogues, it is devoted thematically to the question of social class. In it Andreas opposes dialectically the poetic commonplace of "nobility of character" and the class consciousness of the feudal courts, appealing explicitly to "what people will think."

No matter how worthy the commoner may be, the Chaplain asserts, it is considered, even by common people, a great humiliation and very much out of place if a woman of the higher nobility gives her love to a commoner; the first assumption will be that she is prompted by excessive carnal pleasure (119: 74). We know from other sources that the class consciousness evoked by Andreas reflects a certain social reality: this sentiment was stronger in northern France than in the South and it had gained momentum in the course of the twelfth century.[20]

The dialectical confrontation of this social reality with the poetic theme of "nobility of character" leads to a compromise that attempts to maintain and synthesize the two principles. If a man equally worthy can be found among the nobility, Andreas concludes, he should be preferred; otherwise, the commoner should not be rejected, but his constancy should be tested by many trials before the hope of love is granted him (120–21: 74). This last stipulation displaces the emphasis from that of class to that of deeds, with important consequences for the dialogue to follow.

Doubtless the most striking innovation with respect to the lyric model is the fact that the lady has a chance to respond, a possibility generally denied to the recipient of a love song. In scholastic terms, this transforms the discourse from one of rhetoric to one of dialectic, on the basis of a distinction made in Boethius's *De differentiis topicis*, book 4, which views rhetoric as proceeding by unbroken discourse, dialectic by question and answer.[21] In terms of thematic structure, the purely passive resistance of the lyric lady, which becomes known to the literary public only to the degree in which it is reflected in the lover's arguments, is replaced by the active opposition of a lady free to express her reaction in her own terms.

The possibility of a response to the lover's advances is not unknown in the lyric tradition. The most obvious example is that of the *pastourelle*, which presents a gallant knight and a generally recalcitrant shepherdess engaged in a spirited lyric debate—in ironic inversion of the classic social configuration portrayed in the lyric. The *pastourelle* may well have served as a model for Andreas's fourth and sixth dialogues, which oppose noblemen and middle-class women, as well as contributing to book 1, chapter 11, "The Love of Peasants," but the social situation that it presents is diametrically opposed to that of the third dialogue, modeled, as we have seen, on that of the *canso*. There are also some examples, however, of lyric responses by highborn ladies.

The notion of a possible response by the lady is more or less implied in the structure of the love song, which is presented as a message to be sent to her in the hope of softening her rigor, presumably by eliciting a positive response. Certain of the troubadours expressly mention this possibility. Gaucelm Faidit complains that his lady has not answered his entreaties, while Raimbaut d'Aurenga and Arnaut de Mareuil both ask their respective ladies to answer their *saluts d'amour*.[22] A few texts go even further, presenting a veritable conversation between the troubadour and his lady. This may take the form of a rapid exchange of words within each verse, as is apparently the case in a poem by Peire Rogier,[23] or that of an exchange of one or more verses within each stanza, as in the *tenso* with an anonymous lady sometimes attributed to Albert Marques de Malaspina (P.-C. 296, 1a). It may involve an exchange of whole stanzas, as in the bilingual *tenso* between Raimbaut de Vaqueiras and a Genoese lady,[24] or even that of a long refutation speech, like those which follow two anonymous Old French *saluts d'amour*.[25] In all these cases the lady questions, contradicts, and ridicules the lover's assertions and declarations of passion, just as in

Andreas's dialogues. Whether or not Andreas knew of these lyric antecedents, his work clearly represents a parallel development of a potential inherent in the lyric.

In the third dialogue the lady's response to the lover's first speech addresses point by point the lover's arguments, incorporating the same reservations previously expressed in the authorial commentary. In an initial phase the lady unmasks the lover's artful attenuation of his request through his use of the feudal metaphor. She will, of course, accept any decent offer of service, she says, for to do otherwise would be ungenerous, but the man's words would indicate that he is asking not just to serve but also to be loved. This she does not wish to do, particularly with respect to a man two classes below her own (128–29: 76). She thus introduces for the first time into the dialogue proper the question of social class.

To the lover's hyperbolic threat to die of love unless hope is granted, the lady replies by emphasizing the man's remark that even a deceitful hope would serve the purpose. This, she says, undermines her own reputation by suggesting that she is capable of deceitfulness; it is rather the man who, by even making this suggestion, has shown himself to be guilty of the same vice (130–32: 76). From a rhetorical point of view, the man's introduction of the notion of deceitful hope is indeed difficult to justify. At best it appears as a negative example of the kind of reproach to which one is exposed by a carelessly presented argument. In replying to the lady's objection the man will claim, not altogether convincingly, that he wished thereby merely to express the full depth of his sentiment (137: 78). However, this incident does provide an occasion to discuss one of the most important themes of the vernacular poetry, that of sincerity,[26] which is probably its main function.

Just as the lady has exploited his mention of deceit, so also the lover seizes upon her introduction of considerations of social class to reproach her class prejudices and present the case for nobility of character (133–36: 76, 78). The lady replies by quibbling about the two meanings of "nobility": good character may lend "nobility" (in the moral sense) to a commoner, but only a prince can ennoble (in the social sense) (138: 78). The lover's unshapely legs do not suit him for noble service, she further argues (139–40: 78), echoing a prejudice, common in medieval literature and also, presumably, in feudal society, which associated nobility of birth not only with nobility of character but also with physical beauty.[27] To the first point the lover responds with a tidy syllogism: if character alone ennobles, and if only nobility makes one worthy of the love of a noblewoman, then only character deserves a noblewoman's love (141: 78). On the latter subject he invokes two examples from contemporary society to show the independence of beauty and character, arguing for the superiority of the latter (142–44: 78, 80), as does Andreas at the beginning of book 1, chapter 6 (DA 1.6.3–15: 42, 44).

At this point the lady acknowledges the reasonableness of the man's arguments concerning nobility of character, thus providing a break in the discussion.²⁸ Then, shifting from the general to the particular, she questions on the basis of what good deeds and noble character this lover wishes to press his claim (145: 80).²⁹ The man acknowledges tacitly the paucity of his deeds by asking to be instructed in the art of love (146–47: 80). The lady accedes to this request, not without pointing out the contradiction in asking to be loved on one's merits and then asking to be instructed on how to merit love (148: 80, 82).

The lover's request for instruction marks another generic shift in the dialogue with a corresponding shift in the horizon of expectation. In the long speech of the lady that follows, constituting nearly one-third of the entire dialogue (*DA* 1.6.149–61: 82–84), the contentious style of scholastic debate is replaced by the didactic language of exhortation. Once again, the discourse combines Latin and vernacular models: that of the art of preaching (*ars predicandi*), of which an early example is the treatise of Andreas's contemporary Alain de Lille, with that of the Occitan *ensenhamens*, secular treatises on courtly behavior whose earliest examples date from the same period.³⁰ At the same time, the adversarial relationship of the disputants is transformed into a hierarchical relationship of teacher and disciple, based not only on the civilizing influence of the fair sex but also on the authority of class superiority.

Reflecting both sacred and secular models, the advice of the lady presents a conception of love service whose roots go back to the vernacular poetry but that gives the courtly themes a very different orientation. In the love song, "service" appears to mean little other than loving sincerely and, as a consequence, singing the lady's praises. In the courtly romance, this essentially inner, psychological "service" is replaced by concrete, external actions that more nearly approximate the vassal's service to his lord: courteous social behavior and, especially, exploits of chivalry. These poetic themes are present in the lady's advice to the commoner, but by and large her speech constitutes a reinterpretation of the courtly love ethic in terms of Christian morality.

It begins with a long discussion of the importance of generosity (149–50: 82), a prominent theme in courtly poetry,³¹ but one easily assimilated to Christian charity. The advice to show ardor in battle (155: 82) can be attributed to the courtly romances, and the admonition of fidelity to a single lady (155: 84) reflects a theme ubiquitous in courtly literature. Romance examples can easily be found for the advice (ibid.) to serve all ladies for the sake of one (e.g., Chrétien de Troyes, *Le Chevalier au lion*), an idea already anticipated in the man's very first speech (126: 74), but once again it is not far removed from the notion of Christian charity. Several comments reflect a secular conception of courteous behavior with possible poetic antecedents: the advice to be sociable and pleasant, to talk neither too much nor too little (156–57: 84), and to control one's laughter in the presence of women, although in the latter case the authority invoked is that of

Solomon (153: 82). Otherwise, the lover is advised to avoid blasphemy and foul language (151: 82), as well as lying, cheating, and gaming (159: 84, 154: 82); to turn the other cheek to those who wrong him (159: 84); to reprove evildoers and to forsake their company if they do not mend their ways (152: 82); and to honor the clergy rather than mock them and to attend church regularly (160–61: 84).

From the point of view of acquiring love, which was that originally adopted in the dialogues, the efficacy of this advice would doubtless depend on the piety of the woman being wooed. The dialogues offer not only rhetorical models for would-be lovers but also ethical models for the lovers' ladies, with those of the higher nobility setting a particularly high standard. Not content to resist all advances, the lady of the third dialogue imposes Christian moral conduct of the highest order as a prerequisite for the granting of hope. This curious dual function of the dialogues is in the best tradition of medieval pedagogy, which freely combined instruction in moral philosophy with the teaching of the *trivium*, particularly grammar and rhetoric.[32]

Gratefully accepting the lady's advice, the man renews his appeal to be granted hope. This is refused, however, and the dialogue ends, like the vernacular love song, with the initial situation unaltered (*DA* 1.6.162–65: 84, 86). The lady's intransigence on this point can be better understood if we remember that in Andreas's adaptation of the medieval commonplace regarding the stages of love, the granting of hope represents the first stage.[33] It is true that the man of the eighth dialogue argues that a woman can change her mind without blame, provided she has not yet taken the final step (*DA* 1.6.438: 170), but in book 2, chapter 6, Andreas states that if a woman has given a man the hope of her love or other preliminary favors, and provided he is not found to be unworthy, it is judged a great offense for her to deny him what he has so long anticipated (*DA* 2.6.34: 248). This conclusion is in conformity with the traditional view of the stages of love in which the first stages lead more or less inevitably to the last.[34] We should also remember that early in the dialogue the lady rebuffed the suggestion that she grant hope deceitfully (130–32: 76), and that in her advice to the commoner she warned against making false promises (157: 84), so it seems hardly likely that she herself would fall into that same trap.

Before leaving the third dialogue we must raise the question of its ideological function, that is, in Jauss's terms, its relationship to the real world. The application to courtly poetry of the scientific apparatus of scholasticism, normally used to describe the world, has the result of bringing that poetry closer to a certain everyday reality. The question to which the passage responds may be formulated as follows: "To what degree is courtly poetry compatible with real life?" This question may be further broken down into two components: on the aesthetic level, "What becomes of the discourse of the lyric lover when confronted with the lady's reply?"; on the moral level, "To what degree can courtly poetic values be reconciled with the class mentality of feudal society and with Christian morality?"

The poetry of courtly love is based on a game,[35] with well established rules, which erects a fictional nobility in place of true nobility and a fictional morality in place of true morality. Like any game, it is susceptible to being taken seriously. Whatever may be the degree to which it reflected medieval social practice, it always carried with it at least the potential for becoming a formative influence on that practice.

The confrontation of courtly poetry with feudal and Christian values has as its first effect to bring out the potentially subversive character of the game, which calls into question the social hierarchy underlying the organization of medieval society. In Andreas's third dialogue that subversive tendency is immediately neutralized, however; indeed, it is "coopted" into a sublimating synthesis that transforms the sexual impulse into deeds of chivalry and, especially, acts of Christian charity.

Notes

1. Hans Robert Jauss, *Towards an Aesthetic of Reception*, trans. Timothy Bahti (Minneapolis: University of Minnesota Press, 1982).
2. Andreas Capellanus, *On Love*, ed. and trans. P. G. Walsh (London: Duckworth, 1982) (hereafter *DA*). References are to book, chapter, paragraph, and page numbers.
3. Alfred Karnein, De amore *in volkssprachlicher Literatur: Untersuchungen zur Andreas-Capellanus-Rezeption in Mittelalter und Renaissance* (Heidelberg: Winter, 1985). For a critique of Karnein, see Don A. Monson, "Andreas Capellanus and the Problem of Irony," *Speculum* 63 (1988): 539–72; esp. 547–54.
4. Jauss, *Towards an Aesthetic*, 3–45. Cf. idem, *Literaturgeschichte als Provokation* (Frankfurt: Suhrkamp Verlag, 1970).
5. On the place of Andreas's treatise within the development of early scholasticism, see Don A. Monson, *Andreas Capellanus, Scholasticism, and the Courtly Tradition* (Washington, DC: Catholic University of America Press, 2005).
6. Don A. Monson, "Auctoritas and Intertertextuality in Andreas Capellanus' *De amore*," in *Poetics of Love in the Middle Ages*, ed. Moshé Lazar and Norris J. Lacy (Fairfax, VA: George Mason University Press, 1989), 69–79; idem, *Andreas Capellanus, Scholasticism*.
7. The paucity of metadiscursive genre theory in the Middle Ages contrasts sharply with the abundant and flourishing array of genres observable in discursive practice, including a good deal of generic experimentation, often leading to "transgressive," hybrid forms and the creation of new genres. Combining classical and medieval, Latin and vernacular models of discourse, Andreas takes the process of generic experimentation and syncretism to a new level.
8. The subject of audience expectation raises the thorny question of Andreas's audience, about which there is no consensus. Leaving aside the debate over whether the *De amore* was written at the court in Champagne or in Paris, we can doubtless assume on the part of the Chaplain's intended audience no less

cultural complexity than that observable in the treatise. Like Andreas himself, those who comprised his first public must have been both clerics and courtiers.
9. Ovid, *Ars amatoria*, 1.437–86, 607–30.
10. Richard McKeon, "Literary Criticism and the Concept of Imitation in Antiquity," *Modern Philology* 34 (1936–37): 1–35. Cf. *Rhetorica ad Herennium*, 1.2.3; Quintilian, *Institutio oratoria*, 10.2.1; Geoffrey of Vinsauf, *Poetria nova*, vv. 1705–8.
11. Edmond Faral, *Les Arts poétiques du XIIᵉ et du XIIIᵉ siècle* (Paris: Champion, 1924), 86–89. Cf. *Rhetorica ad Herennium*, 4.8.11; John of Garland, *Parisiana poetria*, ed. and trans. Traugott Lawler (New Haven, CT: Yale University Press, 1974), 38–41. The application to both sexes of the doctrine of levels of style is attributable to the rhetorical principle that persuasion depends on the qualities of both the speaker and the audience; see Aristotle, *Rhetoric*, 1.2.3–6; Cicero, *De inventione*, 1.16.22; *Rhetorica ad Herennium*, 1.4–5.8; Quintilian, *Institutio oratoria*, 6.2.8–24.
12. Normally we would expect to find nine dialogues, corresponding to the number of possible combinations of men and women from various classes. One dialogue has been left out, however, that which should have come in sixth place, opposing a nobleman to a woman of the higher nobility, so that the actual number is eight.
13. J. Boutière and A. H. Schutz, eds., *Biographies des troubadours*: *Textes provençaux des XIIIᵉ et XIVᵉ siècles*, 2nd ed. (Paris: Nizet, 1973), VI, A–B, 20–28. Whether or not the *vida* is of historical value with regard to Bernart's biography, it indicates a medieval reception of troubadour poetry in which the theme of social disparity figures prominently. This theme is expressed only sporadically in the vernacular lyric, leading some scholars to downplay its significance. For a discussion see William D. Paden, Jr., et al., "The Troubadour's Lady: Her Marital Status and Social Rank," *Studies in Philology* 72 (1975): 28–50; Don A. Monson, "The Troubadour's Lady Reconsidered Again," *Speculum* 70 (1995): 255–74; Paden, "The Troubadour's Lady as Seen through Thick History," *Exemplaria* 11.2 (1999): 221–44; Monson and Paden, "The Troubadour's Lady: An Exchange," *Exemplaria* 14.2 (2002): 485–517.
14. Glynnis M. Cropp, *Le Vocabulaire des troubadours de l'époque classique* (Geneva: Droz, 1975), 141–45. On classical antecedents, see Ernst Robert Curtius, *European Literature and the Latin Middle Ages*, trans. Willard R. Trask (Princeton, NJ: Princeton University Press, 1973), 179–80.
15. On the *ars dictaminis* see James J. Murphy, *Rhetoric in the Middle Ages* (Berkeley: University of California Press, 1974), 194–269. On the influence of this art on the troubadour *canso*, see Don A. Monson, "Lyrisme et sincérité; sur une chanson de Bernart de Ventadorn," in Hans Erich Keller et al., eds., *Studia occitanica in memoriam Paul Remy*, 2 vols. (Kalamazoo: Medieval Institute Publications, 1986), 1:143–59. For a more general discussion of the influence of Latin rhetoric on the vernacular love song, see Roger Dragonetti, *La Technique poétique des trouvères dans la chanson courtoise* (Bruges: De Tempel, 1960).
16. Heinrich Lausberg, *A Handbook of Literary Rhetoric*: *A Foundation for Literary Study*, trans. Matthew T. Bliss, Annemiek Jansen, and David E. Orton; ed. David E. Orton and Dean Anderson (Leiden: Brill, 1998), 882–86: 393–94. Cf. *Rhetorica ad Herennium*, 4.27.37.
17. *De inventione*, 1.15.20–21, 1.16–17.23–25. Cf. *Rhetorica ad Herennium*, 1.6.9–7.11; Lausberg, *A Handbook* (n. 16, above), 280–81: 132–33.
18. For examples of the nautical metaphor, see Alfred Pillet and Henry Carstens,

Bibliographie der Troubadours (Halle: Niemeyer, 1933) (hereafter P.-C.) 31, 1, vv. 43–48 (Arnaut Peire d'Agange); 70, 44, vv. 37–40 (Bernart de Ventadorn); 71, 1, vv. 26–30 (Bertolome Zorzi); 80, 29, vv. 33–38 (Bertran de Born); 82, 4, vv. 31–35 (Bertran Carbonel); 106, 18a, vv. 1–6 (Cadenet); 154, 5, vv. 9–16 (Folquet de Lunel); 194, 15, vv. 58–59 (Gui d'Ussel); 242, 60, vv. 35–38 (Giraut de Bornelh); 281, 6, vv. 27–30 (Lamberti de Buvalel); 304, 1, vv. 1–4 (Jofre de Foixa); 366, 31, v. 39 (Peirol); 370, 8, vv. 11–12 (Perdigo); 379, 1, vv. 1–7 (Pons d'Ortafas); 404, 9, vv. 13–14 (Raimon Jordan); 437, 2, vv. 17–24 (Sordel); 461, 8a, vv. 1–6 (anon.). Cf. Ovid, *Ars amatoria*, 1.410–12, 2.2.9–10. Andreas also develops this image at *DA* 1.4.3–4: 38, 1.6.358: 142, and 2.6.22: 244. On love and death in vernacular poetry, see Marie-Noëlle Toury, *Mort et "fin' amor" dans la poésie d'oc et d'oïl aux XIIe et XIIIe siècles* (Paris: Champion, 2001). Andreas also develops this image in four other dialogues: *DA* 1.6.76–77: 60; 191–92: 94; 202, 205–8: 98, 100; 522: 194, 196.

19. On the feudal metaphor, see Eduard Wechssler, "Frauendienst und Vassalität," *Zeitschrift für französische Sprache und Literatur* 24 (1902): 159–90; idem, *Das Kulturproblem des Minnesangs* (Halle: Niemeyer, 1909), 140–82; Silvio Pellegrini, "Intorno al vassallaggio d'amore dei primi trovatori," *Cultura neolatina* 4–5 (1944–45): 21–36; rpt. in idem, *Studi rolandiani e trobadorici* (Bari: Adriatica, 1964), 178–91; Rita Lejeune, "Formules féodales et style amoureux chez Guillaume IX d'Aquitaine," in *Atti del VIII congresso internazionale di studi romanzi, Firenze, 1956*, 2 vols. (Florence: Sansone, 1959), 1: 227–48; rpt. in idem, *Littérature et société occitane au moyen âge* (Liège: Marche Romane, 1979), 103–20; Dragonetti, *La Technique poétique* (n. 15, above), 61–113; Ingrid Kasten, *Frauendienst bei Troubadors und Minnesänger im 12. Jahrhundert* (Heidelberg: Winter, 1986), 53–76, 142–202.

20. Marc Bloch, *Feudal Society*, trans. L. A. Manyon, 2 vols. (Chicago: University of Chicago Press, 1961), 2:320–44; Jean Frappier, "Vues sur les conceptions courtoises," *Cahiers de Civilisation Médiévale* 2 (1959): 135–56, esp. 145–46.

21. *Boethius's De topicis differentiis*, trans. Eleanore Stump (Ithaca, NY: Cornell University Press, 1978), 79–80; cf. Migne, *Patrologia latina*, 64:1205–6. Rhetoric and dialectic also differ, according to Boethius in the same passage, in that dialectic uses complete syllogisms, whereas rhetoric is content with enthymemes, or imperfect, abbreviated syllogisms. Throughout Andreas's dialogues, the formal techniques of dialectic are interspersed with those of rhetoric and adapted to the informal requirements of a rhetorical situation. This is not the *disputatio in forma* that became current following the introduction of the *logica nova*, but rather the much freer *disputatio extra formam*.

22. Gaucelm Faidit, *S'om pogues partir son voler* (P.-C. 167, 56), v. 59; Arnaut de Mareuil, *Dona, gensor qe no sai dir*, v. 205; Raimbaut d'Aurenga, *Donna, cel qe.us es bos amics*, vv. 7–8.

23. Especially *Ges non puesc en bon vers fallir* (P.-C. 356, 4), in which the identity of the poet's interlocutor is ambiguous, however: it could be a dialogue of the poet with himself, with a friend, or with the beloved. This poem was imitated in *Ailas, com mor!—quez as, amis?* (P.-C. 242, 3) by Giraut de Bornelh, where the interlocutor is clearly a friend, and in the romance *Flamenca*, where it forms the basis for a long conversation carried on between the lovers in the church, at the rate of one word each Sunday or feast day. Cf. *Das Leben und die Lieder des Trobadors Peire Rogier*, ed. Carl Appel (Berlin: Reimer, 1882), 13–16; *The Poems of the Troubadour Peire Roger*, ed. Derek E. T. Nicholson (Manchester: Manchester University Press, 1976), 21–26.

24. *Domna, tan vos ai preiada* (P.-C. 392, 7). Cf. Simon Gaunt, "Sexual Difference and the Metaphor of Language in a Troubadour Poem," *Modern Language Review* 83 (1988): 297–313.
25. Paul Meyer, "Le salut d'amour dans les littératures provençale et française," *Bibliothèque de l'Ecole des Chartes* 28 (1867): 124–70, here 147–49; O. Schultz-Gora, "Ein ungedruckter Salu d'amors nebst Antwort," *Zeitschrift für romanische Philologie* 24 (1900): 358–69.
26. See Monson, "Lyrisme et sincérité" (n. 15, above).
27. For example, Old French *gent* and Old Occitan *gen*, from Latin *genitus*, "[well] born," combine the notion of nobility with those of social grace, moral excellence, and physical beauty. See Glyn S. Burgess, *Contribution à l'étude du vocabulaire pré-courtois* (Geneva: Droz, 1970), 134–40; Cropp, *Le Vocabulaire* (n. 14, above), 155–57.
28. This acceptance by the woman of the higher nobility (*nobilior*) of the general claim of nobility of character recalls the opinion attributed to Alienor of Aquitaine by the nobleman in the fourth dialogue (although none of the Love Cases decided by Alienor in book 2, chapter 7, addresses this question), namely that if a noblewoman and a *plebeia* are of equal merit, their love is equally worth seeking (*DA* 1.6.185: 92). By contrast, the woman of the simple nobility (*nobilis*) asserts in the second dialogue that no one should transgress the limits of his rank, and that every good man should seek the love of some good woman in his own class (*DA* 1.6.108: 70). Does this difference in attitude reflect a greater sensitivity on the part of the simple nobility to the threat posed by the rising power of the bourgeoisie? I am indebted to Eugene Vance for this suggestion.
29. The shift from the general to the particular coincides with a shift from dialectic to rhetoric. According to Boethius's *De differentiis topicis* (n. 21, above), rhetoric and dialectic differ in subject matter in that dialectic examines *theses*, or general questions not involved in circumstances, whereas rhetoric is concerned with *hypotheses*, that is, particular questions surrounded by circumstances.
30. On the *ars predicandi*, see Murphy, *Rhetoric* (n. 15, above), 269–355; on the *ensenhamens*, see Don A. Monson, *Les "Ensenhamens" occitans: Essai de définition et de délimitation du genre* (Paris: Klincksieck, 1981). Cf. Jean-Charles Payen, "Un Ensenhamen trop précoce: L'Art d'aimer d'André le Chapelain," in Ernstpeter Ruhe and Rudolf Behrens, eds., *Mittelalterbilder aus neuer Perspektive* (Munich: Fink, 1985), 43–58.
31. Erich Köhler, "Reichtum und Freigebigkeit in der Trobadordichtung," in idem, *Trobadorlyrik und höfischer Roman* (Berlin: Rütten & Loening, 1962), 45–72; Glynnis M. Cropp, "L'Expression de la générosité chez les troubadours," in Keller et al., *Studia occitanica* (n. 15, above), 2:255–68.
32. Philippe Delhaye, "L'Enseignement de la philosophie morale au XIIe siècle," *Mediaeval Studies* 11 (1949): 77–99; idem, "'Grammatica' et 'Ethica' au XIIe siècle," *Recherches de théologie ancienne et médiévale* 25 (1958): 59–110; Curtius, *European Literature* (n. 14, above), 57–61.
33. In their classical formulation, there are five stages of love, the first of which is sometimes omitted: "sight" (*visus*), "conversation" (*alloquium*), "physical contact" (*contactus*), "kissing" (*oscula*), and "consummation" (*factum*). See Curtius, *European Literature* (n. 14, above), 512–14; Lionel J. Friedman, "Gradus amoris," *Romance Philology* 19 (1965): 167–77; Peter Dronke, *Medieval Latin and the Rise of European Love-Lyric*, 2 vols. (Oxford: Clarendon Press, 1968), 2:488–89; Frank R. Akehurst, "Les étapes de l'amour chez Bernard de Ventadour," *Cahiers de Civilisation Médiévale* 16 (1973): 133–47; idem, "Words and

Acts in the Troubadours," in Lazar and Lacy, *Poetics of Love* (n. 6, above), 17–28. In the first dialogue (*DA* 1.6.59–64: 56), Andreas reduces the number of stages to four: "the giving of hope" (*spei datio*), "the granting of a kiss" (*osculi exhibitio*), "the enjoyment of an embrace" (*amplexus fruitio*), and "the yielding of the whole person" (*totius personae concessio*). This schema is repeated at the beginning of the eighth dialogue (*DA* 1.6.438: 170) and in somewhat modified form in the subsequent discussion of "pure" and "mixed" love (*DA* 1.6.470–75: 180).

34. Cf. Ovid, *Ars amatoria*, 1.669–70: "Oscula qui sumpsit, si non et cetera sumet, / haec quoque, quae data sunt, perdere dignus erit." ("He who has taken kisses, if he takes not the rest, deserves to lose what has already been given.")

35. Don A. Monson, "The Troubadours at Play: Irony, Parody and Burlesque," in Simon Gaunt and Sarah Kay, eds., *The Troubadours: An Introduction* (Cambridge: Cambridge University Press, 1999), 197–211.

Virgilian Hauntings in Boccaccio's De casibus virorum illustrium

KAREN ELIZABETH GROSS

This is an essay in ghost-hunting. Boccaccio's *De casibus virorum illustrium*, a text crowded with wailing and obstreperous spirits, is haunted by a presence that never makes itself explicitly heard: the *Aeneid*, and more specifically, Anchises's pageant of future Roman worthies. Virgil's shade is not a noisy ghost. His spirit is a silent one, never insistently clamoring for attention, but quietly pervading the whole enterprise of the *De casibus* nonetheless. He is glimpsed in influences and resonances, not in explicit allusion. But he is there, providing an unrecognized Virgilian moment in the Latin Middle Ages, one that connects Boccaccio to Virgil and the *De casibus* to the *Aeneid*.

I will first point out some ways in which Boccaccio's text echoes Virgil's structurally and thematically, examining how exactly the *De casibus* resembles the *Aeneid*. Boccaccio presents himself as an Aeneas figure, making his way through a world of phantasm, propelled by a purpose larger than his own. Then I will consider the circumstances in which Boccaccio read Virgil and why his evocation of an epic poem in a historical treatise would not be unexpected. Virgil is more than simply the preeminent *auctore* for Boccaccio: his poetry provides the archetype of how human knowledge can be acquired and structured. I will conclude by meditating upon the implications of this pairing of the *De casibus* with the *Aeneid*, of what it means to have the inspiration for a collection of exemplary biographies be an interview in the underworld between a father and a son soon to found an empire.[1]

The *De casibus virorum illustrium* is part of Boccaccio's "post-Petrarch" phase, after the "Phylostropos" (or "loving converter," as Boccaccio fondly calls Petrarch in his fifteenth eclogue) encouraged the younger poet to turn away from vernacular and lyric works and instead to compose volumes of history and moral instruction in Latin.[2] Consisting of over 150 biographies, mostly of political rulers and their rise and fall, the *De casibus*'s litany of lives is frequently punctuated by exhortatory asides urging the renunciation of vice, and by playful fables, such as Fortune's and Poverty's wrestling match at the side of the road (3.1). But the main purpose of the *De casibus* is to recall sensuous rulers to the straight path, to humble those princes who are glutted by success or debauchery with examples of the inevitability of changes in fortune, so that, descending the Great Chain of Being, "they will recognize God's power, the shiftiness of Fortune, and their own insecurity" (*Dei potentiam, fragilitatem suam, et Fortune lubricum noscant*).[3] Boccaccio is eclectic in his selections: the *De casibus* stretches from Adam and Eve to King John of France, captured at Poitiers in 1356, and thus differs from the final form of Petrarch's *De viris illustribus* by its inclusion of Scriptural, non-Italian, and modern lives, as well as accounts of notable (and notorious) women.[4] Yet despite the diversity of Boccaccio's examples, all follow the template of the Fall. This repetitive abundance is intentional, assisting those especially stubborn or thickheaded readers to grasp his point, for "as a constant flow of water will penetrate the hardest stone, so an adamantine heart is softened by long narration" (48; *uti assiduo aque casu durissimus perforator lapis, sic et adamantinum cor talium longa narratione molliatur*; 2.pr.3).

The *De casibus* is frequently judged to be a turning away from Virgil's influence, if only because Boccaccio writes of the historical, modest Dido, choosing suicide to preserve her chastity, rather than the Aeneidic Dido, destroying herself in despair from unrequited passion (a figure who proved to be rich in allusive potential for Boccaccio's earlier erotic works, such as the *Amorosa Visione* and the *Elegia di Madonna Fiammetta*).[5] Critical focus only upon Boccaccio's treatment of Dido, however, occludes how Virgilian the *De casibus* actually is. I should emphasize here that I am interested in global similarities, not local verbal citations, between the *Aeneid* and the *De casibus*. There are a few direct quotations of Virgil appearing in some passages dealing with Trojan figures, as in the *De casibus*'s story of Priam (1.13).[6] Jonathan Usher has examined in detail syntactical and verbal borrowings in the *De casibus* from the *Culex*, another poem relating travels through the underworld that was attributed to Virgil in the Middle Ages.[7] What I address here, though, are structural resonances between the *De casibus* and the *Aeneid*,[8] not least of all Boccaccio's colloquia with the dead, and what implications these resonances raise about how Boccaccio understood the interactions between poetry and history, between the living and the dead.

I. Fortune, Providence, and the Aeneidic *De casibus*

There are three aspects of the *De casibus* that I wish to consider as particularly Virgilian moments: the overall structure of the work as a replication of the *katabasis* of *Aeneid* 6, Petrarch's miraculous manifestation as deus ex machina in *De casibus* 8, and the relation between Fortune and the pageants of souls. More than being only subtle expressions of Boccaccio's erudition, these evocations of the *Aeneid* comment upon Boccaccio's conception of the entire project of writing history.

What initially begins as private thought ("In my mind I ran over the lamentable catastrophes of our ancestors" [2]) soon takes on a spatial or visionary quality existing outside Boccaccio's self ("By now the human race, multiplied by many generations, filled almost all the earth. . . . now I saw an army of mourners milling around me" [9]). Images of travel, as well as of the author's helplessness in steering the narrative, regularly punctuate the text: along with the expected metaphors of resting after a day's journey at the division of books (for example, 1.19.2–3), and the figure of his text being a bark at sea finally reaching the destined landing at the *De casibus*'s conclusion (9.27.4),[9] Boccaccio frequently justifies the ordering of his stories by referring to his writing as an enormous, if unpredictable, itinerary ("It was really enough for us to enter Thebes once, but the great misfortune of Jocasta made it necessary to return there again" [11]; "I had in mind to return to Asia, but the clamor of some Italians called me into Italy, where I did not want to go" [81], to list just two of several incidents). While he himself is not wandering through the underworld—he has neither Sibyl nor Virgil as guide—Boccaccio converses with shades who parade through his bedroom in great numbers, crowds wailing and pressing forward for their stories to be told, or else turning shamefully away in hopes of being unrecognized, as does Appius Claudius (3.8.6). Boccaccio often acts as arbiter in quarrels, as in that among Tiberius, Caligula, and Valeria (7.3), or passes a Dantean moral censure on the shades, as when he is so disgusted by the bestiality of Thyestes and Atreus that he refuses to continue writing their stories (1.9.23).

Nearly all of the figures who process past Aeneas in the underworld (including the short-lived Marcellus) make an appearance in the *De casibus*. In fact, Anchises's pageant in Elysium is the origin for the compositional structure of the *De casibus*: a man charged with pious duty is shown a parade of shades, all great generals and rulers. There are Dantean elements in Boccaccio's presentation: Boccaccio is visited by figures from the past, not by those of the future, as were those shown to Aeneas; the miserable souls whom Boccaccio encounters are vicious, or at least fallen, figures. Yet to recognize Dantean features is to acknowledge the Virgilian origin,[10] a source that is more evident in the *De casibus* as the project is self-consciously classical, not least of all because it is written in Latin and not the *volgare*. Moreover, although denunciations against certain vices interrupt the progress of the *De casibus*, the shades in Boccaccio's history are primarily seen as representatives of human folly in its ambitious dependence upon Fortune, not as embodiments of different particular sins.

One of the most striking Aeneidic echoes is the apparition of Petrarch at the opening of *De casibus* 8. Boccaccio, pausing as always from his labors between books, is suddenly overwhelmed with sloth. Despairing at the effort required to complete his task, as well as mocking his own attempts to achieve fame through his writing, Boccaccio slips into despondent lethargy, allowing his memory to "take flight" in a moment of forgetfulness akin to Dante's at the opening of the *Commedia*. Suddenly, in an incident reminiscent of Mercury's two appearances to Aeneas (*Aen.* 4.259–78 and 4.554–72), a laureated Petrarch manifests himself in Boccaccio's bedroom, gently chiding him as the "famous Professor of Lassitude" (*ociorum professor egregie*; 8.1.7), and instructing him on the merits of fame and those who seek it. Like the god, Petrarch arrives at a time when the hero has been distracted from his main purpose. Both appeal to fame and familial responsibility (to Ascanius and later descendants of Rome in Mercury's case; to all of the illustrious living before and after the *De casibus* in Petrarch's). And, in the second vision of Mercury, the Olympian castigates Aeneas for slumbering in the face of all he has yet to accomplish. Boccaccio's allegorical interpretation of Virgil's Mercury in the *Genealogia deorum gentilium* further suggests that such an association of Petrarch with the divine messenger is probable:

But after showing the enticements of lust, he [Virgil] points the way of return to virtue by bringing in Mercury, messenger of the gods, to rebuke Aeneas, and call him back from such indulgence to deeds of glory. By Mercury, Virgil means either remorse, or the reproof of some outspoken friend, either of which rouses us from slumber in the mire of turpitude, and calls us back into the fair and even path to glory. Then we burst the bonds of unholy delight, and, armed with new fortitude, we unfalteringly spurn all seductive flattery, and tears, prayers, and such, and abandon them as naught.

Tandem ostenso quo trahamur in scelus ludibrio, qua via in virtutem revehamur, ostendit, inducens Mercurium, deorum interpretem, Eneam ab illecebra increpantem atque ad gloriosa exhortantem. Per quem Virgilius sentit seu conscientie proprie morsum, seu amici et eloquentis hominis redargutionem, a quibus, dormientes in luto turpitudinum, excitamur, et in rectum pulchrumque revocamur iter, id est ad gloriam. Et tunc nexum oblectationis infauste solvimus, quando, armati fortitudine, blanditias, lacrimas, preces, et huius modi in contrarium trahentes, constanti animo spernimus, ac vilipendentes omictimus.[11]

If Petrarch is Mercury, then Boccaccio becomes Aeneas, embarking on a textual odyssey. Certainly Petrarch invokes the same language of travel that permeates the entire *De casibus*: "You have begun your journey, and now that you have almost reached the end of it, you stop, turned aside by a fatuous opinion" (*Cepisti cursum et dum iam vicinus termino devenisses, stulta seductus ignavia, subsistis*; 8.1.12: 204). The precise nature of the empire Boccaccio is entrusted with founding will come into sharper focus when we consider how filial responsibility affects literary composition. For the moment, it is sufficient to recognize that for Boccaccio his friend's interruption, reminding him of the higher purpose of his labors, was intended as a reinvention of *Aeneid* 4, and thus casts Boccaccio's enterprise as not only a scholarly exercise or a civic duty (an adaptation of the mirror for princes), but also as a divinely charged mission.

The final element of the *De casibus* that I believe speaks to the *Aeneid* is an aspect that most readers might find to be the biography collection's most medieval quality, rather than a classical one. Boccaccio's insistence upon the inevitability of fall—of Fortune's pervasiveness in touching all who seek to excel—accords with the fated destiny of the Romans as presented by Anchises to Aeneas in the underworld. Here it is interesting to contrast Boccaccio's enterprise with Petrarch's *De viris illustribus*, as both projects were worked upon concurrently. Petrarch's task, as he says in his preface, is to describe "illustrious men, not lucky ones" (*neque fortunatos sed illustres*), or, in his evocation of a Suetonian anecdote about Augustus, to see "kings, not corpses" (*reges . . . non mortuos*),[12] and his belief that events are willed, not fated, is behind his assertion that "the profitable goal of the historian is to point up to the readers those things that are to be followed and those to be avoided" (*fructuosus historici finis est, illa prosequi que vel sectanda legentibus vel fugienda sunt*).[13] While Boccaccio concurs with this pedagogical purpose, the shared commonality in human nature that he recognizes is not free will as much as the unavoidability of man's reliance upon chance due to a will distorted through the Fall. The result is that men (to borrow an image from one of the fables in the *De casibus*) repeatedly unchain Misfortune from its stake, and through their choice of false goods receive unhappiness.

At first it may seem that, if we were to compare Petrarch and Boccaccio to ancient epic poets, Petrarch is the one more like Virgil ("For what is all of history but the praise of Rome?" Petrarch asks[14]), and Boccaccio is more akin to Lucan, replacing sublunar providence with the caprice of Fortune.[15] Certainly their divergent political allegiances might imply that they would find inspiration in different *auctores*, Petrarch perhaps drawing from Aeneas's imperial enterprise to appeal to his northern Italian tyrant-patrons, and Boccaccio despondently viewing the disintegration of the Republic in Lucan's epic as a commentary on the fallen state of contemporary Italian governments.[16] Petrarch's history is a celebration of the exceeding virtue and nobility of heroic ancients, just as the *Aeneid* was intended to increase Augustus's fame.[17] Boccaccio's *De casibus* is not primarily an exercise in exaltation of the Roman spirit, but, like Lucan's *Pharsalia*, a grim series of incidents underscoring the violence and passions that undergird not only the Roman Empire but the human condition. Pompey, in fact, represents for Boccaccio the most dramatic demonstration of Fortune's powers: "I do not believe that any mortal ever fell from so high a pinnacle" (156; *Neminem reor mortalium ex tam sublimi vertice corruisse*; 6.10.2). Instead of a parade of the future greatness of Rome, Boccaccio gives a pageant of the worthlessness of human ambition.

And yet, without going so far as to attribute to Boccaccio the reading of a pessimistic, angst-ridden Virgil similar to that of most twentieth-century scholarship,[18] I think Anchises's assembly of noble Romans in the underworld is closer to Boccaccio's than to Petrarch's idea of an encyclopedic biography, for the illustrious souls of Elysium are great because the gods have willed it so, not because of their personal achievements; they are "the glory henceforth to attend the Trojan race, held in store by fate" (*Dardaniam prolem quae deinde sequatur / gloria*; *Aen.* 6.756).[19] In a sense they are simply the lucky men. For in Boccaccio's world, *fatum* and *fortuna*, fate and chance, are not opposing forces, as they are represented in Lucan. Rather, both are terms that humans give to the mysterious operations of God unfolding within time. Fortune, according to Boccaccio, is simply the misguided name of God's plan on earth; those who put their faith in unstable goods and ambition rather than virtue and God misattribute their changing states to the anonymous force *fortuna* instead of the constant waywardness that accompanies sin (*De casibus*, Proem 6). This configuration accords with the Boethian sentiments underscoring the entire *De casibus*, in its criticisms of temporal pleasures, its lament for the mutability of this world, and (particularly in *De consolatione philosophiae* 4.pr.6) its explanation of the connections among chance, fate, and Providence.[20] Indeed, Boethius would have held close Virgilian connotations for Boccaccio as well: not only was Boethius extensively cited in fourteenth-century commentaries on Virgil,[21] but the *De consolatione* itself was understood to be deeply evocative of the *Aeneid*, both at the syntactical and the larger structural level.[22] Dante's Virgil offers a similar conception of Fortune, ascribing to her a purpose in her mutability, unapparent to humans but ordained by God, who placed her as steward over material goods (*Inferno* 7.70–96).

Furthermore, while it is true that Father Anchises indicates those who will lead great triumphs and trophies into Rome, his list includes several ambiguities (including precisely which individual is to be invoked by family names)[23] and concludes on a tragic note, that of the youth Marcellus, the unfulfilled promise. That the list of worthies should end in grief, that Virgil at this juncture ceases to report direct dialogue between father and son, that the remaining conversation prophesies the bloodshed awaiting Aeneas upon landing in Italy—all this is suggestive to me of the limits of even Rome's prosperity. Augustus himself shall not be immune to misfortune, a lesson with which Boccaccio would concur.

II. Clio, Calliope, and Virgil: The Definitions of History and Poetry

These echoes present us with the odd inconsistency of Boccaccio's evocation of epic poetry—an epic containing inaccuracies that he himself acknowledges and corrects, no less—in a prose historical treatise that has frequently been praised by critics as marking Boccaccio's engagement with the new humanist learning, the *De casibus* advertising its self-conscious status as a history through its rewritings of Livy and Valerius Maximus.[24] Scholarly fastidiousness would suggest that history and poetry are two separate categories. In the *Genealogia* Boccaccio certainly distinguished between the two genres, as in his observation that poetic license permits the narration of events in medias res, "for poets are not like historians, who begin their account at some convenient beginning and describe events in the unbroken order of their occurrence to the end. Such, we observe, was Lucan's method, wherefore we think of him rather as a metrical historian than a poet."[25] In this distinction he follows Servius (In *Aen.* 1.382), who represents only one figure in a lengthy grammarians' school debate over Lucan's status.[26] Boccaccio certainly identifies his *De casibus* as history.[27] And as he begins with Adam and Eve no one can accuse him of starting out of sequence.

It is true that Boccaccio merged his twin interests in the past and the poetic from his earliest literary endeavors: his youthful *zibaldoni*, or notebooks, included translations of Valerius Maximus, Livy, and Orosius alongside his transcription of the epistolary exchanges of eclogues between Dante and Giovanni del Virgilio, as well as a verse *cento* describing Roman history. Similarly his three antique fictions—*Il Filostrato*, *Il Filocolo*, and the *Teseida*—all demonstrate thoughtful depictions of the pagan world in ways that Boccaccio most likely considered to be historically accurate.[28] But the *De casibus* is traditionally thought to be a more sophisticated and erudite engagement with classical letters, avoiding what some view as an uneasy marriage between classicism and fiction represented by the exuberant romances. In order for us to appreciate why for Boccaccio the writing of the *De casibus* would resonate so of Virgil, and why he would interrupt a history to include a defense of pagan poetry (3.14), we must understand what Virgil represented to Boccaccio and how the medieval reception of the ancient poet contributed to the generic distinctions between the two literary modes of historical and poetic writing.

Virgil was, of course, the leading *auctor* of the Middle Ages, revered as a source of wisdom both in his verse (to the superstitious extent of fortune-telling with the *sortes Virgilianae*) and in his own biography (his life accruing legends depicting him as a magus).[29] He is, as Boccaccio calls him in his fourth epistle, *altissimus poeta*,[30] and his poetry was thought to contain all knowledge in microcosm: "For in fact," as Macrobius explains in the *Saturnalia* (a text Boccaccio owned),[31] "if you look closely into the nature of the universe, you will find a striking resemblance between the handiwork of the divine craftsman and that of our poet."[32] No surprise, then, that allegorical interpretations of the *Aeneid*, beginning with Fulgentius's *Vergiliana contentia*,[33] attempted to reveal the truths cloaked under the pleasing veil of poetic fiction. And book 6 particularly lent itself to exposition, singled out by Servius himself as a rich lode for allegorical mining: "for certainly, all of Virgil is filled with knowledge, and that book holds preeminence" (*Totus quidem Vergilius scientia plenus est, in qua hic liber possidet principatum*).[34] Allegorical interpretations are, however, only one facet of the complex reception of the *Aeneid* in the Middle Ages: there was also the grammarian's Virgil, read in part as a fount of historical facts about antique cult and legal practices, and in part as a source for moral education, which coincides with later epideictic interpretations of Virgil associated with Italian humanists, commending the behavior and habits of Aeneas.[35] And what is Boccaccio's *De casibus* if not an exercise in epideictic rhetoric, in the praise and blame of past rulers?

Virgil's authority as a teacher of ethics was not the only motivation for Boccaccio's evocation of the *Aeneid* in the *De casibus*, however. Even more suggestive is that Boccaccio's understanding of the relationship between history and poetry must surely be derived in part from the categorization of *historia* and *fabula* in the commentary on the *Aeneid* by Servius Grammaticus. As Daniel Dietz notes, for Servius *historia* encompasses both real occurrences in the past (*res gesta, factum*, which is our modern notion of "history") and that which seems probable, reasonable, and natural, including the euhemeristic (*argumentum, secundam naturam*), leaving for *fabula* only falsehood, improbability, and poetic fiction.[36] Yet what appears to be a complete condemnation of all poetry in actuality opens the space for certain poetry, particularly epic, to be read as a type of *historia*, thereby containing *argumentum* and wisdom. If allowances are made for poetic license (*poetica licentia*), and if mythological or divine happenings that at first appear improbable can be explained away through a euhemeristic or natural interpretation, then an epic poem can qualify as history in that it mingles reality and fiction.[37] Virgil, then, is a historian as well as a poet, and ought to be most lauded as his writing contains hidden truths as well as surface beauties.[38] Hence why in Canto 5 of Boccaccio's *Amorosa Visione* the seven ladies representing the Liberal Arts are surrounded by poets and historians seated together on the lawn, and Virgil is the first and most elaborately described of this company.

Boccaccio's articulation of the relationship between poetry and history would also have been indebted to another text associated with the *Aeneid* in the Middle Ages, Macrobius's *Commentarii in Somnium Scipionis*. According to Macrobius, proper fiction (*fabula*) that encourages commendable behavior in the reader "rests on a solid foundation of truth" (*fundatur veri soliditate*) that is "presented beneath the modest veil of allegory" (*sub pio figmentorum velamine honesties . . . enuntiatur*).[39] Boccaccio's theory of poetry relating high truths veiled by fiction, as discussed in *De casibus* 3.14, is immediately recognizable in this configuration.[40] And while Macrobius never explicitly addresses the connections between *historia* and *fabula*, the assignment of the Muses to different spheres (*Commentarii* 2.3.1–4) does offer an oblique comment upon this debate. Clio and Calliope, the first and the last of the nine sisters, embody the sororal relationship between history and epic poetry. Together the daughters of Jove represent an ascent to wisdom, commencing with history and culminating in epic. As Boccaccio observes in the *Genealogia* (citing almost verbatim Fulgentius, *Mitologiarium libri* 1.15),

We indeed say that the nine muses represent the stages of learning and knowledge. The first is Clio as the first thought of learning. For *Clios* in Greek means *fame*, and since no one seeks knowledge unless he may advance the worthiness of his fame, therefore the first is named *Clio*, that is, the *thought of pursuing knowledge*. . . . The ninth is Calliope, that is, she of the excellent voice. Therefore, this shall be the order. First is the desire for learning . . . ninth to make known agreeably what you single out.

Nos vero novem Musas doctrine atque scientie dicimus modos, hoc est: prima Clio quasi prima cogitatio discendi; Clios *enim grece* fama *dicitur, et quoniam nullas scientiam querit, nisi in qua fame sue protelet dignitatem, ob hanc rem prima* Clio *appellate est, id est* cogitatio querende scientie. . . . *Nona Caliope, id est optime vocis. Ergo hic erit ordo. Primum est velle doctrinam . . . nonum bene proferre quod elegeris.* (Gen. 11.2)

This mythographic interpretation of the Muses illustrates a sentiment akin to that of the allegorical tradition of interpreting Aeneas's descent to the underworld as a progression through the "stages of learning and knowledge," particularly in the commentary ascribed to Bernardus Silvestris.[41] Boccaccio appears to have especially associated this passage from Fulgentius with Virgil, as he had also copied it into his Miscellanea Laurenziana alongside a set of verses on the Muses from the *Appendix Virgiliana*.[42] If we return now to Macrobius's identification of the celestial spheres with individual muses, the appropriateness of history presiding over the lowest realm (which Macrobius himself silently ignores) becomes strikingly clear: the earth, as the starting point for the soul's return to the empyrean, is aligned with the first stage in the ascension to knowledge; the world is also the setting for those mortal events of which Clio sings; she is, as her name indicates, fame, and therefore she is bounded by the meniscus of this sphere (a lesson Scipio himself learns in his communion with his grandfather, gazing down at the tiny orb). Tempted by personal ambition (Clio), one initiates a journey to wisdom that culminates with making known with "pleasing voice" (Calliope) what knowledge has been selected and attained. For Boccaccio this cosmology would have provided a celestial antecedent for the use of an epic poet in the writing of history. An instructional compendium like the *De casibus* reenacts this hierarchy, relating the fame of fallen kings and appealing to the reader's desires for advancement, while presenting in engaging style only those carefully chosen examples that corroborate the author's lesson of Fortune's instability. The best history, in fact, would be epic poetry like Virgil's.

Macrobius was not simply another convenient late antique *auctor* opportunely chanced upon by Boccaccio; both of Macrobius's major treatises circulating in the Middle Ages, the *Commentarii* and the *Saturnalia*, were rich with Virgilian associations. The bulk of the *Saturnalia* was dedicated to a systematic exposition of Virgil's expertise in subjects ranging from cultic observances to oratory. The *Commentarii* made frequent citations from the *Aeneid*. Structurally, *Aeneid* 6's resonances with the *Somnium Scipionis* (consisting of an interview between a son and a deceased paternal figure, with lessons on the limitations of the Roman Empire and the relationship between the soul and the body) would naturally have linked Macrobius with Virgil.[43] In a more localized sense for Boccaccio, fourteenth-century commentators on Virgil were greatly indebted to Macrobius, especially in explaining cosmological and Platonic elements of *Aeneid* 6. Petrarch was particularly diligent in transcribing passages from the *Commentarii* into his personal manuscript of Virgil's *corpus*, the Codex Ambrosianus (which Boccaccio certainly would have read during his 1350 and 1351 visits to the poet laureate); of Petrarch's twenty-five citations from Macrobius, over half are in reference to Aeneas's descent to the underworld.[44]

This context demonstrates the degree to which nearly any critical reading for Boccaccio was steeped in Virgil. Boccaccio's theory of poetry and its operations is a melding of concepts as discussed by Macrobius and Servius in explicitly Virgilian settings. Not simply the fine points of genre distinctions, however, but epistemology itself was comprehended by Boccaccio within a specifically Virgilian context. How knowledge is defined, into what categories it is divided, the very process of learning—Boccaccio's articulation of any of these concepts, through the assembling of his authorities, would have repeatedly led him back to Virgil. If he at times seems to be suggesting that the writing of the *De casibus* is his own Aeneidic wandering, subject to the buffets of Fortune, this is more than simply the *De casibus* becoming an allegory of its own production. It is a testament to the all-pervasive hold of Virgil's poetry over the wonderfully allusive and erudite mind of Boccaccio. Explicit quotations need not be present in order to recognize Virgil's influence. At this level of saturation, the text itself can be absent or above discussion; the *Aeneid* and its tradition permeate the very substance of language and thought. It becomes a ghost, not felt materially but still undeniably present. Only in this broader context of how, for Boccaccio, truth and fiction can assist each other is his inclusion of a defense of poetry in the *De casibus* understandable. To write a history that would effect a moral change in its reader meant writing a Virgilian history.

III. Fathers, Sons, and the Tomb

One implication raised by refracting Boccaccio's *De casibus* through the prism of *Aeneid* 6 is that the obligation of the living to the dead is to write their stories, to enshrine in these literary assemblies of great men their memories for future generations. The recounting of lives connects souls across the gulf of time. As Anchises mourns for the downcast Marcellus, "Grant me to scatter in handfuls lilies of purple blossom, to heap at least these gifts on my descendant's shade and perform an unavailing duty" (*manibus date lilia plenis, / purpureos spargam flores animaque nepotis / his saltem accumulem donis, et fungar inani / munere*; *Aen.* 6.883–86). At the heart of this simple pronouncement lies a beautifully poignant paradox that embodies the ties joining generations beyond an individual's lifetime: the sire of the new Roman *gentis*, rather than receiving his own memorial, desires to perform funerary rites for the lost promise of Augustus's heir, destined for a too-brief tenure on earth ages into the future. And fame, the perpetuation of the memory of others, is one way in which this relationship is acknowledged and celebrated. Hence Boccaccio describes his *Trattatello in laude di Dante* as providing a worthy tomb for the exiled poet through his biography (sec. 6). As the apparition of Petrarch in the *De casibus* explains,

Fame makes very long our too brief span of mortal life, and as if she gave us another life, she bears witness to the honors earned by one who is dead. It is by this means that we praise and honor Abraham, Moses, Aristotle, Virgil, Scipio Africanus, and the Catos as if they were actually present. We feel a great pleasure within our souls for the fame that they receive from us, for we believe by our labors we will be able to earn the same thing from those who come after us. And thus, in hope, we anticipate a future glory. (204)

Hec [Fama] brevissimum mortalis vite tempus facit amplissimum et, quasi vita alia, defunctorum posteriati meritos testator honores. . . . Cuius rei evidentissimum argumentum est quod suo robere literis infixo: . . . Abraham . . . , Moysen . . . , Homerum . . . , Aristotilem . . . , Affricanum . . . , Catones aliosque insignes viros, quos quasi perenni viriditate ipsa in hodiernum usque deduxit perpetuos. Quos, ea agente, noscimus laudamus et colimus magnamque anni voluptatem sentimus, dum id quod illi suscipiunt a nobis, nos labore nostro apud futuros posse suscipere credimus; et sic futuram gloriam spirants anticipamus. (8.1.11–12)

This dynasty of mutual admiration is the empire that Boccaccio-the-Aeneas seeks to found: a *gens* connected through time by the celebration of the illustrious ("just as those who came before us were of use to us, so will we be of advantage to those who come after" [206]; *ut tanquam preteriti labore suo profuere nobis, sic et nos nostro valeamus posteris* [8.1.26]). It is a literary empire linked by renown.

And yet there seems to be an inherent contradiction at this moment: what does it mean to construct a *fallen* empire, to seek everlasting fame in the midst of an enterprise condemning ambition and illustrating the mutability of this life? We seem to be presented with a contest between Boethius and Petrarch. For if I have earlier likened Petrarch's sudden manifestation in *De casibus* 8.1 to Mercury's descent to Aeneas, surely the other literary allusion intended is to Lady Philosophy appearing to Boethius, castigating him for lethargy and his self-forgetfulness. But Boethius was counseled to relinquish his desires for personal fame and to accept the uselessness of history in commemoration (2.pr.7), "For if you think that fame can lengthen life / By mortal famousness immortalized, / The day will come that takes your fame as well, / And there a second death for you awaits" (2.met.7.23–26; *Quodsi putatis longius vitam trahi / mortalis aura nominis, / cum sera vobis rapiet hoc etiam dies, / iam vos secunda mors manet*).[45] Lady Philosophy mocks the very type of literary project in which Boccaccio is engaged, as well as its fictional promise to animate the dead. The actual Petrarch occasionally conceded this instability of fame, as in the *Secretum* (first dialogue), in the *De remediis utriusque fortune* (1.117), and in the *Trionfi*, when the pageant of Fame is ultimately superseded by that of Time. Boccaccio's Petrarch, however, argues that the quest for renown is not a worthless enterprise; with an evangelical fervor he insists that renown for virtue is not simply desirable, but crucial to prove one's membership among the saved: "then we will have immortal fame; then we will believe that in the worldly campaign, we will have fought on God's side, not on the side of sin" (206; *ut videamur hac in peregrinatione mortali Deo et non vitiis militasse*; 8.1.26).

If these positions are indeed reconcilable, if Boccaccio can praise *gloriam famamque* while also writing a *contemptus mundi*, then perhaps we should look to the ghost of Dante in *De casibus* 9.13 for a possible resolution. When Dante refuses to allow Boccaccio to tell his story, and pushes forward Walter, Duke of Athens, as a subject instead, he explains that he himself has no place among this crowd of miserable shades, for he was not conquered by Fortune. We realize that Dante is of the same category as those illustrious whom Boccaccio's Petrarch urges us to follow, those who have achieved fame through virtue. Dante should be admired for withstanding the revolutions of Fortune's wheel stoically; heedless of the mutable goods of this world, he persevered in exile, his lasting legacy a collection of moral philosophy and a salvific vision of heaven. We should not confuse, then, the false fame achieved through the pursuit of instable goods with the spiritual fame attained by those who understand the blind operations of Fortune. And while the *De casibus* certainly includes biographies of Fortune's victims who nevertheless ought to be praised (e.g., Dido, Cicero, Zenobia), we must never forget that "although there may be great virtue in one who is rising in fortune, yet he must fall eventually" (209; *etsi multa sit virtus, ascendenti tamen quandoque cadendum est*; 8.6.9). If the destination is to be an empire of the illustrious virtuous, then the *De casibus* is the journey to lead to that promised place, for by its repeated examples it directs the readers to a deeper understanding of Fortune's machinations, freeing them to distinguish virtue from false goods. This is the obligation Boccaccio feels toward his readers, both those contemporary princes consumed by sensuality, alluded to in the proem, and also those readers yet to come: "But it is not enough to have awakened those who were asleep, unless they have also been led into the clear light. They must develop strength of belief," he writes, "then we will have fulfilled our promise that through the stories of our overthrown ancestors, their faith has increased" (111; *Sane, cum eduxisse soporatos in vigiliam satis non sit, ni in lucem deducantur integram, in solidationem credulitatis iam sumpte procedendum est, ut, dum promissa sequemur, fides etiam maiorum deiectorum copia amplietur*; 4.pr.4). At this juncture, Boccaccio is concerned for his descendants, those later generations who will come to the *De casibus* with hardened hearts.

Rather than helplessly scattering purple lilies, as does Anchises, Boccaccio offers *florilegia* of instruction. Because he begins his history with Adam and Eve, his empire is not bounded by nation: all the dead are our ancestors, all those to come our descendants. Within this framework, the various exhortatory asides (praising chastity, condemning greed, and the like) are not intrusive pieties, "medievalizing" sermons that interrupt what should be a classical catalogue of worthies similar to Petrarch's *De viris illustribus*; instead they become the real substance of the *De casibus*, housed within an architecture of lives.

Reading *Aeneid* 6 through a *De casibus* lens helps to smooth this same contradiction as raised in Aeneas's colloquium with his father. Anchises, like a good Neoplatonist, describes the bliss of the souls in the Elysian Fields and the degradations that await them once they drink of Lethe and are joined with a corporeal form;[46] yet he then with no sense of irony introduces the parade of glorious Romans yet to be and glowingly describes the magnitude of their achievements. If Anchises is to be criticized for being a bad philosopher, presented by Virgil in a setting intentionally reminiscent of Scipio's interview with his grandfather but empty of the underlying stoic message of the triviality of fame,[47] Boccaccio's Petrarch provides that absent justification for praise. Petrarch's celebration of reputation, in fact, oddly suggests that fame can assist in the soul's Neoplatonic return to the empyrean: "with the greatest luster renown leads the spirit of those who merit it up to the heavens, as if they were on a paved highway" (204; *Hec [fama] morientium corporum animas, quasi per stratum iter, summa cum claritate deducit in cellos*; 8.1.10). This is a similar function to that which Macrobius assigns to music at funerals (*Commentarii* 2.3.6), and perhaps Petrarch even intends a connection between a poet's *carmen* and the harmonies of the spheres. Perhaps, too, there is an allusion here to Apollo's address to Ascanius in *Aen.* 9, when the god of poetry congratulates Aeneas's son for his valor while situating him within a familial line: "thus is the path to the stars, you son of gods and sire of gods-to-be" (*sic itur ad astra, / dis genite et geniture deos*; 9.641–42).

Boccaccio's Petrarch does more than simply mimic classical attitudes toward fame's transcendence, though: he attaches a purgatorial purpose to the writing of history. By preserving fame, biography is the literary humanistic equivalent to the chantry chapel, a method by which the living can intervene and assist the dead. (This suggestion that the dead's happiness and fortune continue to be affected by the living may also in part derive from Aristotle's *Nicomachean Ethics*, 1.11.) In this way the present generation is the tender custodian to those who have grown still. Thus the *De casibus* is as much Boccaccio's response to Dante's *Purgatorio* as to Petrarch's *De viris illustribus*: *Purgatorio* is the *cantica* exploring both how prayer can intercede across the gulf of mortality and how artistry—visual, verbal, musical—offers moral guidance and consolation, often beyond the grave (Statius's conversion to Christianity through reading Virgil's fourth eclogue being the supreme example, *Purg.* 22). Boccaccio grafts this notion of the communion of souls onto the antique cult of fame, which the Petrarchan *De viris illustribus* consciously sought to revive. Rather than empty into metaphor the apotheosis to the stars and the siring of gods, Boccaccio replaces euhemerism with intercession, and taking a cue from Dante, he looks to Virgil as the primary guide for this project harmonizing classical fame with Christian moral instruction.

More than simply memorializing the dead, then, Boccaccio sees biography as part of a larger responsibility: keeping the dead present to us as our teachers and parents. For the dead survive not just textually but spatially: it is a crowded world, with an afterlife peopled with the damned, the blessed, and (perhaps the majority) the maculated saved undergoing purgation—dimensions where the souls of the dead are sentient and active: the souls of Virgil, of Dante, of Boccaccio's own father, Boccaccino di Chelino.

Boccaccio's poetic career was fraught with paternal tension. His trademark chattiness reveals his ambivalence toward his father, a recurring figure who creeps into his writings. We are given the image of a "cold-hearted, harsh, stingy old man" from the *Commedia della Ninfale* (44); a picture of Boccaccino clawing the pile of gold to no avail in the *Amorosa Visione*'s Triumph of Wealth (Canto 14); a veiled pastoral account of his treacherous seduction and abandonment of Boccaccio's mother in *Filocolo* 5.8 (and perhaps repeated in the *Commedia della Ninfale* 23).[48] Even if these representations are somewhat recuperated in Eclogue 14 (*Olympia*) by the affectionate rejoicing with which Boccaccino welcomes into heaven his granddaughter, Boccaccio's deceased, illegitimate daughter Violante,[49] Boccaccino remains a failed businessman, deeply disappointed by his son's decision not to follow in the banking career he had chosen for him. He also remains charged with his son's self-perceived failure to fulfill his poetic aspirations:

Whatever the vocation of others, mine, as experience from my mother's womb has shown, is clearly the study of poetry. For this, I believe, I was born. . . . If my father had only been favorable to such a course at a time of life when I was more adaptable, I do not doubt that I should have taken my place among the poets of fame. But while he tried to bend my mind first into business and next into a lucrative profession, it came to pass that I turned out neither a business man, nor a canon-lawyer, and missed being a good poet besides.
Verum ad quoscunque actus natura produxerit alios, me quidem, experientia teste, ad poeticas meditationes dispositum ex utero matris eduxit et meo iudicio in hoc natus sum. . . . Nec dubito, dum etas in hoc aptior erat, si equo genitor tulisset animo, quin inter celebres poetas unus evaissem, verum dum in lucrosas artes primo, inde in lucrosam facultatem ingenium flectere conatur meum, factum est ut nec negociator sim, nec evaderem canonista, et perderem poetam esse conspicuum.[50]

Boccaccio was always conscious of his disobedience, so different from Aeneas's honoring of Anchises's wishes, no matter how misguided they were (think only of the troubles caused by Anchises's mistaken interpretation of the Delian prophecy [*Aen.* 3.90–171]). And the Virgilian tradition particularly for Boccaccio would have been one saturated with loving exchanges between fathers and sons: Macrobius had dedicated both the *Saturnalia* and the *Commentarii in Somnium Scipionis* to his own son Eustachius for his education; Petrarch's Codex Ambrosianus was a gift from Petrarch's father, Petracco de Parenzo;[51] Boccaccio's literary hero Dante insisted that "it is appropriate for one to love one's elders, from whom one has received being, nature, and education, so as not to seem ungrateful" when citing Aeneas's memorial to Anchises.[52] Boccaccino left no such literary testament to his son, and Boccaccio maintained no such respect for his father. One wonders if Boccaccio had written a *Secretum meum* like Petrarch's how much of his confession would have been devoted to exonerating his lack of fealty to Boccaccino.

This disloyalty consisted of Boccaccio's transferring his *pietas* from his mercantile biological father to his different spiritual fathers. Dante, of course, was one such paternal presence for Boccaccio, and when they meet in *De casibus* 9.13 Boccaccio is aghast at the thought that he has not fulfilled his filial duty by including a suitable biography of Dante within his encyclopedic collection: "You know, greatest father, that my powers are too weak for such a burden" (*Scis, pater optime, quam fragiles tanto oneri michi vires sint*).[53] Boccaccio's protestation reveals his anxiety that he does not possess the heroism of Aeneas, for I believe that a phrase linking "father" and "burden" (particularly the use of *oneri*) cannot but evoke Aeneas's flight from the flaming towers of Troy, with Anchises hoisted upon his back and with hands clasped with young Ascanius, trebling his steps to keep up with his father on his short little legs. "Fearing alike for my companion and my *burden*" (*comitique* onerique *timentem*; *Aen.* 2.729): this image of three generations sustained by one body is a metonymy for Rome, its Trojan past and triumphant future linked by the Dardan Diaspora, but it becomes also a figure for Boccaccio's biographical project, the labor required to effect moral change in future readers while transporting past fathers from ruins. The history of Dante, of one who has escaped the destruction of Fortune's wrath, is the *onus* Boccaccio fears he will be asked to carry and be found wanting in strength.

Dante reciprocates the familial exchange, "Stop, my son, and do not squander your words so volubly in my praise. Show me some of your thrifty nature. I know your skill, and know what I have earned" (227; *Siste, fili mi, tam effluenter in laudes mea effundere verba, et te tam parcum tuarum ostendere. Novi ingenium tuum; et quid merear novi*). In truth, Boccaccio was not meager with his words as he drafted his *Trattatello in laude di Dante* in 1351 and revised it in 1360, thus composing it simultaneously with the first redaction of the *De casibus*.[54] Boccaccio's reverence for Dante even elicited praise from another of his literary fathers, Petrarch:

You expressly add as justification for your praise [of Dante] that he was your first guide and the light of your youthful studies. This is proper, grateful, accurate, and, to speak candidly, fitting acknowledgment; for if we owe everything to the creators of our bodies and much to our benefactors, what do we not owe to the parents and fashioners of our minds? How much more deserving of our gratitude are those who cultivated our minds than those who tended to our bodies is realized by whoever has a just perspective on both, for he will recognize the one as an immortal gift and the other as a perishable and mortal one.

Inseris nominatim hanc huius officii tui excusationem, quod ille tibi adolescentulo primus studiorum dux et prima fax fuerit. Iuste quidem, grate memoriter et, ut proprie dicam, pie; si enim gentoribus corporum nostrorum omnia, si fortunarum auctoribus multa debemus, quid non ingeniorum parentibus ac formatoribus debeamus? Quanto enim melius de nobis meriti sint qui animum nostrum excoluere quam qui corpus, quisquis utrique iustum precium ponit, intelligent, et alterum caducum et mortale fatebitur. (Fam. 21.15)[55]

(In this same letter, however, Petrarch is at great pains to defend himself to Boccaccio against the charge of envy: Petrarch himself refuses to acknowledge Dante as any such literary father to him, admitting he never owned a manuscript of Dante's work for fear of being drawn under his influence at an impressionable age.)

The sire most deserving of gratitude for an immortal gift, however, was Virgil. Not only was Virgil familiar as a parent through Dante's *Commedia*, in which he is lovingly referred to as both father and mother, but Virgil was particularly responsible for Boccaccio's decision to pursue poetry. As Filippo Villani relates, while Boccaccio was in Naples about his father's business he made a pilgrimage, alone and unhappy, to Virgil's tomb. At that moment, contemplating the Mantuan poet, Boccaccio renounced both Mammon and Boccaccino: "When Giovanni had thought admiringly about the grave and its contents for some time, he suddenly began to blame and lament his fortune, which forced him to devote himself to hated commerce. Thus, seized by a sudden love for the Pierian Muses, he returned home scorning all that was commerce, and gave himself to studying poetry ardently."[56] Villani can be forgiven the romance of this episode, as Boccaccio's early writings demonstrate his particular devotion to Virgil's resting place: a number of his early letters from Naples are dated from his tomb (*data sub monte Falerno apud busta Maronis Virgilii*; see epistles 1, 2, 4) and in *Il Filocolo* Florio and his companions make a similar journey to the mausoleum (4.14). Perhaps Villani even had in mind Boccaccio's second epistle from 1339, in which he describes how, while staying in "Napoli virgiliana," he arose one morning and strolled carefree to Virgil's tomb; suddenly he had a vision of a woman of surpassing beauty amid lightning and thunder. Boccaccio became enthralled by Fortune and her fickle wheel, but thankfully through divine intervention he was released, instructed to seek the assistance of a famous learned man, knowledgeable in all sciences and arts. If the addressee of this *ars dictaminis* exercise is indeed Petrarch, whom in 1339 Boccaccio knew only by reputation,[57] then even at this early stage in his career Boccaccio is creating the succession of poetic generations that he outlines in the fourteenth book of *Genealogia deorum gentilium*.

Boccaccio would not have been alone in the fanciful attribution of conversion to Virgil's tomb. Its cult was rich in legend, for among the miracles and magics associated with the place was the tradition that St. Paul had sojourned to Naples to convert Virgil if still alive, only to be greeted by either (depending upon the version) his ashes or copper automata guarding the poet's shade as he read by torchlight.[58] How fitting that the persuasive apostle of the Gentiles should seek out the poet embodying the apogee of pagan wisdom and prophecy! How appropriate that St. Paul, who while corporeal had been blessed with a vision of the afterlife,[59] should desire the salvation of Aeneas's author! "*Io non Enëa, io non Paulo sono*," Dante protests to Virgil before embarking on his own otherworldly journey (*Inf.* 2.32). This tradition was certainly known to Petrarch: on a flyleaf of the Codex Ambrosianus he had copied verses from the service of the feast day commemorating St. Paul's conversion, which describe the Apostle's grief upon reaching Virgil's tomb, too late to offer saving grace.[60] And while Boccaccio would not yet have met Petrarch in 1339, much less have read his personal manuscript, as a resident in Naples for over a decade he would have known this legend, and his own conversion to poetry would have been adumbrated by these shared associations among Virgil, St. Paul, and Dante.

Pius Boccaccio writes the *De casibus* as an act of filial responsibility to his poetic father. In doing so, he grafts himself into the family tree, joining the line of succession Virgil himself consciously commenced with his homage to his epic progenitor, Ennius.[61] Even though the *De casibus* is a history, Boccaccio wistfully reminds his reader that "I wish to be and take great pains that I may be a poet. . . . If the highest type of man is a poet, then his poetry is the highest achievement" (106; [*poeta*] *esse quidem opto et pro viribus ut sim studeo. . . . et si optimus homo sit, poesis optima apparebit*; 3.14.10, 14). That a defense of the morality of pagan poetry—and a defiant avowal of his own devotion to that cause—should appear here suggests that even the *De casibus*, a prose history, will show a family resemblance to the *Aeneid*. Perhaps if Boccaccio were to have made use of the same anecdote that Petrarch had from Suetonius, he would have said that he looks into the pages of the past for "fathers, not corpses."

Notes

1. Vladimiro Zabughin briefly surveys Virgil's influence upon Boccaccio, although he does not mention the *De casibus virorum illustrium*: *Vergilio nel Rinasci-*

mento italiano di Dante a Torquato Tasso, I: Il Trecento ed il Quattrocento, ed. Stefano Carrai and Alberto Cavarzere (1921; reprint, Trent: 2000), 39–43. The study of Virgil's influence upon Boccaccio's writings by Lao Paoletti mainly focuses upon Boccaccio's *Eclogues*: "Virgilio e Boccaccio," in R. Chevallier, ed., *Présence de Virgile: Actes du Colloque des 9, 11 et 12 Décembre 1976*, Caesarodunum 13 (Paris: Société d'édition "Les belles letters," 1978), 249–63. Francesco Bruni discusses Boccaccio's familiarity with the *Aeneid* and medieval Florentine redactions that reorder Trojan material in *Boccaccio: L'invenzione della letteratura mezzana* (Bologna: Società editrice il Mulino, 1990), 100–109; he particularly examines Boccaccio's imitations of Aeneas's dream of Hector (*Aen.* 2.270–79) in *Filocolo* and *Elegia di madonna Fiammetta*. Charles G. Osgood provides a brief survey of Boccaccio's use of ancient grammarian biographies of Virgil in "Boccaccio's Knowledge of the Life of Vergil," *Classical Philology* 25 (1930): 27–36. Giuseppe Velli details Boccaccio's borrowings from *Aeneid* 6 in his *Teseida* as well as his commentary upon Dante's *Commedia*: "L'Apoteosi di Arcita: Ideologia e coscienza storica nel 'Teseida,'" *Petrarca e Boccaccio: Tradizione, memoria, scrittura*, Studi sul Petrarca 7 (Padua: Editrice Antenore, 1979), 122–55 (132–45).

2. For the relationship between Boccaccio and Petrarch, see Giuseppe Billanovich, "Il piú grande discepolo," *Petrarca letterato, I: Lo scrittoio del Petrarca* (Rome: Edizioni di Storia e Letteratura, 1947), 57–294 (117–19 specifically discusses Petrarch's use of Virgil in the laureation interview and the impressions it may have made upon Boccaccio); Vittore Branca, *Boccaccio: The Man and His Works*, trans. Richard Monges (New York: New York University Press, 1976), 86–127. Branca argues elsewhere that this shift to more serious Latin works did not stifle Boccaccio's innate genius as a storyteller and that we ought to regard the *De casibus* as the predecessor for the historical novel: "Il Romanzare storico del Boccaccio," in Siegfried Loewe et al., *Literatur ohne Grenzen: Festschrift für Erika Kanduth* (Frankfurt: Peter Lang, 1993), 65–71.

3. Latin quotations from the *De casibus* are taken from the edition by Pier Giorgio Ricci and Vittorio Zaccaria, volume 9 of *Tutte le opere di Giovanni Boccaccio*, gen. ed. Vittore Branca, 13 vols., I Classici Mondadori (Milan: Mondadori, 1983); their text provides a complete facing page Italian translation. English quotations are based upon Louis Brewer Hall's abridged translations, *The Fates of Illustrious Men* (New York: Frederick Ungar Publishing, 1965), with my silent emendations. Latin quotations are accompanied with book and chapter citations; English translations are followed with the page number of Hall's version.

4. Giuseppe Chiecchi demonstrates how the rhetorical style of Boccaccio's narration is nearly as diverse as his examples, "Sollecitazioni narrative nel *De casibus virorum illustrium*," *Studi sul Boccaccio* 19 (1990): 103–49. Petrarch may have originally intended his collection to have a similarly inclusive structure. From 1351 to 1353 (roughly contemporaneous with both Boccaccio's visit and the starting of the *De casibus*) Petrarch planned for his *De viris illustribus* to stretch from Adam to possibly the present and drafted a long preface to accompany it. Petrarch rejected this "all-ages" plan, however, and in its final form the *De viris illustribus* encompassed only Romulus to Titus, with a different, shorter preface; see Benjamin J. Kohl, "Petrarch's Prefaces to *De viris illustribus*," *History and Theory* 13 (1974): 132–37 (133–34). The 1351–53 version, complete from Adam to Caesar, can be found (with Italian translation) in Francesco Petrarca, *Prose*, ed. G. Martellotti et al. (Milan and Naples: Riccardo Ricciardi, 1955), 218–67. The later version is partially available in the critical edition

(containing only Romulus through Cato); Francesco Petrarca, *De viris illustribus*, ed. Guido Martellotti, vol. 1 (Florence: G. C. Sansoni, 1964); the complete Romulus to Trajan Latin text, with Trecento Italian translation by Donato Albanzani, is in Francesco Petrarca, *De viris illustribus*, ed. Luigi Razzolini, 2 vols. (Bologna, 1874).

5. Billanovich, *Restauri boccacceschi* (Rome: Edizioni di Storia e Letteratura, 1945), 135–43, and *Petrarca letterato*, I, 153–56; Paoletti, "Virgilio e Boccaccio," 252 and n. 13; Laura D. Kellogg, *Boccaccio's and Chaucer's Cressida* (New York: Peter Lang, 1995), 105–23. For a more nuanced understanding of Boccaccio's use of the chaste Dido, his relation to Virgil, and his debt to Petrarch, see Craig Kallendorf, *In Praise of Aeneas: Virgil and Epideictic Rhetoric in the Early Italian Renaissance* (Hanover and London: University Press of New England, 1989), 58–76, which is a variation of his article "Boccaccio's Dido and the Rhetorical Criticism of Virgil's *Aeneid*," *Studies in Philology* 82 (1985): 401–15. (See also 191, n. 12, in Kallendorf, *In Praise of Aeneas*, for a fuller list of the criticism on Boccaccio's use of the Dido story.) For the transmission of the chaste Dido accounts, see Mary Louise Lord, "Dido as an Example of Chastity: The Influence of Example Literature," *Harvard Library Bulletin* 17 (1969): 22–44, 216–32; and Marilynn Desmond, *Reading Dido: Gender, Textuality and the Medieval Aeneid*, Medieval Cultures 8 (Minneapolis and London: University of Minnesota Press, 1994), esp. 55–73 for Boccaccio.

6. Particularly *Aen.* 2.403 and 2.526 in the accounts of Cassandra being pulled by her hair into slavery and the death of Polites.

7. "Echoes of the *Culex* in Boccaccio's *De casibus*," *Giornale Italiano di Filologia* 53 (2001): 237–54, and "A Quotation from the *Culex* in Boccaccio's *De casibus*," *Modern Language Review* 97 (2002): 312–23. Boccaccio's knowledge of the *Appendix Vergiliana* is reviewed by Mary Louise Lord, "Boccaccio's *Virgiliana* in the 'Miscellanea Latina,'" *Italia medioevale e umanistica* 34 (1991): 127–97. Giuseppe Velli discusses in particular Boccaccio's familiarity with the *Moretum*: "Cultura e 'imitatio' nel primo Boccaccio," *Petrarca e Boccaccio*, 61–96 (61–71).

8. In this my aims are similar to those of Barbara Nolan's in her studies of Boccaccio's *Il Filostrato* and *Teseida*, in which she sought to recognize the influence of the works of Ovid as well as the French *romans antiques* and medieval commentaries upon the *Heroides* not through explicit allusion but in character development: "They are pervasively present, but in a muted, oblique way" (121); see chapters 4 (119–54, 314–27) and 5 (155–97, 327–38) of *Chaucer and the Tradition of the* Roman Antique (Cambridge: Cambridge University Press, 1992).

9. Boccaccio was particularly fond of this image, using it as well in *Il Filostrato* 9.3–4, *Teseida* 12.86, and *Il Filocolo* 5.97.

10. Dante's reliance upon the *Aeneid* in conceiving his journey through the afterlife is most obviously evident by his having Virgil as his guide and by his protestation that he is not Aeneas (*Inf.* 2.23); for Dante's specific rewriting of *Aen.* 6 in his meeting with Cacciaguida in *Par.* 15–17, see Jeffrey T. Schnapp, *The Transfiguration of History at the Center of Dante's* Paradise (Princeton, NJ: Princeton University Press, 1986), 130–49.

11. *Genealogia deorum gentilium*, 14.13.16, edited with facing page Italian translation by Vittorio Zaccaria as volumes 7 and 8 of *Tutte le opere di Giovanni Boccaccio*, gen. ed. Branca (Milan: Mondadori, 1998); English translation from *Boccaccio on Poetry*, trans. Charles G. Osgood, Library of Liberal Arts (1930; reprint, New York: Liberal Arts Press, 1956), 69.

12. The paraphrase of Suetonius is from *Divus Augustus*, 18, reporting a remark of

Augustus's upon being asked if he wished to see the tombs of the Ptolemies after he had shown obsequies to the grave of Alexander.

13. From his first, longer preface to the *De viris illustribus* (1351–53), which Boccaccio surely would have known at the time of writing the *De casibus*. Francesco Petrarca, *Prose*, 140.
14. "*Quid est enim aliud omnis historia, quam Romana laus?*"; from *Invective contra eum qui maledixit Italie* in Petrarca, *Prose*, 790; facing page translation found in Francesco Petrarca, *Invectives*, ed. and trans. David Marsh, I Tatti Renaissance Library 11 (Cambridge, MA: Harvard University Press, 2003), 417.
15. Velli (*Petrarca e Boccaccio*) traces Lucan's influence upon Boccaccio's earlier vernacular writings, particularly *Il Filocolo* (75–90) and *Teseida* (125–28).
16. For Petrarch's and Boccaccio's politics in writing their encyclopedic biographies, see David Wallace, *Chaucerian Polity: Absolutist Lineages and Associational Forms in England and Italy*, Figurae: Reading Medieval Culture (Stanford, CA: Stanford University Press, 1997), 300–307; and Massimo Miglio, "Boccaccio biografo," in Gilbert Tournoy, ed., *Boccaccio in Europe: Proceedings of the Boccaccio Conference, Louvain, December 1975* (Louvain: Leuven University Press, 1977), 149–63. Warren Ginsberg, *Chaucer's Italian Tradition* (Ann Arbor: University of Michigan Press, 2002), 190–227, attempts to read the *De casibus* less schematically, as a text seeking to blend "autocratic, Petrarchan models of self-government" and "associational forms of communal life." None discusses Virgil or Lucan in relation to Petrarch or Boccaccio. Maria Teresa Casella contrasts Boccaccio's and Petrarch's histories and their reliance upon Livy and Valerius Maximus: *Tra Boccaccio e Petrarca: I volgarizzamenti di Tito Livio e di Valerio Massimo* (Padua: Editrice Antenore, 1982), 61–88.
17. The assumption by medieval commentators that Virgil wrote to promote Augustus was ultimately derived from Servius; see Christopher Baswell, *Virgil in Medieval England: Figuring the* Aeneid *from the Twelfth Century to Chaucer*, Cambridge Studies in Medieval Literature 24 (Cambridge: Cambridge University Press, 1995), 19, 64–68.
18. For instance, W. R. Johnson's superb *Darkness Visible: A Study of Vergil's* Aeneid (Berkeley and Los Angeles: University of California Press, 1976); R. A. Brooks, "*Discolor Aura*: Reflections on the Golden Bough," *American Journal of Philology* 34 (1953): 260–80; Adam Parry, "The Two Voices of Vergil's *Aeneid*," *Arion* 2.4 (1963): 66–80. Both Brooks's and Parry's essays are reprinted in Steele Commager, ed., *Virgil: A Collection of Critical Essays* (Englewood Cliffs, NJ: Prentice Hall, 1966), 143–63 and 107–23 respectively.
19. Quotations from the *Aeneid* are from P. Vergili Maronis, *Opera*, ed. R. A. B. Mynors (Oxford: Clarendon Press, 1969); translations (occasionally modified by me) are from the Loeb Classical Library edition, trans. H. Rushton Fairclough, rev. G. P. Goold (Cambridge, MA: Harvard University Press, 1999).
20. Howard R. Patch places Boethius's configuration within the larger medieval tradition in *The Goddess Fortuna in Mediaeval Literature* (1927; reprint, New York: Octagon Books, 1974), 18–20, 77–79; see also his "Fate in Boethius and the Neoplatonists," *Speculum* 4 (1929): 62–72.
21. Particularly those commentaries of Nicholas Trevet and Benvenuto da Imola on Virgil's *Eclogues*; see Mary Louise Lord, "The Uses of Macrobius and Boethius in Some Fourteenth-Century Commentaries on Virgil," *International Journal of the Classical Tradition* 3 (1996): 3–22, esp. 9–11.
22. Baswell, *Virgil in Medieval England*, esp. 121–23 and 359–60, n. 141–42.
23. D. C. Feeney, "History and Revelation in Vergil's Underworld," in Philip Har-

die, ed., *Virgil: Critical Assessments of Classical Authors*, 4 vols. (London and New York: Routledge, 1999), 4:221–43; reprinted from *Proceedings of the Cambridge Philological Society* 32 (1986): 1–24.

24. Branca, "Missions of Civil Diplomacy and Works of Humanistic Erudition (1352–1360)," *Boccaccio: The Man and His Works*, 109–14; Miglio, "Boccaccio biografo"; Billanovich, *Restauri boccacceschi*, 137–38; Louis Brewer Hall, "Introduction," Giovanni Boccaccio, *The Fates of Illustrious Men*, x–xi. For Livy in the Trecento see Giuseppe Billanovich, "Petrarch and the Textual Tradition of Livy," *Journal of the Warburg and Courtauld Institute* 14 (1951): 137–208, which should be read in conjunction with his later refinement of this subject, vol. 1, pt. 1, *Tradizione e fortuna di Livio tra medioevo e umanesimo*, in *La tradizione del testo di Livio e le origini dell'umanesimo*, Studi sul Petrarca 9 (Padua: Antenore, 1981), esp. 57–122. For Valerius Maximus see Casella, *Tra Boccaccio e Petrarca*, which examines the vernacular rendering of Valerius Maximus *Facta et dicta memorabilia* and an Italian translation of the third decade of Livy attributed to Boccaccio; see also the series of articles in *Studi sul* Boccaccio 10 (1977–78) by Casella ("Nuovi ardomenti per l'attribuzione del volgarizzamento di Valerio Massimo al Boccaccio," 109–22), Emilio Lippi ("Una Redazione Particolare Del Volgarizzamento Liviano," 27–40), and Adriana Zampieri ("Una Primitiva Redazione Del Volgarizzamento Di Valerio Massimo," 41–54, and "Per L'edizione Critics Del Volgarizzamento Di Valerio Massimo," 55–108).

25. *Nam poete non, ut hystoriographi faciunt, qui a quodam certo principio opus exordiuntur suum, etcontinua atque ordinate rerum gestarum descriptione in finem usque deducunt (quod cernimus fecisse Lucanum, quam ob causam multi eum potius metricum hystoriographum quam poetam existimant)*; from *Genealogia* 14.13.14; *Boccaccio on Poetry*, 67.

26. Eva Matthews Sanford, "Lucan and His Roman Critics," *Classical Philology* 26 (1931): 233–57; Berthe Marie Marti, "Literary Criticism in the Mediaeval Commentaries on Lucan," *Transactions and Proceedings of the American Philological Association* 72 (1941): 245–54; Guido Martellotti, "La difensa della poesia nel Boccaccio e un giudizio su Lucano," *Studi sul Boccaccio* 4 (1967): 265–79.

27. For a study on the importance of this distinction, particularly for modern critics who mistakenly classify Boccaccio's and other *de casibus* texts as tragedies, see Paul Budra, A Mirror for Magistrates *and the* de casibus *Tradition* (Toronto: University of Toronto Press, 2000), 14–17.

28. For the *zibaldoni*, see below, n. 42. On his vernacular fictions see James McGregor, *The Image of Antiquity in Boccaccio's* Filostrato, Filocolo, *and* Teseida (New York: Peter Lang, 1991) and *The Shades of Aeneas: The Imitation of Virgil and the History of Paganism in Boccaccio's* Filostrato, Filocolo, *and* Teseida (Athens, GA: University of Georgia Press, 1991); and David Anderson, *Before the Knight's Tale: Imitation of Classical Epic in Boccaccio's* Teseida (Philadelphia: University of Pennsylvania Press, 1988).

29. Domenico Comparetti, *Vergil in the Middle Ages*, trans. E. F. M. Benecke (1895; reprint, Princeton, NJ: Princeton University Press, 1997); John Webster Spargo, *Virgil the Necromancer: Studies in Virgilian Legends*, Harvard Studies in Comparative Literature 10 (Cambridge, MA: Harvard University Press, 1934). For a summary of grammarians' lives surviving in the Middle Ages along with these more fantastic legends, see Fabio Stok, "Virgil between the Middle Ages and the Renaissance," *International Journal of the Classical Tradition* 1 (1994): 15–22, and his *Prolegomeni a una nuova edizione della Vita Vergilii di Svetonio-Donato*, Bolletino dei classici, supplement no. 11 (Rome: Accademia nazionale

dei Lincei, 1991); these antique accounts are to be found in Giorgio Brugnoli and Fabio Stok, eds., Vitae Vergilianae antiquae: *Scriptores graeci et latini* (Rome: Instituto Polygraphico, 1997). Boccaccio himself seemed to give little adherence to the more fantastic legends, mentioning them only in passing in his commentary on the *Commedia* (Osgood, "Boccaccio's Knowledge of the Life of Vergil," 36), although Zabughin suggests otherwise, *Vergilio nel Rinascimento italiano di Dante a Torquato Tasso*, 39–40 (69–70). The thirty-five essays in the special issue of *Studi Medievali* 5 (1932), *Vergilio nel Medio Evo*, record medieval reception of Virgil in England, Ireland, Holland, Portugal, Spain, France, and Italy, as well as his influence upon several individual authors.

30. *Epistole*, ed. Ginetta Auzzas, in volume 5 of *Le Opere di Giocanni Boccaccio*, gen. ed. Vittore Branca, 13 vols. (Milan: Mondadori, 1992), 531.
31. Boccaccio's copy of the *Saturnalia* was bound with Macrobius's *Commentarii Somnium Scipionis* and is included in the inventory of his books bequeathed to the Augustinian friars' Parva Libraria at Santo Spirito in Florence; see Antonia Mazza, "L'inventario della parva libraria di Santo Spirito e la biblioteca del Boccaccio," *Italia medioevale e umanistica* 9 (1966): 1–71 (19, item II.1), and Anderson, *Before the Knight's Tale*, 55 and 89 n. 40, who also notes that Coluccio Salutati wrote to Boccaccio in 1372, asking for a copy of the *Saturnalia*.
32. *quippe si mundum ipsum diligenter inspicias, magnam similitudinem divini illius et huius poetici operas invenies*; *Saturnalia* 5.1.19. Ambrosii Theodosii Macrobii, *Saturnalia*, ed. James Willis, Bibliotheca Scriptorum Graecorum et Romanorum Teubneriana (Leipzig: B. G. Teubner Verlagsgesellschaft, 1970), 243; translation from *The Saturnalia*, trans. Percival Vaughan Davies, Records of Civilization (New York: Columbia University Press, 1969), 285.
33. Fulgentius, *Opera*, ed. R. Helm, rev. Jean Préaux (1898; reprint, Stuttgart: Teubner, 1970); translated by Leslie George Whitbread as *The Exposition of the Content of Virgil According to Moral Philosophy* in *Fulgentius the Mythographer* (Columbus: Ohio State University Press, 1971), 103–54. For an introduction to Fulgentius's importance, see Robert Edwards, "Fulgentius and the Collapse of Meaning," *Helios*, n.s., 3 (1976): 17–35, and "The Heritage of Fulgentius," in Aldo S. Bernardo and Saul Levin, eds., *The Classics in the Middle Ages: Papers of the Twentieth Annual Conference of the Center for Medieval and Early Renaissance Studies*, Medieval and Renaissance Texts and Studies 69 (Binghamton, NY: Center for Medieval and Renaissance Studies at the State University of New York at Binghamton, 1990), 131–51.
34. J. W. Jones, Jr., "Allegorical Interpretation in Servius," *Classical Journal* 56 (1960–61): 215–26, and "The Allegorical Traditions of the *Aeneid*," in John D. Bernard, ed., *Vergil at 2000: Commemorative Essays on the Poet and His Influence* (New York: AMS Press, 1986), 107–32 (111). For a useful introduction to what Servius bequeathed to the Middle Ages, see Peter K. Marshall, *Servius and Commentary on Virgil*, Occasional Papers no. 5, Center for Medieval and Renaissance Studies, Binghamton, New York (Asheville, NC: Pegasus Press, 1997). Other examples of allegorical readings of Virgil in the Middle Ages include the commentary attributed to Bernardus Silvestris (see below, n. 41), John of Salisbury's *Policraticus* 8.24–25 (discussed in Seth Lerer, "John of Salisbury's Virgil," *Vivarium* 20 [1982]: 24–39), and Petrarch's letter to Frederigo Aretino (*Sen.* 4.5). For Petrarch's allegorizing in his personal copy of Virgil, the Codex Ambrosianus (Milan, Biblioteca Ambrosiana, Sala dal Prefetto, Scaf. 10, no. 27), see Mary Louise Lord, "Petrarch and Vergil's First *Eclogue*: The Codex Ambrosianus," *Harvard Studies in Classical Philology* 86 (1982): 253–76, esp. 260–61.

35. For the grammarians' Virgil, see Baswell, *Virgil in Medieval England*, esp. 11–13, 47–53; for epideictic criticism, see Kallendorf, *In Praise of Aeneas*.
36. Daniel B. Dietz, "*Historia* in the Commentary of Servius," *Transactions of the Philological Society* 125 (1995): 61–97, esp. 66–69.
37. Dietz, "*Historia* in the Commentary of Servius," 88; Anderson (*Before the Knight's Tale*, 146–54) discusses how Servius's definition of *metrum heroicum*, and its relation with truth and fiction, was used by Boccaccio in composing the *Teseida*.
38. *miscet philosophiae figmenta poetica et ostendit tam quod est vulgare, quam quod continet veritas et ratio naturalis*; comment on *Aen.* 6.719, from George Thilo and Hermann Hagen, eds., *Servii Grammatici qui feruntur in Vergilii Carmina Commentarii*, 3 vols. (1878–84; reprint, Hildesheim: Georg Olms Verlagsbuchhandlung, 1961), 3:99. (Dietz also cites this passage, 94.)
39. *Commentarii in Somnium Scipionis*, ed. James Willis (Leipzig: B. G. Teubner Verlagsgesellschaft, 1970), 1.2.9, 1.2.11; *Commentary on the Dream of Scipio*, trans. William Harris Stahl, Records of Western Civilization (1952; New York: Columbia University Press, 1990), 85.
40. "Poetry is a celebrated body of knowledge, elevated and beautiful, requiring skill. Only by the aid of poetry is it possible, within the limits of human weakness, to follow in the footsteps of Holy Writ. For as scripture reveals the secrets of the Divine Spirit and the prophecies of things to come under the guise of figures of speech, so poetry tries to relate its lofty concepts under the veils of fictions" (106; *Est quidem de se inclita plurimum artificiosa sublimis et ornate facultas, sola, in quantum humane imbecillitati possible est, sancta pagine vestigial sequi conata. Nam prout illa divine mentis archana prophetis futurisque sub figuram tegmine reseravit, sic et hec celsos suorum conceptus sub figmentorum velamine tradere orsa est*; *De casibus* 3.14.12–13). Boccaccio makes similar declarations in the *Trattatello in laude di Dante*, sec. 9–10, and more expansively in *Genealogia* 14.10–13.
41. *Commentum quod dicitur Bernardi Silvestris super sex libros Eneidos Virgilii*, eds. Julian Ward Jones and Elizabeth Frances Jones (Lincoln: University of Nebraska Press, 1977); English translation was published as by Bernardus Silverstris, *Commentary on the First Six Books of Virgil's* Aeneid, trans. Earl G. Schreiber and Thomas E. Maresca (Lincoln: University of Nebraska Press, 1979). For bibliography, see the notes in David L. Pike, "Bernard Silvestris' Decent into the Classics: The *Commentum super sex libros Aeneidos*," *International Journal of the Classical Tradition* 4 (1998): 343–63. An edition of a related twelfth-century commentary can be found in Christopher Baswell, "The Medieval Allegorization of the 'Aeneid': MS Cambridge, Peterhouse 158," *Traditio* 41 (1985): 181–237, whose findings are qualified by Julian Ward Jones, Jr., "The So-Called Silvestris Commentary on the *Aeneid* and Two Other Interpretations," *Speculum* 64 (1989): 835–48.
42. Item 40 listed in Bianca Maria Da Rif, "La Miscellanea Laurenziana XXXIII 31," *Studi sul Boccaccio* 7 (1973): 59–124. The Miscellanea Laurenziana is one of three autograph notebooks once belonging to Boccaccio: Florence, Biblioteca Laurenziana, MSS 29.8 (Zibaldone Laurenziano) and 33.31 (Miscellanea Laurenziana or Miscellanea Latina), and Florence, Biblioteca Nazionale, B. R. 50 (Zibaldone Magliabechiano). The Zibaldone Laurenziano is a collection of texts made by Boccaccio during his school days and studies in Naples, dating c. 1339 to the late 1340s; the Miscellanea Laurenziana and Zibaldone Magliabechiano were compiled in the early to mid-1340s, and thus after Boccaccio had returned to Florence. For a list of their contents, see Aldo Maria Constant-

ini, "Stuido sullo Zibaldone Magliabechiano," *Studi sul Boccaccio* 7 (1973): 21–58, and da Rif, "La Miscellanea Laurenziana XXXIII 31." See also Filippo Di Benedetto, "Considerazioni sullo Zibaldone Laurenziano del Boccaccio e restauro testuale della prima redazione del 'Faunus,'" *Italia medioevale e umanistica* 14 (1971): 91–129, and the essays collected in Michelangelo Picone and Claude Cazalé Bérard, *Gli Zibaldoni di Boccaccio: Memoria, scrittura, riscrittura: Atti del Seminario internazionale di Firenze-Certaldo (26-28 aprile 1996)* (Florence: Franco Cesati, 1998). A fascinating codicological study of the Zibaldone Laurenziano and the Miscellanea Laurenziana (made from the same palimpsest) is Virginia Brown, "Boccaccio in Naples: The Beneventan Liturgical Palimpsest of the Laurentian Autographs (MSS 29.8 and 33.31)," *Italia medioevale e umanistica* 34 (1991): 41–126, briefly summarized as "Between the Convent and the Court: Boccaccio and a Beneventan Gradual from Naples," in Picone and Bérard, eds., *Gli Zibaldoni*, 307–14. For Virgilian materials in the Miscellanea Laurenziana, see Lord, "Boccaccio's *Virgiliana* in the Miscellanea Latina" (see above, n. 7), and Robert Black, "Boccaccio, Reader of the *Appendix Vergiliana*: Miscellanea Laurenziana and Fourteenth-Century Schoolbooks," in Picone and Bérard, eds., *Gli Zibaldoni*, 113–28; for Virgil's influence upon the *Elegia di Costanza* in Zibaldone Laurenziano, see Velli, "L'Elegia di Costanza e l'ars combinatoria del Boccaccio," *Petrarca e Boccaccio*, 112–21.

43. For Virgil's rewriting of this incident from Cicero's *Republic*, see Feeney, "History and Revelation in Vergil's Underworld," 221–25.

44. Lord, "The Use of Macrobius and Boethius in Some Fourteenth-Century Commentaries on Virgil"; for a list of Petrarch's citations from Macrobius, see Lord's appendix, 14–22.

45. *De consolatione philosophiae*, ed. L. Bieler (Turnholt: Brepols, 1957); translation from *The Consolation of Philosophy*, trans. V. E. Watts (New York: Penguin Books, 1969), 76.

46. Michael Murrin, *The Allegorical Epic: Essays in Its Rise and Decline* (Chicago: University of Chicago Press, 1980), 27–34.

47. Feeney, "History and Revelation in Vergil's Underworld," 224. Murrin rightly points out, however, that modern critics should employ caution when fixedly applying terms such as "Platonic" and "Stoic" to early Empire writers, who often held a syncretic view like that of the New Academy, relying upon a skeptical epistemology to defend Platonic positions concerning the relationship between the body and soul (*The Allegorical Epic*, 27–50).

48. Vittore Branca discounts that the mistreated shepherdess is intended to represent Boccaccio's mother (*Giovanni Boccaccio, profile biografico* [Florence: Antenore, 1977], 8), but one must admit that the rest of the narrative presented by the character Fileno is intended to allude to Boccaccio's own circumstances; even if the charge is fictional, it is curious that Boccaccio would seem to invite such slander about his father. Certainly Filippo Villani (only a generation later than Boccaccio) repeated the story of an abandoned French mother in his life of Boccaccio (*Vitae Dantis, Petrarchae, et Boccaccii a Philippo Villanio* [Florence, 1826], 68–69).

49. A touching testimony to Boccaccio's devotion to Violante (d. c. 1355) was the now-lost altarpiece commissioned by him for the church of Santi Michele e Jacopo in Certaldo: a surviving set of sixteenth-century sketches of the piece depict in the donor positions himself and a small girl, the latter releasing a tethered goldfinch to fly to the Christ Child seated on Mary's lap (an extremely unusual iconography, perhaps symbolic of her soul soaring to heaven); see

Robert Williams, "Boccaccio's Altarpiece," *Studi sul Boccaccio* 19 (1990): 229–40, which discusses its relationship with *Olympia*.
50. *Genealogia* 15.10.6–8; *Boccaccio on Poetry*, 131–32. This sentiment was hinted at in *Il Corbaccio* as well: "Far more than your father would have wished, then, right from your childhood you liked studies pertaining to sacred philosophy, and especially that part dealing with poetry, which perhaps you have pursued with more fervor of spirit than with heights of genius"; *gli studii addunque alla sacra filosofia pertinenti, infino dalla tua puerizia, più assai che il tuo padre non arebbe voluto, ti piacquero, e massimamente in quellaparte che a poesia appartiene; la quale per avventura tu hai, con più fervore d'animo che con alteza d'ingegno, seguita.* Italian edited by Giorgio Padoan in vol. 5, pt. 2, of Giovanni Boccaccio, *Tutte le Opere*, ed. Vittore Branca (Milan: Mondadori, 1995), 463; translation from *Corbaccio, or The Labyrinth of Love*, trans. and ed. Anthony K. Cassell, 2d rev. ed. (Binghamton, NY: Center for Medieval and Early Renaissance Studies at the State University of New York at Binghamton, 1993), 23.
51. Lord, "Petrarch and Vergil's First *Eclogue*: The Codex Ambrosianus," 256–57; Giuseppe Billanovich, "Tra Dante e Petrarca," *Italia medioevale e umanistica* 8 (1965): 20–24. Petrarch, of course, had stormy relations with his own father, who once burned Petrarch's books for distracting him from his legal studies (Ernest Hatch Wilkins, *Life of Petrarch* [Chicago: University of Chicago Press, 1961], 5).
52. *convienesi amare li suoi maggiori dalli quail ha ricevuto ed essere e nutrimento e dottrina, sì che esso non paia ingrato*; *Il Convivio* IV.26.10. Dante Alighieri, *Convivio*, ed. Franca Brambilla Agento, 2 vols. (Florence: Casa Editrice Le Lettere, 1995), 2:431. Translation from *Dante's* Il Convivio *(The Banquet)*, trans. Richard H. Lansing, Garland Library of Medieval Literature 65 (New York and London: Garland Publishing, 1990), 226.
53. Ginsberg (*Chaucer's Italian Tradition*, 197–207) also reads the *De casibus* as a drama of fathers and sons, noting that Dante's appearance follows the story of the Templars, based upon the account of events Boccaccio received from his own father; Ginsberg further sees the *De casibus*'s Dante and Petrarch as competing father figures, providing different models of civic duty. He makes no mention of Virgil.
54. The *De casibus* survives in two versions: redaction A was drafted in 1355–60, which later was expanded into B in the years before his death in 1375; among the additions to the second redaction were a dedication to Mainardo Cavalcanti and further citations to Homer (newly available in Latin after 1363 thanks to Boccaccio's sponsorship of Leontinus Pilatus). Appendix II of the critical edition of the *De casibus* (1101–7) contains the notable differences of redaction A from B (the latter of which formed the basis for the modern text). On the relationship between the two versions see Pier Giorgio Ricci, "Studi selle opere Latine e volgari del Boccaccio," *Rinascimento*, ser. 2, 2 (1962): 3–31 (11–20), reprinted as chapter 15, "Le due redazioni del 'De casibus,'" in Ricci's *Studi sulla vita e le opere del Boccaccio* (Milan: Riccardo Riccardi Editore, 1985), 179–88. Ricci's findings were corroborated and expanded by Vittorio Zaccaria, "Le due redazioni del 'De casibus,'" *Studi sul Boccaccio* 10 (1977–78): 1–26.
55. Francesco Petrarca, *Le Familiari*, ed. Vittorio Rossi et al., 4 vols. (Florence: G. C. Sansoni, 1942), 4:94. Translated in *Letters on Familiar Matters:* Rerum familiarium libri *XVII-XXIV*, trans. Aldo S. Bernardo (Baltimore and London: The Johns Hopkins University Press, 1985), 202–7.
56. *una dierum forte accidit, utproficisceretur solus ad locum, ubi Maronis cineres humati*

fuerunt, cuius sepulcrum cum Ioannes defixo contuitu perpensius miraretur, et quid intro clauderet, atque ossium famam suspenso meditaretur animo, suam coepit illico, et accusare, et deflere fortunam, qua cogebatur invitus mrecaturis sibi improbis militare; subitoque Pieridum tactus amore, ad domum reverses, neglectus ex toto mercibus, flagrantissimo studio in poesim se concessit; from *Vitae Dantis, Petrarchae, et Boccaccii a Philippo Villanio*, 69–70. English version (made from a Quattrocento Italian translation rather than the Latin original) by Hugh Skubikowski, in Giovanni Boccaccio, *The Decameron*, ed. and trans. Mark Musa and Peter E. Bondanella (New York: W. W. Norton, 1982), 188–91.

57. If 1339 is the accurate date, the letter would have been two years before Petrarch's coronation and over a decade before their first meeting; the attribution is suggested by the epistle's editor, Ginetta Auzzas, in *Tutte le opere di Giovanni Boccaccio*, 5.754, n. 1.
58. Spargo, *Virgil the Necromancer*, 20, 103–5. In stark contrast is the fate of Ovid's grave: while Virgil's tomb was garlanded with legend, and Livy's reputed sarcophagus found among fanfare in Padua in the fourteenth century, Ovid's resting place was never known, as he died in exile on a hostile coast. This didn't preclude stories, though: see J. B. Trapp, "Ovid's Tomb: The Growth of a Legend from Eusebius to Laurence Sterne, Chateaubriand, and George Richmond," *Journal of the Warburg and Courtauld Institute* 36 (1973): 35–76; and, for Livy, B. L. Ullman, "The Post-Mortem Adventures of Livy," *Studies in the Italian Renaissance* (Rome: Edizioni di Storia e Letteratura, 1955), 55–79.
59. The apocryphal Apocalypse of St. Paul, a fourth-century book purporting to reveal details of the vision to which the apostle only alludes in 2 Corinthians 12:2–4.
60. *Ad maronis mausoleum ductus fudit super eum pie rorem lacrime Quem te, inquit, reddidissem si te vivum invenissem poetarum maxime*; as transcribed in Lord, "Petrarch and Vergil's First *Eclogue*," 258–59. Lord notes that this inscription is an exception from the predominantly classical nature of the rest of Petrarch's marginalia. See also Bernard M. Peebles, "The *Ad Maronis mausoleum*: Petrarch's Virgil and Two Fifteenth-Century Manuscripts," in Charles Henderson, Jr., ed., *Classical, Medieval and Renaissance Studies in Honor of Berthold Louis Ullman*, 2 vols. (Rome: Edizioni di Storia e Letteratura, 1964), 2:169–98. Comparetti (*Vergil in the Middle Ages*, 98) also reproduces the verses.
61. See Philip Hardie, *The Epic Successors of Virgil: A Study in the Dynamics of a Tradition, Roman Literature and Its Contexts* (Cambridge: Cambridge University Press, 1993), esp. 98–105. Petrarch, of course, perpetuates this lineage in Book 9 of his *Africa*, in which Ennius has a vision of the "new poet" who will better sing Scipio's praises.

Reinventing the Ideal Sovereign in Christine de Pizan's Livre des fais et bonnes meurs du sage roy Charles V

DAISY DELOGU

Composed in 1404, some twenty-five years after the death of its subject, Christine de Pizan's *Livre des fais et bonnes meurs du sage roy Charles V* marks a turning point in the literary career of this prolific author. Initially known for her poetry as well as for her prominent role in the literary quarrel surrounding the *Roman de la rose*, Christine had more recently composed two moral-historical-autobiographical texts in verse—the *Chemin de long estude* (1403) and the *Livre de la mutacion de fortune* (1404). The *Livre des fais* is Christine's first prose, historical-political work, but not her last. Indeed, the *Livre* initiates the second phase of Christine's literary production, which henceforth would be characterized by predominantly prose works that dealt in a serious manner with the moral, philosophical, and political issues of her day, including the *Livre du corps de policie* (1406–7), the *Livre des fais d'armes et de chevalerie* (1410), and the *Livre de la Paix* (1412–13), as well as what is today perhaps her best-known work, the *Livre de la cité des dames* (1404–5).[1]

Although the quality of Christine's poetic production has long been recognized, until quite recently the *Livre des fais*, indeed the historical-political corpus of Christine de Pizan, received little critical attention.[2] This was in part due to Christine's status as a female author.[3] As recently as 1974, Gianni Mombello assessed Christine as a political thinker in the following manner: "Nous nous garderons donc de lui attribuer ou de lui demander des idées originales dans ce domaine, dans lequel son activité inlassable s'est bornée à répéter des notions plus ou moins connues et acceptées, à peine nuancées, çà et là, par sa sensibilité de femme."[4] Mombello was actually very sympathetic to Christine on the whole, and his belief that she was a well-intentioned autodidact who simply restated the ideas of the few authors she had read is fairly representative of criticism in this area up until the last decade or so. The 1992 volume *Politics, Gender,*

Medievalia et Humanistica, New Series, Number 31 (Paul Maurice Clogan, ed.), Rowman & Littlefield Publishers, Inc., 2005.

and Genre: The Political Thought of Christine de Pizan (ed. Margaret Brabant [Boulder: Westview, 1992]) opened the door to a reevaluation of the author's political thought, including her substantial originality, and many scholars have since continued this line of inquiry.[5] In particular, Kate Langdon Forhan's *The Political Thought of Christine de Pizan* (Aldershot: Ashgate, 2002) has substantially enriched scholarship in this area. Moreover, recent editions and translations of several of Christine's prose works have made possible considerable advances in the research concerning this part of her corpus.[6] The present work is intended to contribute to the growing awareness of Christine's impact not just as a poet or moralist, but as a creative and influential political writer as well.

The *Livre des fais* was written during a period of considerable political instability.[7] In 1404 the reigning king, Charles VI, had suffered for over a decade from intermittent bouts of insanity. Referred to as "absences," the king's episodes became longer and more frequent over time and rendered him effectively dysfunctional as a ruler. This void at the center of the power structure made possible the development of an intense and bitter rivalry between the king's younger brother, Louis d'Orléans, and his cousin, Jean sans Peur, which eventually errupted in civil war. On the international front, the peace talks with England that had been ongoing throughout much of the 1390s had come to an end with the deposition and death of Richard II, the succession of Henry IV, and the return to power of the war party. Finally, the Great Schism of the West was in its twenty-sixth year. Against this tumultuous backdrop Christine de Pizan composed her biography of the previous ruler, Charles V, the Wise, whose reign from 1364 to 1380 represented a golden age of reconquest and recovery.[8]

The *Livre des fais* is a curious text, one that unites in a surprising manner a variety of canonical discourses.[9] On one hand the *Livre* is a biographical and historical work in which Christine describes and memorializes Charles V and his reign. At the same time Christine articulates a new ideal of sovereignty that she posits as an exemplum for the princes of her generation, and in particular for the dauphin, Louis de Guyenne. It was generally accepted in the Middle Ages that narratives depicting good conduct had the power to incite virtue in their readers or listeners, and Christine was clearly a proponent of this precept.[10] Accordingly, what better way to improve the moral fiber of Louis de Guyenne and the other princes of the blood than by detailing the virtuous character and conduct of their forefather? Christine's innovative combination of historically specific detail with scholarly theoretical reflection allows her to create a privileged space in which to examine the person, image, and function not just of Charles V, but of kingship in general.

The present work will examine some of the ways in which Christine's depiction of Charles V's character and acts serves to modify and revitalize the notion of the ideal sovereign. I will focus first on the principle of order, as exemplified by the description of the king's mounted excursions and by the visit of the Holy Roman Emperor, Charles IV. Next, I will examine Kate Forhan's conception of "mediated monarchy," particularly as it applies to the return to war with England and to the Schism. Then, I will explore how Christine's reformulation of chivalry permits her to arrive at the unexpected conclusion that Charles was indeed a "vray chevalereux" (I/243) [true knightly one].[11] Finally, I will look at the way in which Christine's rich and complex vision of *prudence* makes this quality the hallmark of the ideal monarch.

Charles V's Sense of Order

The ideal of order in the *Livre des fais* is not simply a question of tidiness or aesthetics but is a moral order, associated with notions of justice, moderation, propriety, and rectitude, and is related to, indeed illustrative of, the authority immanent in the office of the king. In Charles V's outings on horseback all of these elements are brought to bear in a display that clearly communicates a message about the French king. Christine writes:

L'acoustumée maniere de son chevauchier estoit *de notable ordre* à tres grant compagnie de barons et gentilzhommes bien montez et en riches habiz, lui assis sus paleffroy de grant eslite, tout temps vestu en habit royal, chevauchant entre ses gens, si loings de lui et par tel et si *honnorable ordennance*, que, à l'aourné maintien de *son bel ordre*, bien peust savoir et cognoistre tout homme, estrangier ou autre, lequel de tous estoit le roy." (I/50, emphasis added)

[The customary manner of his outings on horseback was noteworthy for the order of a great company of nobles and gentlemen well mounted and richly dressed, he {i.e., the king} seated on a choice palfrey, at all times clothed in royal garb, riding amongst his men, who were far enough from him and in such honorable order, that, from the magnificent aspect of his fine order, well might any man, foreign or otherwise, know and recognize which of them was the king.]

The king's excursions on horseback constitute a visual discourse in which the preeminence of the king is highlighted by several factors: the distinctive royal garb that he always wears, the quality of his horse, and the physical distance that is maintained between the king and all others, which reflects the moral and political distance that separates the king from the rest of the nobility. Anyone, even a foreigner, could recognize the king, says Christine.[12] This is not because the features of Charles V were known far and wide, but because the display of Charles V's authority made clear to all onlookers who occupied the office of the king. Thus the king's outings are designed to inspire the proper combination of respect, honor, admiration, love, and even fear in his subjects that Charles recognized was one of the exigencies of kingship. Charles appreciated, as did Christine, that authority is part spectacle.[13]

Christine further observes that Charles's outings on horseback were not designed for his personal pleasure, but to "donner exemple à ses successeurs à venir que par solemnel ordre se doit tenir et mener le tres digne degré de la haulte couronne de France" (I/51) [provide the example for his future successors that by solemn order must maintain and conduct itself the very worthy rank of the lofty crown of France]. Christine's use of the expression "haulte couronne de France" is very significant, for this statement points to one of the essential aspects of kingship that was being articulated during the reign of Charles V, and throughout the whole of the later Middle Ages: the distinction between the person and the office of the king, or *le roi* and *la couronne*. Jacques Krynen, in his work on evolving notions of kingship over the latter half of the Middle Ages, has observed that "[l]a couronne en vient à être considérée comme le siège abstrait et permanent du pouvoir. Le roi n'en est que l'administrateur passager."[14] In *The King's Two Bodies* Ernst Kantorowicz traces in detail the evolution of the juridical notion that the king was possessed of two bodies: one natural and mortal, the other political and immortal. As part of this discussion he examines the emergence of the Crown as a notion distinct from both king and kingdom: "as opposed to the pure *physis* of the king and to the pure *physis* of the territory, the word 'Crown,' when added, indicated the political metaphysis in which both *rex* and *regnum* shared, or the body politic (to which both belonged) in its sovereign rights."[15] Thus when Christine speaks of "le tres digne degré de la haulte couronne de France" she is not referring simply to the personal dignity of Charles V, or of any king of France, but to something that transcends the individual king, and which it is the king's duty to preserve and uphold. One reason why this distinction is particularly useful at the time of the *Livre des fais*'s composition is the weakness and inadequacy of Charles VI. While the reigning French king may be manipulated from within and threatened from without, by constructing authority such that it resides in the office rather than the person of the king, Christine safeguards the integrity of royal power.

The king's order or orderliness occupies an equally prominent place in the account of the emperor Charles IV's visit to Paris in 1378, where it is used once again to communicate the authority of the king of France, this time with respect to the emperor. In the king's procession "estoit l'ordennance si bien faitte que nulle presse n'y faisoit grief" (II/99) [order was so well maintained that no crowd oppressed it]; "la sage ordenance du roy" (II/100) [the wise order of the king] organized the meeting between Charles and the emperor; and the king's guard "se ordenerent en moult belle ordennence" (II/101) [arranged itself in very fine order].[16] The many entrances, processions, gift-giving ceremonies, dinners, and entertainments—of which Christine highlights the exemplary organization—illustrate Charles's power, as well as his graciousness, wealth, and generosity. The emperor's visit provided Charles with an opportunity to impress his authority upon his own nobles and subjects, and also to demonstrate the authority of the king in his kingdom, which was in no way subordinate to that of the emperor. A legal formula developed in the late twelfth century affirmed that *rex in regno suo est imperator regni sui*, the king is emperor in his kingdom. This formula was invoked by the French in the fourteenth century as part of a theory of royal territorial sovereignty intended to maintain French freedom from both papal and imperial claims of political and juridical dominance.[17] Christine summarizes the French position in her conclusion to the famous story of the black horse sent by Charles to the emperor for the latter's entrance into Paris: "ne fu mie sanz avis envoié de cellui poil, car les empereurs, de leur droit, quant ilz entrent es bonnes villes de leur seigneurie et de l'Empire, ont acoustumé estre sus chevaulx blans, si ne voult le roy qu'en son royaume le feist, affin qu'il n'y peust estre notté aucun signe de dominacion" (II/97) [nor was a horse of that color sent unadvisedly, for the emperors, by right, when they enter the good towns of their sovereignty and of the empire have a custom of riding white horses, which the king did not wish the emperor to do in his kingdom, so that no sign of domination might be observed]. The image of Charles V entering his capital mounted on a white horse, accompanied by the emperor on a black one, evidently struck the medieval imagination. Françoise Autrand has remarked that despite the vast quantity of detail concerning the imperial visit provided by both the *Grandes Chroniques de France* and by the *Livre des fais*, later historians and chroniclers seem to have retained principally this image as the one that emblematized the entire imperial visit ("Mémoire et cérémonial" 91). Moreover, as Claire Richter Sherman has observed, the entry into Paris formed the subject of one of the illuminations of the *Grandes Chroniques*, thereby further impressing this scene onto the imagination and memory of medieval readers.[18]

In addition, it is likely that Charles's careful organization of the emperor's visit, which highlighted so effectively the sovereignty of France vis-à-vis the empire, had another intended audience besides the emperor: Edward III of England.[19] By staging a formidable demonstration of French sovereignty Charles was able to convey a message about the inviolability of the king's sovereignty throughout his lands, including the disputed regions of Gascony and Aquitaine.[20] By renarrating this episode in detail and by interpreting its events for her readers, Christine is able to reiterate Charles V's message to the reigning English king at a moment when the French were once again seriously threatened by their English foes.

Mediated Monarchy

Despite her emphasis on the king's authority, Christine's vision of monarchy does not appear to be absolutist. Rather, she depicts Charles V's rule as what Kate Forhan characterizes as a "mediated monarchy." Kate Forhan, citing James Blythe, says that "'Giles [of Rome] . . . does substantially dilute the king's unlimited power by requiring him to take counsel with the wise few'" (42).[21] Forhan goes on to observe that "[t]his is exactly the emphasis that we shall see with Christine de Pizan. While monarchy is best, it is a mediated monarchy because the wise king listens to the experts, and acts accordingly" (42–43). Since Giles of Rome's *De Regimine Principum*—or more probably Henri de Gauchy's French translation thereof—formed one of Christine's principal sources for the *Livre des fais*, it is not surprising to see her view of monarchy and the powers of the king influenced by his. Another work that Christine would very likely have consulted is Nicole Oresme's translation and commentary of Aristotle's *Politics*, in which Oresme argued for the rights of a properly constituted (i.e., aristocratic) multitude to counsel the king.[22] In Christine's text, the importance of seeking and accepting counsel is best illustrated by two episodes: the Gascon appeals and the Schism.

At the heart of the so-called Gascon appeals was the issue of the disputed sovereignty over Gascony and Aquitaine. The treaty of Brétigny, which followed the French defeat at Poitiers (1356) and the imprisonment of Jean II by the English, required the French to relinquish their claim to sovereignty of Gascony and Aquitaine in return for Edward III's abandonment of his claim to the French throne. However, formal renunciations on both parts had never been made. In May of 1368 when the count of Armagnac appealed certain actions of Prince Edward of Aquitaine to Charles V of France, the issue of sovereignty was brought to the forefront. By appealing to Charles V of France, the Gascon lord acknowledged the French king's continued sovereignty over the disputed regions. In turn, accepting the appeals in the French court was tantamount to a declaration of war with England. Before taking such action, Charles sought advice from all quarters. He received the Gascon lord d'Albret honorably "par le conseil de ses sages, sanz lequel ne faisoit aucune chose" (I/125) [upon the advice of his wise men, without whom he did nothing]. With regard to the legal basis for breaking the treaty of Brétigny, Charles consulted scholars from the law schools of Bologna, Montpellier, Toulouse, and Orléans, as well as the most noted clerks from the court at Rome.[23] Charles did not limit his advisors to members of his family, or even to members of the nobility, but consulted legal specialists on a question of legal interpretation. Though this may seem like an obvious approach, in fact Charles's selection of counselors based on their knowledge and capabilities regardless of their rank is one of the features of his genius as a ruler, and one that is especially appreciated by Christine.[24] As she twice observes in her *Livre du corps de policie*, "un chascun expert en son art on doit croire" (37, 69) [one should believe he who is expert in his art].[25] Finally, having established his legal rights with the help of his learned advisors, Charles reaches out to a broader and more representative community of his subjects before taking the final step toward war, and "par le conseil des nobles, clers et bourgois renvoya deffier le roy Edouart d'Angleterre" (I/127–8) [upon the advice of nobles, clerics, and bourgeois sent his challenge to king Edward of England].[26] Thus Charles includes all three estates in a decision that would affect them all—the resumption of hostilities.

Similar care is taken by Charles, and highlighted by Christine, in making the decision that contributed to the Great Schism. In April 1378, following the death of Pope Gregory XI, the cardinals assembled in Rome to elect a new pope. At that time, they chose the bishop of Bari, Bartolomeo Prignano, who became Pope as Urban VI. However, in September of that year, claiming that the election had been performed under duress (since it was conducted as the rioting Romans chanted *romano lo vogliamo*), a group of thirteen cardinals who were assembled at Fondi repudiated the election of Urban VI and proceeded to elect Robert of Geneva, who took the name Clement VII. Thus was born the Schism, which would last for two generations. Before rejecting the election of Pope Urban VI and accepting that of Clement VII, Charles, who "ne voult en aucune maniere y proceder de sa propre voulenté, mais tousjours, en toutes choses, par deliberacion des plus sages" (II/141) [did not wish in any way to proceed of his own volition, but always, in all things, by deliberation of the wisest], sought the opinions of clerks and scholars from throughout France and abroad. Upon consideration of the evidence presented, Charles declared his adherence to the papacy of Clement VII, and he urged his allies to do the same. Not surprisingly, given the context of the Hundred Years War, papal loyalties broke down largely along the lines of political allegiance, and for decades prohibited a successful conclusion to the papal schism.[27] Since Charles was subsequently accused of contributing to the Schism by his actions, Christine is especially mindful to point out that he did not act rashly or unilaterally, but only after due consideration of the issues and upon the advice of his clergy and council.[28]

With regard to the idea that Charles exemplified "mediated monarchy," it is important to note that his consultations were not legally mandated, but proceeded from his own inclination and personal virtue. Christine writes: "non obstant que de sa seigneurie et autorité peust faire et ordener de tout à son bon plaisir, quant venoit à conseillier sus l'estat du royaume, il appelloit à son conseil les bourgois de ses bonnes villes, et meismement des moyenes gens, et de celz du commun, affin qu'il leur moustrast la fiance qu'il avoit en eulx" (II/28) [despite the fact that of his own sovereignty and authority he could do and order all at his pleasure, when it came to questions that touched the state of the kingdom, he called to his council the bourgeois of his good towns, and even average people, and commoners, so that he might show them the confidence that he had in them]. Thus in theory Christine articulates an absolutist view of Charles's authority as king. In this respect she differs from Nicole Oresme, who believes counsel of the king to be a right, not a privilege, of a properly constituted group chosen for this purpose. Yet in the exercise of kingship,

Christine advocates discussion with the appropriate individuals and bodies, as well as consideration of the views of the king's subjects.

It is important to distinguish between two types of counsel depicted in the *Livre des fais*. On one hand, there is the advice offered by experts with respect to specific situations, as in the cases of the Gascon appeals and the Schism, discussed previously. On the other hand, Christine notes that in situations that touched the well-being of the kingdom, Charles called to his council "les bourgois de ses bonnes villes, et meismement des moyenes gens, et de celz du commun, *affin qu'il leur moustrast la fiance qu'il avoit en eulx*" (II/28, emphasis added). The purpose of these consultations was not to obtain the advice and opinions of the middle and lower classes per se, but rather to display Charles's confidence in them and his concern for their needs. Such studied consideration of the views of all and sundry allowed Charles to implicate the collectivity of his subjects in his important decisions, making it all the more difficult for them to oppose his actions or to lament the results, whether with respect to the war with England, to new taxes, or other.

Charles as *vray chevalereux*

Yet another aspect of Christine's new monarchical ideal involves a reformulation of the conventional vision of chivalry. Traditional notions of the royal ideal demanded that the king be militarily adept, an exemplary knight at the head of his army. Showing the bookish and frail Charles V to be a model of chivalry, a "vray chevalereux" (I/243) [true knightly one], was a tall order; Christine does so by redefining the very notion of chivalry. First, she demonstrates chivalry to be an intellectual, rather than a physical, endeavor. Since Christine realizes that such a perspective is completely at odds with the knightly tradition, she preempts and responds to possible criticisms of her characterization of Charles's chivalry. She first refutes the possible accusation of cowardice, which some might claim had prevented Charles from personally participating in his battles, as his father and grandfather had. Christine observes that Charles did participate successfully in military campaigns prior to his coronation. Thereafter, illness precluded his personal involvement in military undertakings. Christine then affirms that in any event, prudence and wisdom are more essential to chivalry than physical performance, and she cites the military historian and theoretician Vegetius in support of her assertion: "dit Vegece que plus doit estre louée chevalerie menée à cause de sens que celle, qui est conduitte par effett d'armes" (I/1323) [Vegetius says that chivalry conducted by means of wisdom is more to be praised than that driven by the effect of arms]. Her mention of Charles's Valois predecessors, Jean II and Philippe VI, further supports her argument, for though they led their armies into battle their lack of prudence and tactical acumen caused them to suffer what at the time were the two greatest losses of the Hundred Years War.[29]

Christine makes intellect the basis for chivalry by focusing not on military activity, but on end results. Thus we can see that Charles was a model of chivalry "par la fin de ses glorieuses conquestes" (I/118) [from the result of his glorious conquests]. Christine's relative disinterest in the means of success is reflected in her narration of the reconquest. She provides almost no detail concerning the various military campaigns, for what matters is that towns and castles were won and that subjects "turned French." At one point she remarks that "comme tout dire et narrer seroit longue chose, qui mielx y fist, qui fu capitaine, et qui y ala, et par qui ce vint, à tout dire en brief, tant sagement et prudemment y pourvey nostre sage roy" (I/129) [since to tell and narrate everything would be a long affair—who fought best, who was captain, who went there, by whom it was done—to tell all briefly, so wisely and prudently did our king attend to matters] that the city and castle of Crotoy were taken. The fact of the victory, and Charles's role as the directing force thereof, are the essential points, not the individuals who participated in the campaign or the deeds they performed.[30]

Christine goes on to compare Charles's successes to those of the Romans, models of military achievement, and in so doing she effects the second significant reformulation of the notion of chivalry. The Romans, Christine writes:

plus acqueissent seigneuries et terres par leur sens que par force, semblablement le fist nostre roy, lequel plus conquesta, enrichi, fist aliences, plus grans armées, mieulx gens d'armes paiez et toute gent, plus fist bastir edifices, donna grans dons, tint plus magnificent estat, ot plus grant despense, moins fist de grief au peuple et plus sagement se gouverna en toute policie, et plus largement [fu] furnie toute despense que n'avoit fait roy de France . . . depuis le temps Charlemaine. (I/133)
[acquired more sovereign territories and lands by their wisdom than by force; similarly acted our king, who conquered more, enriched, made alliances and great armies, better paid his men at arms and all people, had more edifices constructed, gave great gifts, maintained a more magnificent rank, had greater financial obligation yet burdened his people less and more wisely governed himself in all public affairs, and more generously provided for all expenses than had any other king of France . . . since the time of Charlemagne]

Here, Christine vastly expands and essentially transforms the idea of chivalry, which is not restricted to military undertakings but embraces all successful and effective government. This reformulation is illustrated by Charles's ability not only to raise and pay great armies and to (re)conquer lands, but also to construct public works, maintain an impressive household, and avoid burdening his people with taxes. Kate Forhan has remarked on this conversion of chivalry from a military value to one that connotes good government in a broad sense. In the *Livre des fais* she perceives the elaboration of "a revitalized notion of chivalry that reconstructs the fundamental duty of kings, and focuses on peace. Christine inverts or subverts the traditional image of the king as warrior by uncoupling chivalry . . . from warfare entirely."[31] I would argue that Christine does not entirely uncouple chivalry and warfare but that she relegates the latter to one small corner of the former, and that chivalry in the *Livre des fais* is more akin to what we might call the essence of sound and beneficial government. Forhan further states that "true chivalry is not explicitly military, but in fact can prevent or avoid military engagement, thus serving the common good by protecting the weak and by recognizing the value of all the prince's subjects" (144). Thus the chivalrous king is not the one who successfully leads his armies in battle, but the one who uses negotiation and diplomacy to achieve his ends, who establishes and maintains peace, and whose primary concern is the *res publica*—the prosperity of the state and its people.

In establishing Charles V as the model for a new kind of chivalry, Christine also relies on a traditional paradigm of chivalry—the emperor Charlemagne. In the quote above, Charles V is presented as the equal and fourteenth-century version of his namesake, Charlemagne, the warrior-king par excellence. The medieval image of Charlemagne was so rich and multifaceted that it could be used to advance various—even conflicting—aims.[32] For her part, Christine chooses to emphasize the aspect of Charlemagne's legacy that will most effectively legitimize Charles V: the emperor's intellect, and his role in promoting France in general, and Paris in particular, as centers of learning. In the *Livre des fais* Charlemagne is not only a successful founding father and famous knight, but also an intellectual, a sort of double and soul mate of Charles V. This parallel is made most explicit in chapter 13 of book 3, in which Christine speaks of "comment le roy Charles amoit l'Université des clers, et comment elle vint à Paris" (II/46) [how the king Charles loved the University of clerics, and how the University came to Paris]. Her discussion of Charles V's love for the university, the "fille du roi" [daughter of the king], and the respect and privileges he accorded it, lead naturally to an account of the history of its foundation, under none other than Charlemagne. According to Christine, the University of Paris was founded by Alcuin under the aegis of Charlemagne, a cultured sovereign who "fist translater les estudes des sciences de Romme à Paris, tout ainsi comme jadis vindrent de Grece à Romme" (II/47) [transferred the seats of learning from Rome to Paris, just as formerly they came from Greece to Rome].[33] His close resemblance to Charlemagne allows Charles V to carry on, while revitalizing, the tradition of the wise and successful French monarch. By foregrounding the intellectual aspects of sovereignty and the necessity of all types of knowledge for effective governing, Christine creates a new vision of the ideal sovereign, illustrated by both Charles V and Charlemagne, in which, as Jacques Krynen writes, "[l]e chevalier preux cède la place au stratège."[34]

The *prudent ordeneur*

The most striking aspect of Christine's new ideal, as we have already seen relative to order and to chivalry, is the importance of wisdom for the king. The consequence of this quality is highlighted by the very structure of the *Livre des fais,* for book 3, which discusses wisdom, is as long as books 1 and 2 combined. The value of intellectual qualities is also evidenced by Charles's sobriquet—the Wise—given to him by Christine. As Kate Forhan writes, by the later Middle Ages there was a realization that "more [was] necessary for good government beyond the exercise of individual virtue. This enlargement of perspective focused attention on two virtues in particular, which were increasingly emphasized. Wisdom and prudence become the royal virtues par excellence" (83–84).

In the *Livre des fais* Christine identifies prudence as one of the elements of wisdom, and situates it "es parties de l'ame, là où advient prattique, qui apertient aux choses ouvrables" (II/21) [in the parts of the soul, there whence comes practice, which belongs to workable things]. She then separates the quality of prudence into its constitutive parts, invoking the authority of Cicero for her division: "prudence par memoire des choses passées porvoie aux futures, car, selon Tulle [i.e., Marcus Tullius Cicero] ou IIe des siennes Rethoriques, «les parties d'elle sont mises: memoire, intelligence et pourveance»" (II/21) [prudence, by the memory of past things, provides for future ones, for, according to Tullius in II of his *Rhetoric,* "the parts of {prudence} are: memory, intelligence, and foresight"]. In order to appreciate the significance of the prudence ascribed to Charles, it is necessary to differentiate the Middle French conception of prudence from our own modern English definition of the word. Today, prudence can carry a connotation of narrow-mindedness or Puritanism, and can also imply care with regard to small matters. The Middle French idea of prudence was at once broader and more vital. Liliane Dulac defines prudence as the "sagesse et science des choses pratiques,"[35] while Kate Forhan first identifies prudence as "moral wisdom" (107) and later expands her explanation to include "foresight, expertise, shrewdness and . . . even . . . deceit" (164).[36] Both authors emphasize the practical nature of prudence, making it something like applied wisdom.

Christine offers three examples of Charles V's prudence. The first illustrates the role of memory and foresight, and in particular how the memory of past events allows the prudent person to amend the course of future ones. "[P]our le bien de la couronne de France et de la commune utilité" (II/22) [for the good of the crown of France and the common utility], Charles codified the laws of succession, stipulating for example that the eldest son of the king was to succeed to the throne, that women could neither rule nor transmit the throne, and that a king's personal rule would begin at fourteen. These laws addressed and clarified questions of succession that had arisen during the final years of Capetian rule, and that had furnished the pretext for the Hundred Years War.[37]

Christine next discusses a major public works project that was planned but never implemented: the construction of a canal between the Loire and Seine rivers, which would have allowed merchandise to be transported by boat from Paris to the Loire valley. Though the king's untimely death precluded the execution of this project, its planning shows Charles to be "tres ameur et desireux du bien et proffit commun" (II/25) [very loving and desirous of the common good and profit].

Finally, Christine shows how Charles sought to assure his subjects' love and loyalty, and how this strengthened his own position: "comme il fust perfait ameur de ses subgiez, avisoit en toutes manieres de les tenir en amour et dilection vers lui, pour ce voult vers eulx tenir tel maniere que de touz estas se tenissent pour contens des ordenances" (II/28) [as he loved his subjects perfectly, he sought in all manners to maintain their love and happiness toward him, for this reason he wished to conduct himself such that all estates esteemed themselves satisfied with his edicts].[38] Although Christine presents Charles's conduct as benevolent, the result of his love for his people, she recognizes, as did he, that the most successful kings are those who seek to obtain and retain the consent of all of their subjects—not simply those who are the most powerful—with respect to important directives of the kingdom. This consent was achieved, as we have seen, through consultation.[39] In addition, Christine's subtle acknowledgment of the role of self-interest in governing, the awareness that consideration for the prosperity and contentedness of the kingdom assures the power and authority of the ruler, gives her text an original, and decidedly modern, outlook.[40] John of Salisbury and Giles of Rome, authors of two of the most influential medieval *miroirs du prince* and significant sources of the *Livre des fais*, both view self-interest as a characteristic of the tyrant, not of the ideal monarch. Yet the hallmark of Charles's prudence, and the secret to his success as a king, is the recognition that in serving his kingdom he is serving his own political ends.[41]

A close examination of the depiction of monarchy in the *Livre des fais*, such as the one undertaken here, reveals that certain details of Christine's vision of the ideal sovereign do not always cohere. Questions remain— who may counsel the king? is the authority of the king absolute? what is the role of *nobles, clers et bourgois* in the governing of the kingdom?—to which the text does not provide definitive answers. These tensions and uncertainties make Christine's text particularly compelling. The *Livre des fais* provides a snapshot of an unfolding transformation in the understanding of kingship and the relationship between the king and his subjects. On one hand, Christine continues to couch the relationship of Charles to his people in terms of individuals rather than offices or institutions, as an affective rather than a political rapport. All of her examples of the king's prudence insist upon his concern for his subjects and present

Charles as "perfait ameur de ses subgiez" (II/28) [perfect lover of his subjects]. His benevolent conduct is depicted as the result of personal virtue, in accordance with the *miroir du prince* tradition, which requires the ideal sovereign to love and protect the people entrusted to his care. Yet at the same time Christine's vocabulary—which includes terms such as *la couronne, l'utilité commune, le bien et proffit commun, l'estat du royaume*—points to a certain understanding of the state as a concept, and, in accordance with newly popularized Aristotelian notions of good government, identifies care of the *res publica* as the primary obligation of kingship.[42]

In the *Livre des fais* Christine both continues and revitalizes traditional ideas concerning the character, actions, and function of the king. She integrates Charles V and the Valois dynasty into the Capetian and Carolingian past, while at the same time postulating a new ideal of kingship that emphasizes the duties of the king toward his subjects and the common good, the establishment and maintenance of peace as an element of chivalry, and the importance of wisdom both for the king and for his advisors. Equally as significant, Christine's work responds to the political demands of her day by highlighting the legitimacy, indeed the glory, of the Valois. The *Livre des fais* makes the Valois dynasty newly canonical; with the advent of Charles V, the Valois can boast their own model sovereign, one fit to join the ranks of Saint Louis, Philippe Auguste, and Charlemagne. After the *Livre des fais*, the royal example to aspire to will no longer be Capetian or Carolingian, but Valois.

Notes

1. In the prologue to the *Livre des fais* Christine recognizes the innovative nature of her new work, which she characterizes as a "nouvelle compilacion menée en stille prosal et hors le commun ordre de mes autres choses passées" (I/5) [a new compilation carried out in a prose style and out of the common order of my other past things]. All textual citations are from Suzanne Solente's edition in two volumes (Geneva: Slatkine Reprints, 1977). The volume numbers provided refer to S. Solente's publication of the text and do not reflect Christine's tripartite division of her work.
2. Cary Nederman has observed that "until quite recently, scholars have systematically ignored or dismissed the body of Christine's political writings" ("The Mirror Crack'd: The *Speculum Principum* as Political and Social Criticism in the Late Middle Ages," *The European Legacy* 3.3 [1998]: 28).
3. Although not entirely, other factors certainly came into play. On one hand Christine's political writings, like those of many of her contemporaries, were perceived by many modern critics as fundamentally traditional, and therefore not worthy of study. In addition, it must be said that for many years the entire fourteenth and fifteenth centuries were relatively undervalued by literary critics, who viewed this period as one lacking in creativity and literary merit. Works such as Johan Huizinga's *The Waning of the Middle Ages: A Study of the Forms of Life, Thought and Art in France and the Netherlands in the XIVth and XVth*

Centuries (New York: Doubleday Anchor Books, 1954 [1924]) and Barbara Tuchman's *A Distant Mirror: The Calamitous Fourteenth Century* (New York: Knopf, 1978) illustrate this negative perception of the late Middle Ages. Daniel Poirion's seminal book *Le Poète et le Prince, l'évolution du lyrisme courtois de Guillaume de Machaut à Charles d'Orléans* (Paris: Presses Universitaires de France, 1965) led to a dramatic reevaluation of many late medieval authors and texts.

4. "Quelques aspects de la pensée politique de Christine de Pizan," in *Culture et politique en France à l'époque de l'Humanisme et de la Renaissance*, ed. Franco Simone (Turin: Accademia delle Scienze, 1974), 52.

5. Edited volumes on Christine now regularly include articles on her political works. See for example *The City of Scholars: New Approaches to Christine de Pizan*, ed. Margarete Zimmermann and Dina De Rentiis (New York and Berlin: Walter de Gruyter, 1994); *Une Femme de lettres au Moyen Age: études autour de Christine de Pizan*, ed. Liliane Dulac and Bernard Ribémont (Orléans: Paradigme, 1995); *Christine de Pizan 2000: Studies on Christine de Pizan in Honour of Angus J. Kennedy*, ed. John Campbell and Nadia Margolis (Amsterdam and Atlanta: Rodopi, 2000); *Au Champ des escriptures*, ed. Eric Hicks (Paris: Honoré Champion, 2000); and *Christine de Pizan: A Casebook*, ed. Barbara Altman and Deborah McGrady (New York and London: Routledge, 2003).

6. An English translation of the *Livre du corps de policie* was published by Kate Langdon Forhan in 1994 (*The Book of the Body Politic* [Cambridge: Cambridge University Press]), while a new critical edition of the same text was published by Angus Kennedy in 1998 (Paris: Champion); a modern French edition of the *Livre des fais* was produced by Eric Hicks and Thérèse Moreau in 1997 (Paris: Éditions Stock); and an edition and English translation of the *Livre des fais d'armes et de chevalerie* was produced by Sumner and Charity Cannon Willard in 1999 (*The Book of Deeds of Arms and of Chivalry* [University Park: Pennsylvania State University Press]).

7. For general historical context, see C. T. Allmand, *The Hundred Years War* (Cambridge: Cambridge University Press, 1988); Françoise Autrand, *Charles VI, la folie du roi* (Paris: Fayard, 1986); Alain Demurger, *Temps de crises, temps d'espoirs* (Paris: Éditions du Seuil, 1990); Jean Favier, *La Guerre de Cent Ans* (Paris: Fayard, 1980); and Jean Favier, *Le Temps des principautés* (Paris: Fayard, 1984). With respect to the Great Schism of the West, see Jean Favier, ed., *Genèse et débuts du Grand Schisme d'Occident (1362–1394)* (Paris: Éditions du Centre national de la recherche scientifique, 1980), and Edouard Perroy, *L'Angleterre et le grand Schisme d'Occident* (Paris: Librairie J. Monnier, 1933).

8. On the reign of Charles V, see, in addition to those works mentioned previously, Françoise Autrand's *Charles V: le sage* (Paris: Fayard, 1994).

9. The hybrid nature of the *Livre des fais* has certainly not escaped its readers, although the elements that constitute this hybrid vary somewhat from one author to the next. Joël Blanchard remarks that "[l]e *Livre* est en effet animé par un double dessein: le souci pédagogique . . .; [et] le désir de rappeler les moments importants de la vie d'un roi" ("Christine de Pizan: tradition, expérience et traduction," *Romania* 11 [1990]: 214); Liliane Dulac notes that the *Livre* is an important historical work, as well as "un traité de morale et de politique à l'usage des princes" ("De l'art de la digression dans *Le Livre des fais et bonnes meurs du sage roy Charles V*" in *The City of Scholars*, 148); Kate Forhan sees the work as both a biography and a study on rulership (*The Political Thought of Christine de Pizan*, 157); Eric Hicks and Thérèse Moreau characterize the work as a mirror and a panegyric (Introduction, *Le Livre des Faits et Bonnes Mœurs du*

roi Charles V le Sage, 16–17); Judith Laird views the Livre as panegyric and history ("Autobiographical Revelations of Christine de Pizan in her Le Livre des fais et bonnes meurs du sage roy Charles V," South Central Bulletin 14 [1997]: 56); Suzanne Solente, in the introduction to her edition of the work, affirms that the Livre was intended to "rendre hommage à la mémoire du grand souverain" as well as to "former une sorte de guide ou de manuel à l'usage d'un roi de France" (xxvii).

10. See for example chapter 13 of Christine's Livre du corps de policie, in which she affirms (following Valerius Maximus) that "plus meuvent a desirer venir a honneur et vaillance et amer vertu exemples que simples paroles" [examples inspire a greater desire to come to honor and courage and to love virtue than simple words] (Le Livre du corps de policie, ed. Angus Kennedy, 23).

11. Translations of Christine's texts are my own.

12. Christine's affirmation that Charles's kingship was somehow apparent to onlookers is not original. On the contrary, the recognizability of the king is a frequently encountered literary topos. By inscribing Charles in a tradition of transparent kingship, Christine reaffirms the legitimacy not only of Charles's rule, but of the entire Valois dynasty. It must be remembered that Valois rule had been challenged by the king of Navarre under the reign of Jean II (1350–64), and that the supposed illegitimacy of the Valois succession constituted the main pretext for the Hundred Years War.

13. Liliane Dulac notes very perceptively with respect to Christine's tentatives to establish her credibility as a political writer that the establishment of authority includes the presumption that one already has authority. She writes: "[i]ci, [i.e., in writing] comme ailleurs, il y a une part de fiction dans l'exercise du pouvoir" ("L'autorité dans les traités en prose de Christine de Pizan: Discours d'écrivain, parole de prince," in Une Femme de lettres au Moyen Age, 16). This insight applies equally well to Charles's staging of his own monarchical power and authority, and points to one of the many parallels between Christine and her biographical subject.

14. L'Empire du roi, idées et croyances politiques en France XIII^c–XV^c siècle, (Paris: Gallimard, 1993), 68.

15. (Princeton, NJ: Princeton University Press, 1957), 314.

16. Françoise Autrand has aptly pointed out with respect to Christine's account of the emperor's visit that "[l]'idée dominante du récit paraît donc être celle de l'ordre" ("Mémoire et cérémonial: La visite de l'empereur Charles IV à Paris en 1378 d'après les Grandes Chroniques de France et Christine de Pizan," in Une Femme de lettres au Moyen Age, 96).

17. On the topic of the formula rex in regno suo est imperator regni sui, along with the related formula, rex qui superiorem non recognoscit, see chapter 3 of Joseph Canning's A History of Medieval Political Thought, 300–1450 (London and New York: Routledge, 1996).

18. See Claire Richter Sherman's Imaging Aristotle, Verbal and Visual Representation in Fourteenth-Century France (Berkeley: University of California Press, 1995), 11. It should be remembered that Charles V oversaw the production of the Grandes Chroniques, and therefore the large amount of textual space dedicated to the emperor's visit, as well as the image chosen to illustrate it, demonstrate the significance of the visit and of that particular moment for Charles and his reign.

19. As Françoise Autrand has written: "peut-être les matines de Noël chantées à Cambrai, le silence des cloches à l'entrée des villes et le cheval noir de Charles

IV formaient-ils un message destiné au roi d'Angleterre plutôt qu'à l'empereur" ("Mémoire et cérémonial," 101).
20. Throughout Charles V's reign—and beyond—one of the principal stumbling blocks to peace with England was the issue of sovereignty. The French were willing to make considerable territorial concessions provided that they retain juridical sovereignty over the entirety of the kingdom.
21. Cited from *Ideal Government and the Mixed Constitution in the Middle Ages* (Princeton, NJ: Princeton University Press, 1992), 62.
22. Although Oresme's work was extremely influential, his ideas did not necessarily dominate the court. On the contrary, Charles's reign witnessed a theoretical struggle between proponents of a strong central authority in the person of the king, and a more distributive or consultative vision of monarchy, in which legislative and advisory bodies had a role to play. Jacques Krynen sees this clash as being illustrated by two great works produced under the reign of Charles V and commissioned by the king himself: Nicole Oresme's vernacular translation and commentary of Aristotle's *Politics*, and Évrart de Trémaugon's *Songe du Vergier*. Krynen summarizes the distance between these two works—and the ideologies they represent—as follows: "le fossé qui sépare les deux traités est éloquent: en moins de dix ans, deux ouvrages issus de la commande royale, deux monuments de la production politique médiévale française, ont en effet accouché de deux conceptions radicalement antithétiques de la monarchie. L'une extrait de la philosophie d'Aristote une doctrine de la «posté modérée». L'autre, éprise d'efficacité, est tendue vers l'affirmation de la «puissance absolue». Il n'y a pas de meilleur témoignage du bouillonnement des idées et, sous Charles V, de leur affrontement" (*L'Empire du roi*, 120).
23. See II/119 of the *Livre des fais*.
24. Charles's knack for detecting excellence in others was not limited to intellectual areas, as evidenced by his selection of Bertrand Du Guesclin as constable of France. By birth, Du Guesclin was certainly not the equal of past constables, but his tactical brilliance was largely to thank for the success of Charles's military efforts in the 1370s. The weight accorded to personal merit by Charles V is highlighted in the *Chronique des règnes de Jean II et de Charles V*, wherein it is written that Du Guesclin was selected "pour la vaillance du dit chevalier, car il estoit de mendre lignage que autre connestable, qui par avant eust esté, mais par sa vaillance, il avoit acquises pluseurs grans terres et seigneurie" [for the courage of the said knight, for he was of a lesser lineage than other constables, who had preceded him, but by his courage, he had acquired several great lands and lordship], ed. R. Delachenal (Paris: Société de l'Histoire de France, 1916–20), II/147. As one whose sex, rank, and status would not have been sufficient to command the attention of princes, it was important for Christine to emphasize the notion that individuals should be valued based on their personal gifts and qualities.
25. As she further explains, "c'est a entendre que le bon prince se doit conseillier a diverses gens selon ce qu'il a faire diverses choses. Car du fait de gouverner sa justice, ou les divers cas qui y pevent avenir, de ce ne se doit mie conseillier a ses gens d'armes ne a ses chevaliers, mes aux legistes et clers en ycelles science[s], aussi du fait des armes non mie aux clers; semblablement des autres choses" [that is to say that the good prince owes it to himself to consult various people according to his need to do various things. For, concerning the administration of his justice, or the various cases that can arise, about this he should not at all consult his men-at-arms or his knights, but jurists and clerics in those

disciplines, likewise on military matters he should not seek advice from clerics, and so on with respect to similar things] (37).
26. Charles announced his decision to accept the appeals on December 3, 1368, the same day as the long-awaited birth of a son, the future Charles VI.
27. Indeed, the rival popes became just another instrument of the antagonists in the Hundred Years War, and later in the French civil war.
28. This, despite her personal grief at the results of the Schism. Renate Blumenfeld-Kosinski has noted that "[a]s historian/biographer looking back at the year 1378 Christine approves of Charles's policies, but as the writer living in 1404, she cannot but bemoan the heavy price paid for Charles's course of action" ("Christine de Pizan and the Political Life in Late Medieval France," in *Christine de Pizan: A Casebook*, 16).
29. The French suffered devastating losses at the battles of Crécy (1346) and Poitiers (1356).
30. In her article "De l'art de la digression" Liliane Dulac discusses the primacy of intellectual virtues in the *Livre des fais*. She analyzes the various types of digressions in which Christine engages, including the extensive technical military discussions that occupy so much of book 2. Dulac observes that "[l]a mention des succès appelle immédiatement l'analyse des moyens qui peuvent conduire à pareil résultat, et ces moyens sont d'abord intellectuels: c'est la 'prudence'—sagesse et sciences des choses pratiques—qui fait la 'chevalerie' de ce roi" (153).
31. See Forhan's *Political Theory*, 143. Nadia Margolis states that the *Livre des fais* "reflects the flowering of the new chivalric ideal" ("Christine de Pizan: The Poetess as Historian," *Journal of the History of Ideas* 47 [1986]: 372). However, like Kate Forhan, I believe that Christine goes a long way toward creating, rather than merely reflecting, this new ideal.
32. Robert Morrissey examines the legacy of Charlemagne in *L'Empereur à la barbe fleurie: Charlemagne dans la mythologie et l'histoire de France* (Paris: Gallimard, 1997), in which he writes: "[é]voquer la figure de Charlemagne devient un moyen non seulement de concevoir et de légitimer ses origines, mais aussi de le faire *par rapport* à l'autre" (10, emphasis in original). In the early years of the Valois dynasty, the *other* in question was the king of England, and the task facing the Valois rulers was to construct an unassailably legitimate claim to the French throne in the face of vigorous English opposition.
33. For an insightful analysis of the significance of translation, as well as the role of Christine de Pizan and Charles V as translators, see Lori Walters, "Christine de Pizan as Translator and Voice of the Body Politic," in *Christine de Pizan: A Casebook*, 25–41.
34. *L'Empire du roi*, 213.
35. "De l'art de la digression," 153.
36. Forhan's inclusion of deceit as a component of prudence is interesting, and merits comment. Charles V was famously adept at manipulating language. Christine frequently praises his rhetorical skill, in particular in chapter 43 of book 3, entitled "comment le roy Charles parla au Conseil, present l'Empereur, du tort que le roy d'Angleterre avoit vers lui" (II/116) [how the king Charles spoke to the Council, with the Emperor present, of the wrong that the king of England had perpetrated toward him]. The English naturally had a less favorable opinion of Charles's facility with language, referring to him as the *roi des avocats*. In chapter 26 of book 3 Charles speaks of the relative moral value of dissimulation. In response to some in his entourage, who maintain that dissimulation is a type of treason, Charles replies that "les circonstances

font les choses bonnes ou mauvaises, car en tel maniere peut estre dissimulé, que c'est vertu, et en tel maniere, vice" (II/74) [circumstances make things good or bad, for in one way something can be dissimulated and it is a virtue, and in another way, a vice]. Chapter 23 of Françoise Autrand's *Charles V* offers an insightful discussion of Charles's strategic deployment of language and the law.

37. For a historical overview of the background to and start of the Hundred Years War, see chapters 1 and 2 of Jean Favier's *La Guerre de Cent Ans*, as well as chapter 1 of C. T. Allmand's *The Hundred Years War*. The legal justification for the Valois claim to the throne was founded largely on an article of Salic Law, which was rediscovered and skillfully deployed during the late fourteenth and early fifteenth centuries in a *post facto* attempt to legitimize the succession of Philippe VI. On the history of Salic Law and its application to fourteenth-century successions, see Philippe Contamine, "'Le royaume de France ne peut tomber en fille': Fondement, formulation et implication d'une théorie politique à la fin du Moyen-Age," *Perspectives Médiévales* (June 1987): 67–81.

38. In the *Livre des fais* Christine clearly depicts Charles's efforts to maintain the contentedness of his subjects—including those of modest social standing—in a positive light. On Christine's attitude more generally toward those of the lower classes, and the manner in which her outlook evolved over the course of her career, see Susan Dudash's recent article "Christine de Pizan and the 'menu peuple,'" *Speculum* 78.3 (2003): 788–831.

39. See for example the following previously quoted passage: "quant venoit à conseillier sus l'estat du royaume, il appelloit à son conseil les bourgois de ses bonnes villes, et meismement des moyenes gens, et de celz du commun, affin qu'il leur moustrast la fiance qu'il avoit en eulx" (II/28).

40. This perspective is articulated also in the *Livre des Trois Vertus* (ed. Charity Cannon Willard and Eric Hicks [Paris: Honoré Champion, 1989], which is thought to have been composed at roughly the same time as the *Livre des fais*. In chapter 8 of part 1 Christine discusses the role of the princess in preserving the goodwill of the prince's subjects, and says that the princess should explain to her husband "comment il est neccessaire que prince, se longuement il veult regner en paix et glorieusement, soit améz de ses subgiéz et de son peuple" (33) [how it is necessary that the prince, if he wishes to reign for a long time gloriously and in peace, be loved by his subjects and by his people].

41. See Kate Forhan's *Political Theory* on the subject of *prudence* in Christine's political works, especially 80–85, 100–109, and the conclusion, where she also discusses the ways in which Christine's concept of *prudence* prefigures Machiavelli's *virtù*.

42. With regard to Christine's composite and sometimes contradictory conception of kingship, Jeannine Quillet remarks that "du point de vue de la signification politique du regard qu'elle porte sur le roi, elle reste dépendante à la fois d'une conception ministérielle du pouvoir politique dans la ligne de l'augustinisme politique: le roi est le bon pasteur, le roi très chrétien, défenseur de l'Église; sa «sagesse» en est l'illustration la plus remarquable. Mais en même temps une telle sagesse n'exclut nullement la prise en compte d'une figure de roi prudent, soucieux de délibération et de calcul, habile à négocier pour imposer sa volonté—au pape, à l'Université, à la Bretagne et à la Guyenne, aux Anglais" (*D'une cité à l'autre, problèmes de philosophie politique médiévale* [Paris: Honoré Champion, 2001], 311).

Cupid's Wheel: Love and Fortune in The Knight's Tale

ROBERT STRETTER

In his 1602 edition of *The Canterbury Tales*, Thomas Speght writes that *The Knight's Tale* "discourseth of the deeds of Arms and the love of Ladies," a description that might serve as a general definition of the tale's traditional generic rubric, chivalric romance.[1] Scholars have noted that love, more than arms, is *The Knight's Tale*'s primary focus. J. A. Burrow, for instance, asserts that Palamon and Arcite "are lovers and nothing else, in the best romantic tradition."[2] Chaucer himself describes an early version of the tale as telling "al the love of Palamon and Arcite / Of Thebes."[3] But if one calls *The Knight's Tale* a love story, one must do so reservedly, for Chaucer's treatment of love in the tale differs significantly from how he treats it elsewhere in his work.

The Knight's Tale is indeed about love, but not in the usual sense of an emotional connection between human beings. Chaucer's poem explores instead the overwhelming power of love over individuals. This essay argues that Chaucer, aided by his generic choices, models love in *The Knight's Tale* on traditional representations of fortune, the vicissitudes of which form the other main theme of the narrative. In so doing, Chaucer develops what might be called "amatory fatalism"—love as something that *happens to* the lover and robs him of choice and reason—as a way of understanding by analogy problems of chance, destiny, and Providence. Chaucer's characterization of love, in addition to his problematic portrayal of the pagan gods, calls into question the Boethian reading of fortune as Providence at the end of *The Knight's Tale*, since the particularized sufferings of the lovers resist the generalized consolation of philosophy. The similarities between love and fortune give a human face to an inscrutable cosmos and allow Chaucer to maintain a sympathetic focus on how humans *perceive* experience, regardless of how that experience is ultimately ordered or explained.

Chance and Romance: The Genre of *The Knight's Tale*

Chaucer's portrayal of love and fortune is intimately linked to questions of genre. His approach to love in *The Knight's Tale* is a departure from

Medievalia et Humanistica, New Series, Number 31 (Paul Maurice Clogan, ed.), Rowman & Littlefield Publishers, Inc., 2005.

much of his other poetry on the subject, where he portrays himself as an Ovidian figure who might be dubbed "Love's Storyteller" or the "Clerk of Love." This is the Chaucer of the dream visions, the devotee of the daisy whom Alceste defends in the prologue to *The Legend of Good Women*. This is also the Chaucer of *Troilus and Criseyde*, professing not to be a lover himself but rather one who honors the God of Love by narrating the woes of his servants (I.15–51). And this is the Chaucer whom readers meet in the introduction to the *Man of Law's Tale*, which announces that "he hath toold of loveris up and doun / Mo than Ovide made of mencioun / in his Epistles" (II.53–55). As "Love's Storyteller," Chaucer writes about the religion of love, exploring the mysteries of "Seynt Venus" and Cupid, the God of Love (Pro *LGW* G 313). In *The House of Fame*, Chaucer presents his dream journey as an education necessary for a love poet, a way of acquiring more accurate "tydynges / Of Loves folk" (644–45); so too in *The Parliament of Fowls*, where Venus's temple and a love-debate provide the dreamer with "mater of to wryte" (168). The poet-dreamer's role in these narratives is like that of an anthropologist studying the cult of love. He observes, collects data in the form of stories or examples (*mater*, *tydynges*), and reports what he learns for the edification of his readers. Chaucer's engagement with the religion of love can be clearly seen in the prologue to *The Legend of Good Women*, with its references to saints (Venus, good women), heresies (e.g., Chaucer's translation of the *Roman de la Rose*), repentance, and penance (the *Legend* itself). Chaucer defends himself against charges of heresy by pleading good intentions and, characteristically, ignorance of love; Alceste, Cupid's queen, takes Chaucer's side, listing for the God of Love the works that the poet undertook "in preysinge of your name" (F 416).

Chaucer's approach to love in *The Knight's Tale*, however, is philosophical rather than theological, intricately bound up with his interest in the workings of fortune in a pre-Christian world. The cult of love still figures in the tale: Cupid remains "the god of love" who binds lovers by his "lawe"; the imprisoned Palamon and Arcite profess to "love and serve" Emelye immediately upon seeing her; Palamon promises Venus "thy temple wol I worshipe everemo" and "dye in thy servyse" (1785, 1165, 1143, 2251, 2243). But it is the philosophy of Boethius, rather than the religion of *fin amor*, that sets the tone of the poem. Fortune, which plays a central role in the poem from its very beginning when the Knight receives the lot "by aventure, or sort, or cas" (*GP* 844), had a complex range of signification in the Middle Ages.[4] On a general level, Dame Fortuna in her various incarnations guarantees earthly instability, while in medieval theology and philosophy, "Fortune" is a technical term, part of what R. E. Kaske describes as "the famous 'Boethian hierarchy': Providence, Destiny, Fortune, Nature, and their earthly results."[5] In this discussion, I will use "Fortune" as Chaucer does, which is to say loosely, as a synonym for "aventure, or sort, or cas."[6] Chaucer most often seems to use the term to mean "that which happens to us," thus stressing the passive role of human beings who experience events, while at the same time recognizing that events necessarily raise questions of causality. The cause, depending on whether one takes a pagan or Christian perspective, can be identified as Fate or Providence. With its active pagan deities and its Boethian conclusion, *The Knight's Tale* manages to present both perspectives simultaneously, making it difficult to draw clear distinctions between them. But distinctions at the level of causation are unimportant to Chaucer. His treatment of fortune in *The Knight's Tale*, regardless of fortune's ultimate causes, puts the emphasis on human experience, on how human beings *react* to what their circumstances bring to them.

Why does Chaucer, if he wishes to expound the nature of fortune, choose a chivalric romance rather than something along the lines of the *de casibus* stories told by the pilgrim Monk?[7] One answer lies in the episodic conventions of chivalric romance itself. M. W. Bloomfield links the growth of romance during "the narrative revolution of the twelfth century" to a "resuscitation of interest in Boethius and a re-evaluation of *Fortuna*." Both Fortuna and romance, he argues, serve as figures for "the arbitrariness of life."[8] More recently, Susan Crane and Barbara Nolan have emphasized that *aventure*, the favorite romance term for chance happenings, is the key concept for understanding romance structure: "The linking of episodes *par aventure*," writes Nolan, "is of the essence of medieval romance construction."[9] Crane argues at length in *Gender and Romance in the* Canterbury Tales that "Chaucer's sense of adventure's illogicalities and marvels" links *The Knight's Tale*'s romance form to issues of feminine mystery, an argument that can be extended to the parallel between romance happenstance and mutable fortune.[10] Crane mentions in passing that Chaucer's interest in romance influences his treatment not only of gender, but also of social order and destiny; in fact, the conclusions she draws about romance and gender are readily extrapolated to fortune, which is conventionally associated with femininity.

One might object that if medieval romance is characterized by *aventure*, then fortune is arguably central to almost any romance and thus that Chaucer can scarcely help but reveal what is inherent to the genre. One finds, however, that Chaucer takes great care to emphasize both fortune and *aventure* in *The Knight's Tale*. Jill Mann points out that Chaucer "alter[s] his Boccaccian source in order to emphasize the role of chance in the events of the narrative."[11] Nolan notes that not only does the term *aventure* appear more often in *The Knight's Tale* than in any other tale, it also provides "the mainspring of most . . . of the story's action"; *The Knight's Tale*, in fact, accounts for more than one third of the word's occurrences in the whole of *The Canterbury Tales*.[12] Chaucer's selectivity is further underscored by the fact that he does not always use a fortune-related vocabulary when dealing with romance material. In *The Squire's Tale*, the most obvious "romance" in *The Canterbury Tales*, there is not a single occurrence of the word *aventure*. Significantly, the other two poems with the highest occurrence of the term are *Troilus and Criseyde* and *The Franklin's Tale*;[13] these works, together with *The Knight's Tale*, are what A. C. Spearing has usefully called the "philosophical romances."[14] The philosophical romances all highlight Chaucer's practice of exploring questions of great import to medieval Christians by setting them in a richly imagined pagan world that is free from both the limitations and the advantages of Christian dogma.

It seems likely, then, that Chaucer would have found romance ideally suited to treatments of fortune precisely because of its reliance on fortuitousness and accident (whether expressed as "hap," "cas," "aventure," or "sort") to move the action along. Moreover, conventions of love in romance—sudden passions, amatory complaints, reversals of fortune, and so forth—tend to reinforce these issues of arbitrariness. Yet what Chaucer does in the philosophical romances is unparalleled in medieval English literature.[15] His attention to the philosophical implications of the romance *aventure* convention distinguishes him even from so great an artist as Chrétien de Troyes, whose heroes encounter unduly fortuitous opportunities to prove their knightly worth but reflect little on the strangeness of these occurrences. This is no criticism of Chrétien, who uses the romance form to explore important issues of his own, but it serves to emphasize the new ways in which Chaucer treats conventional material.

Amatory Fortune and Deterministic Love

Howard R. Patch has established that the portrayal of Dame Fortuna as "Goddess of Love" was common in medieval literature, especially among the French poets who influenced Chaucer.[16] In *The Knight's Tale*, however, Chaucer does not directly personify fortune. Instead, he establishes the analogy between love and fortune in two more subtle ways. First, he makes a connection through his choice of language; second, he describes an identical human response to both love and fortune: complaint. The language Chaucer employs in describing the act of falling in love emphasizes the element of chance. Palamon's fatal glimpse of Emelye in the garden, for instance, comes about "by aventure or cas" (1074). Similar examples can also be found in the other two "philosophical romances." Troilus's first sight of Criseyde is also attributed to "cas" (I.271). In *The Franklin's Tale*, "it happed" that Aurelius and Dorigen fall into conversation at a dance (V.960), which leads to his confession of love.[17] Beyond descriptions of love's initial thunderclap, Chaucer uses terms such as "aventure" or "hap" in conjunction with love throughout *Troilus and Criseyde* (e.g., I.784, 896; II.281–88; III.1217). Similar usage of the vocabulary of chance can be found in *The Knight's Tale*, as in the reaction of the ladies of Theseus's court to Palamon and Arcite's love feud: they think it "[g]reet pitee . . . [t]hat evere swich a chaunce sholde falle" (1751–52). The effect of Chaucer's casting the experience of love in terms of fortuitousness is a sense that falling in love is a great improbability, an accident of fortune in which two people happen to be in the same place at the same time.

This amatory fatalism suggests that one can no more escape loving than one can escape the divine "necessitee" that determines human fortune.[18] The scene of Palamon and Arcite's prison rivalry offers a good illustration of this kind of language. As W. A. Davenport observes, Chaucer first establishes firmly the social duty that Palamon and Arcite owe to one another: "The terms of address and identification of the other, *brother, cosyn, knight,* are all reminders of obligation."[19] The traditional duties of friendship, one of which is providing counsel,[20] inform Palamon's assertion, "I . . . tolde thee my wo / As to my conseil and my brother sworn / To forthre me" (1146–48). In his complaint against Arcite, Palamon repeatedly mentions the particular terms of their obligation: the men are to aid each other "in every cas" (1138), a phrase which suggests not only "in all situations," but also hints at "in whatever fortune may bring." Significantly, the only "cas" specified is a love affair.

Love, however, is portrayed as a selfish endeavor, unconducive to same-sex teamwork. As Arcite says, "Ech man for hymself, ther is no oother" (1182). Arcite's self-defense in the face of Palamon's charges of treachery hinges on his interpretation of love as an irresistible force that cancels all other obligations:

> Wostow nat wel the olde clerkes sawe,
> That 'who shal yeve a lovere any lawe?'
> Love is a gretter lawe, by my pan,
> Than may be yeve to any erthely man;
> And therfore positif lawe and swich decree
> Is broken al day for love in ech degree. (1163–68)

Here Arcite depicts love, like fortune, as a celestial power dictating human actions. The proverb Arcite cites comes from *The Consolation of Philosophy* (3.m12), where Boethius intends it as a negative comment on Orpheus's rash love. But to Arcite it is merely an "olde clerkes sawe" that serves his purpose of self-justification. Then comes Arcite's most telling assertion: "A man moot nedes love, maugree his heed; / He may nat fleen it, thogh he sholde be deed" (1169–70). This characterization of love as inevitable sounds very much like Theseus's definition of "necessitee" as "that we may nat eschue" (3042–43). Love acts, in effect, as a naturalistic analogue to the larger forces of destiny in *The Knight's Tale*. That is, if "necessitee" can be interpreted as something imposed on man from outside his power of choice, a grand cosmological barrier to free will, love functions similarly but within the natural, earthly sphere. Arcite suggests that human beings cannot avoid the dictate of love because it is part of their terrestrial nature.[21]

Troilus and Criseyde, which is thought to have been written around the same time as *The Knight's Tale*, offers some parallels that can further elucidate Chaucer's approach to amatory fortune. Take for instance the way Chaucer blends commonplace notions of love and fortune when he chastises Troilus's haughty contempt for love—the equivalent, he implies, of the false security of those who scorn the power of fortune:

> O blynde world, O blynde entencioun!
> How often falleth al the effect contraire
> Of surquidrie and foul presumpcioun . . .
> . . . .
> This Troilus is clomben on the staire,
> And litel weneth that he moot descenden . . . (I.211–13, 215–16)

The subject at hand in this stanza is specifically love, but the rhetoric is familiar from medieval treatments of fortune in general, such as *de casibus* tragedy. The image of ascending and descending a stair is a variation on the ups and downs brought by Lady Fortune's infamous wheel. This portrait of love's power of change may be compared with Chaucer's description of lovers in *The Knight's Tale* as "now up, now doun, as boket in a welle" (1532–35).[22] While the detail might seem minor in *The Knight's Tale*, in *Troilus and Criseyde* Chaucer follows the stair image with an extended point about the inescapability of love, using Troilus as an example of the power of love (like fortune) to affect both great and small. Chaucer's reminder that the "strengest folk ben therwith overcome, / The worthiest and grettest of degree" (*TC* I.243–44) parallels the ubiquitous medieval warnings that even the greatest king can fall if Fortune chooses to spin her wheel.

In *Troilus and Criseyde*, Chaucer also develops the connection alluded to by Arcite between love and natural law. Chaucer presents the "lawe of kynde" as essentially a naturalistic form of determinism, and offers Troilus as an example of the futility of struggling against natural imperatives:

> Forthy ensample taketh of this man,
> Ye wise, proude, and worthi folkes alle,
> To scornen Love, which that so soone kan
> The fredom of youre hertes to hym thralle;
> For evere it was, and evere it shal byfalle,
> That Love is he that alle thing may bynde,
> For may no man fordon the lawe of kynde. (I.232–38)

Chaucer reinforces the complete authority of the "lawe of kynde" by comparing mankind to the horse who must obey "horses lawe" (I.218–24). In *The Knight's Tale*, one recognizes the sort of inevitable love described in *Troilus* when Theseus, having discovered Palamon and Arcite's love quarrel, exclaims:

> The god of love, a benedicite!
> How myghty and how greet a lord is he!

Ayeyns his myght ther gayneth none obstacles.
He may be cleped a god for his myracles,
For he kan maken, at his owene gyse,
Of everich herte as that hym list divyse. (1785–90)

Theseus's statement that Cupid "*may be cleped* a god" because of his power to achieve his will hints that the God of Love may be more a personification of natural imperatives (the "lawe of kynde") than a god in his own right. One way of interpreting these lines would be to say that love has godlike powers over the human heart. Because Cupid, like the personification of Fortune, does not correspond to a planet, he occupies an uncertain position as a heavenly force. Venus, of course, is a planet, but this perhaps makes it all the more noteworthy that complaints about love are directed to Cupid instead of her. Lacking the capacity for planetary influence, the only way in which pagan gods could be "real" within the framework of medieval science, Cupid runs the risk of being diminished to a metaphor or dismissed altogether as an illusion, as Gower does with Fortune in the *Confessio Amantis*.[23]

The sentiments Theseus expresses about love's power draw on the conventional idea of lovers as thralls to Cupid, but in the larger context of fortune that Chaucer explores so attentively in all three of his philosophical romances, one begins to see a more causal and less casual connection between the themes. This comparison of human beings in love to irrational, enslaved animals suggests, for instance, an additional level of meaning for the animal imagery Chaucer uses to describe the rival lovers in *The Knight's Tale* (e.g., 1655–59, 1698–99). These lines are often interpreted to mean that excessive (animal) passion degrades humanity to the level of beasts, which leads one to pass moral judgment, implicitly or explicitly, on Palamon and Arcite. Although such a reading has its merits, Chaucer's association of passion with fortune and destiny may call into question the young knights' powers of choice in the matter. In both *The Knight's Tale* and *Troilus and Criseyde*, love and fortune provide mutually informing models of the human condition as one in which will, choice, and reason are limited by powerful yet intangible external forces.

In *The Knight's Tale*, the impersonal forces associated with fortune influence Chaucer's depiction of love in a way that makes love also appear impersonal and arbitrary. This is why one gets a stronger sense of Palamon and Arcite's frustration in the face of this arbitrariness than one does of their feelings for Emelye. This can also help explain why Chaucer, as Elisabeth Salter writes, "abandons almost completely [Boccaccio's] 'three-dimensional' way of regarding human beings" in *The Knight's Tale*.[24] Indeed, very few psychological details appear in the tale, and the reason is that, unlike *Troilus*, *The Knight's Tale* is not principally about male-female love. Perhaps this is why Chaucer describes it as "the love of Palamon and Arcite," with no mention of Emelye. Chaucer tells the story of what happens to these two men as a result of love; Emelye's primary function is to cause that love, which is why it is only partially accurate to describe the gender dynamics of *The Knight's Tale* as a woman coming between men. The source of the men's conflict is love itself, which is only loosely attached (in this instance) to a particular woman.

Chaucer is interested not only in the effect of love on Palamon and Arcite, but in the threat that an arbitrary, irrational, and irresistible love poses to ideals such as reason, honor, loyalty, and friendship. In spite of lingering positive elements of courtly love, Chaucer places love in stark opposition to the Boethian wisdom that Theseus recommends. Although Theseus does show respect for the God of Love, remembering the time when he was a lover himself (1814), he considers passionate love something to be left behind with age and maturity.[25] So too when he finds the kinsmen fighting in the woods, he does not object to the source of their quarrel, since "he thoghte wel that every man / Wol helpe hymself in love, if that he kan" (1767–68); instead, Theseus emphasizes Cupid's poor treatment of his followers: "See how they blede! . . . / Thus hath hir lord, the god of love, ypayed / Hir wages and hir fees for hir servyse!" (1801–3). The emphasis on the suffering of lovers rather than the joys continues in the temple of Venus, which depicts "[t]he firy strokes of the desirynge / That loves servantz in this lyf enduren" (1922–23).

This darker vision of love is one of the tale's major departures from the sort of love portrayed in the dream poems, and even in *Troilus*. In addition, Chaucer's attention to the negative side of love marks an important change from the *Teseida*, which though it professes to be about the noble deeds done for Mars, is equally about those done for Venus.[26] In Boccaccio, love is portrayed as having an ultimately positive influence on lovers. On his deathbed, Arcita has no regrets about falling in love; in fact, though it cost him his life, he feels that love has made him a better man:

Love taught me to become humble; it made me fearless, it made me gracious and gentle, it made my faith holy and pure. It showed me that I should never hold any creature in contempt, it made me courteous and obedient, it made me valiant and steadfast.[27]

This positive estimation of love is common in courtly romance, and provides a link between the *Teseida* and *Troilus and Criseyde*, which, thematically speaking, have more in common with each other than either does with *The Knight's Tale*.[28]

The malevolent force of love that permeates *The Knight's Tale* can be seen in Chaucer's description of a domineering Cupid who brooks no challengers:

> O Cupide, out of alle charitee!
> O regne, that wolt no felawe have with thee!
> Ful sooth is seyd that love ne lordshipe

Wol noght, his thankes, have no felaweshipe.
Wel fynden that Arcite and Palamon. (1623-27)

The terms "felawe" and "felaweshipe" have an important resonance here, suggesting not only that Cupid does not allow equals (for fear of competitors), but implying also that he threatens, obstructs, and prevents comradeship among the mortals he controls. This depiction of Cupid, as well as the presence of a Venus with whom nothing can "holde champartie" (1949), draws on the tradition of *eros tyrannos* and serves to associate love with tyranny in *The Knight's Tale*. J. D. Burnley writes that in medieval literature "[t]he image of the tyrant, which is a moral and psychological symbol of disorder, extends far beyond the political sphere."[29] Like Creon, the tyrant Cupid lacks any sense of justice and behaves erratically. Moreover, tyranny provides an additional link between love and fortune, another force frequently envisioned as a tyrant. Tyranny, love, and fortune—supported generically by romance's sense of *aventure*—all contribute to *The Knight's Tale*'s atmosphere of instability, chance, and fatalism. A citizen is to a tyrant as a lover is to Cupid and as all mankind is to fortune—completely at the mercy of a powerful and malign whim.

The Mode of Complaint

Love and fortune in *The Knight's Tale* are analogous not only in their unpredictability, their inevitability, and their capacity to bring extreme joy followed by extreme sorrow, but also in the responses they elicit from their victims. Both love and fortune give rise to poetic complaint, a parallel for which Chaucer would have found precedent in French writers. James Wimsatt writes that "[i]t was the idea of Guillaume de Lorris to adapt the Boethian topics and dramatic situation to a love narrative," adding that Guillaume transforms the Boethian "cosmic lament" into "the lover's complaint," just as Machaut later does in his *Remede de Fortune*.[30] In his book *Chaucer: Complaint and Narrative*, W. A. Davenport convincingly demonstrates both Chaucer's interest in and his sophisticated use of complaint rhetoric. The fact that Davenport singles out the philosophical romances—*The Knight's Tale*, *Troilus and Criseyde*, and *The Franklin's Tale*, to which he devotes a chapter each—as prime examples of Chaucer's use of complaint is particularly telling in conjunction with his assertion that the poet's "exploration of the first-person expression of the lover's moods and moral states perhaps led naturally to the expression of more general reflections in religious and philosophical lyrics."[31] The philosophical framework of *The Knight's Tale* provides the perfect setting for just this kind of interaction between complaints about love and those about the more general vicissitudes of fortune.

The intermingling of love and fortune as themes for complaint can be seen from the instant Arcite mistakes Palamon's love-struck cry—"A!" (1078)—for a disconsolate reaction to the misfortune of prison:

> For Goddes love, taak al in pacience
> Our prisoun, for it may noon oother be.
> Fortune hath yeven us this adversitee. (1084–86)

Arcite goes on to emphasize the inevitability of fortune, which cannot be escaped "although we hadde it sworn" (1089), a phrase that provides ironic comment on the durability of sworn brotherhood when confronted by fortune in the form of love. Within the space of ten lines, Chaucer transforms Palamon from a "sorweful prisoner . . . compleynynge of his wo" (1070–72) into a new type of prisoner—a slave to love—with a new cause for complaint. At this point in the narrative, fortune and love are not just similar but identical.

The two themes also comingle in the long, formal complaints that follow Arcite's release from prison. As Davenport points out, Arcite's speech beginning "Allas that day that I was born" (1223) moves from love lament "into the more general phase of Boethian moral complaint concerning Fortune."[32] Arcite worries about fortune's ability to give Palamon romantic access to Emelye: "For possible is . . . / That by some cas, syn Fortune is chaungeable, / Thow maist to thy desire somtyme atteyne" (1240–43).[33] This talk of fortune leads into an explicitly Boethian reflection on the problems of the human condition, and then back again to Arcite's specific amatory dilemma: "Syn that I may nat seen you, Emelye, / I nam but deed" (1273–74). This shifting of the complaint's focus between localized love and generalized fortune renders ambiguous Arcite's assertion, "O deere cosyn Palamon . . . thyn is the victorie of this aventure" (1234–35). Is the *aventure* in question Arcite's release from prison? Or is it the love rivalry itself? By conflating the themes of love and fortune, Chaucer allows it to be both.

Palamon's complaint follows the pattern of Arcite's, beginning with the problem of love, expanding the issue to encompass the heavenly powers he thinks are responsible for fortune, then returning to the case at hand. The triple complaint against Saturn, Juno, and Venus that ends Palamon's lament (1328–33) prefigures Arcite's later accusation of Juno, Mars, and Love (1542–66). Both of these passages contribute to the poem's theme of amatory fatalism by associating love with the forces of destiny, as Davenport realizes when he comments that the complaints "make the results of love part of the determinist view of the historical events." As he explains further, Palamon and Arcite protest "not just against the injustices of love, but against love as a type of the injustices of history and fate."[34] This interaction accounts in part for the dark portrayal of love in *The Knight's Tale*: the opprobrium conventionally heaped on fortune tarnishes the erstwhile ideal of chivalric love.

Love, however, is more than an instance of fortune; it is the most intelligible microcosm of it. Both produce the same apparently inexplicable (to blinkered mortal eyes) cycles of loss and gain. But because love operates within earthly Nature, the inexorable "lawe of kynde," it is considerably more tangible, more humanly accessible, than the arcane operation of general fortune.[35] The human experience of love is more acute, personal, and finally comprehensible than the abstraction "Fortune" because it involves a love object directly linked to the individual's joys and sorrows. Chaucer shows that, by particularizing fortune in this way, love allows mortals to imagine that they can see the shadowy chain of cause and effect. An excellent example comes when Arcite complains about the malevolence of Mars, Juno, and Love. The speech begins on the level of abstract fate as Arcite blames the gods for the tragic destiny of Thebes. He then makes the connection between the ill fortune of his people and his own amatory destiny, complaining that because of love "shapen was my deeth erst than my sherte" (1566). Finally, he latches on to Emelye:

> Ye sleen me with youre eyen, Emelye!
> *Ye been the cause* wherfore that I dye. (1567–68, my emphasis)

One can see clearly how Arcite's thinking goes from the general to the specific. Unlike fortune, Emelye offers a tangible cause for Arcite's suffering. Chaucer's use of love as a model for fortune thus presents a brilliant way of demonstrating how the abstract problems of human suffering can be more keenly felt and perhaps better understood by way of analogy with other types of experience. Conventional lovesickness has been expanded to provide a model of human subjection to fortune.

Human Suffering and the Pagan Gods

The complaints against love and fortune in *The Knight's Tale* pose explicit questions about the nature of causality and justice. Chaucer's focus on the suffering of Palamon and Arcite as lovers has important implications for interpreting Theseus's controversial Boethian speech at the end of the poem. As Theseus attempts to allay the general grief that follows Arcite's untimely death, he claims to solve the problem of seemingly unjust fortune by putting it in the classic Boethian context of divine Providence, which springs from a "Firste Moevere" whom Theseus identifies as "Juppiter, the kyng." Theseus has been traditionally, and, I think, rightly, understood as a force of order, a figure who attempts not only to offer consolation, but also to invoke rituals and ceremonies (such as funeral and marriage) that allow human beings to cope with misfortune and go on living. But Theseus's attempts at closure and consolation, at the creation of a happy ending that reflects the familiar pattern of Middle English romance, are frustrated by the sufferings of Arcite and Palamon as lovers and by Chaucer's depiction of the pagan gods, particularly Saturn.

The actions of the pagan gods seriously complicate Theseus's consolation. In representing the gods, Chaucer makes some significant additions to his source material: he introduces the narrative of cosmic strife, the impotent figure of Jupiter, and the consequent need for a mediator—Saturn—to resolve the conflict. In the *Teseida*, Boccaccio makes clear that Palemone and Arcita conduct their rivalry under the auspices of Venus and Mars, but there is no sense that the contest between the gods is particularly bitter. Just as Boccaccio appeals to both Mars and Venus to inspire him in his poetic undertaking, Palemone and Arcita call on both deities prior to their fight in the woods.[36] Although Palemone eventually fights under the banner of Venus and Arcita pledges himself to Mars, Boccaccio's gods do not themselves seem to be personally involved in the "strif" imagined by Chaucer. In fact, after the young men offer prayers in the temples of their respective deities, Venus and Mars settle things quite amicably between themselves; when Venus courteously insists that she will fulfill her promise to Palemone, Mars concedes graciously: "What you say is true, dear; now do whatever gives you perfect pleasure."[37] Chaucer, however, follows his temple scene with a much more polarized version of events:

> And right anon swich strif ther is bigonne,
> . . . .
> Bitwixe Venus, the goddesse of love,
> And Mars, the stierne god armypotente,
> That Juppiter was bisy it to stente,
> Til that the pale Saturnus the colde
> . . . .
> Foond in his olde experience an art
> That he ful soone hath plesed every part. (2438, 40–43, 45–46)

Chaucer complicates Boccaccio's heavenly power structure not only by adding the animosity between Venus and Mars, but also by establishing a troubled power relationship between Jupiter and Saturn. Intriguingly, Chaucer seems to include Jupiter only to demonstrate his inability to govern the heavens—a detail with serious ramifications for the divine hierarchy as imagined by Theseus.

The importance of these additions for interpreting *The Knight's Tale* should not be underestimated. Boccaccio's heavens are much more placid, much more Boethian and Christian than Chaucer's. In spite of his ostensibly pagan setting, Boccaccio explains in his glosses that the apparent agency of Mars, Venus, and the fury Erinys in bringing about Arcita's downfall is no more than imaginative license; the real source of the "sad destiny" that looms at the start of the ninth book of the *Teseida* is "the sorrowful Providence of God for Arcites."[38] The world of the *Teseida* thus fits perfectly within a Boethian cosmology. But, outside of Theseus's First Mover speech, Chaucer scrupulously avoids such explicit demystification of the causes of fortune in *The Knight's Tale*. Instead, Chaucer deliberately recasts the pagan heavens in a way that subverts Boethian explanation, then gives Theseus a thoroughly Boethian speech. As a result, much of Theseus's "consolation" feels strangely off the mark. How can Theseus be so confident of Jupiter's power and grace when Chaucer has shown a Jupiter unable to resolve the squabble between his children? And, even more troubling, if Jupiter is meant to be the First Mover, how can Saturn assert his control of the heavens?[39]

These questions present a serious interpretive dilemma. The presence of the pagan gods in *The Knight's Tale* adds an additional level of philosophical difficulty for those in search of Boethian unity. Not only must the human condition be reconciled to Providence, but so must the Olympian gods. Spearing states the heart of the problem succinctly: "Theseus believes the world of the poem to be ruled by the benevolent Jupiter; we know that it is ruled by the malevolent Saturn."[40] This dilemma has been the source of much scholarly disagreement, prompting widely varying and often flatly contradictory readings of the gods.[41] The contradictions within *The Knight's Tale* are so profound that scholars have tended to take sides, either with Palamon and Arcite in blaming the gods or with Theseus in defending them. Praise of Theseus and divine order becomes an implicit condemnation of Palamon and Arcite. Consider D. W. Robertson's reading: "In [Theseus's] speech on the God of Love which follows his remarks about mercy for those who are repentant, he demonstrates the fact that he recognizes the folly of the kind of love to which Palamon and Arcite *have subjected themselves*."[42] Alan T. Gaylord, one of the most vigorous defenders of the "good spirits" of *The Knight's Tale*, is even more direct in his condemnation of the knights. Palamon and Arcite's destiny is savage, he argues, only "because [they] sacrificed their chance to rise above it."[43] In the opposing camp are scholars such as A. J. Minnis, who argues that "the Jupiter of *The Knight's Tale* is a moral coward who, after a feeble attempt at peacemaking, relinquishes his proper role to his mischief-making father,"[44] and Elizabeth Salter, who writes that "it becomes very difficult for us to respond uncritically either to a philosophic statement which largely ignores the prominent issue of divine malice or to a happy ending which gives little sign of recognising the unhappiness it builds upon."[45]

A possible solution to this critical polarization is to posit a deliberate dual imagination within the world of the tale, a purposeful tension between two irreconcilable ways of understanding human experience. At the heart of this double perspective is Chaucer's imaginative sympathy with pagan antiquity. As Minnis, Nolan, and Spearing have shown, Chaucer imagined the pagan world very deeply.[46] He presents Palamon, Arcite, and Emelye as seeing the world through genuinely pagan, polytheistic eyes, while Theseus, if not a fledgling Christian, is the pre-Christian equivalent—a monotheist with a belief in absolute order. Recognition of the presence of a carefully imagined pagan worldview in *The Knight's Tale* will necessarily change one's understanding of the gods. It cautions against explaining the gods away as allegory, metaphor, or even planets, whose influence can be accounted for by medieval astrology, and invites us to begin our reading at a more literal level. Thus when Arcite refers to the "wikke aspect and disposicioun / Of Saturne," (1087–88) he is referring to what he understands to be an actual god—a planetary god, certainly, but a god nonetheless. Saturn may be a "figure of speech," as Gaylord suggests, for a medieval Christian interpreter, but in the world of the poem, where the gods have temples, where Emelye performs strange rites, where "[n]ymphes, fawnes and amadrides" inhabit the forests (2928), and where planetary deities bicker in the heavens, there is nothing to suggest that anyone other than Theseus sees the gods as an allegory of divine Providence.

Palamon and Arcite have an essentially phenomenological approach to the world. They respond to the world as they experience it; they feel, and leave philosophizing to others. This comes across clearly in Palamon's poignant conclusion to the speech in which he questions why the innocent suffer: "The answere of this lete I to dyvynys, / But wel I woot that in this world greet pyne ys" (1323–24). These lines capture the essence of Palamon and Arcite's role in the philosophical argument of *The Knight's Tale*. The lovesick knights are the spokesmen for human suffering. Palamon, though perfectly aware that philosophers and theologians (*dyvynys*) attempt to offer answers to the problem of suffering, emphasizes the fact that these theories do little to lessen the visceral experience of "greet pyne" that constitutes his and Arcite's understanding of the world. Theseus's appeal to Boethian theory, however attractive it may seem, can thus never completely address the problem posed by the argument from experience.

By juxtaposing experience to theory in this way, Chaucer sets up a debate about fortune and suffering that parallels the Wife of Bath's famous experience-versus-"auctoritee" debate on the subject of marriage.[47] The conclusion of *The Knight's Tale* depends on this implicit dialectic. In the remainder of this essay, I will argue that Chaucer essentially structures the tale so that Theseus is the voice of Boethian authority while Palamon and Arcite speak for human suffering. But this is no easy schematization, for Chaucer complicates the debate in two significant ways: first, Chaucer makes some of his most direct use of Boethius in the complaints of Palamon and Arcite; second, in his First Mover speech Theseus specifically claims that his providential interpretation of fortune is "preeved *by experience*" (3001, my emphasis).

Because the simplest way to characterize Chaucer's use of the *Consolation of Philosophy* is to say that Palamon and Arcite ask Boethius's questions and Theseus offers Philosophy's answers, it can be tempting to view Chaucer's young pagans as misguided creatures who exist to be taught a lesson. But *The Knight's Tale* is a debate about Providence, not a lecture, as can be seen in the way Chaucer revises the Boethian dialectic in Palamon and

Arcite's love complaints. Chaucer's highly selective use of the *Consolation* in *The Knight's Tale* results in a compassionate emphasis on the questioning sufferer in spite of the answers to the suffering. Chaucer achieves this effect by presenting Boethian questions of suffering in a new context in which they take on special relevance—a world controlled by malevolent pagan gods.[48]

This contextual shift can be observed in the two major instances of Boethian complaint in *The Knight's Tale*. The first comes from Arcite, who reflects on the bitter irony of his release from prison, and is worth examining in detail:

> Allas, why pleynen folk so in commune
> On purveiaunce of God, or of Fortune,
> That yeveth hem ful ofte in many a gyse
> Wel bettre than they kan hemself devyse?
> Some man desireth for to han richesse,
> That cause is of his mordre or greet siknesse . . .
> . . . .
> We witen nat what thing we preyen heere;
> We faren as he that dronke is as a mous.
> A dronke man woot wel he hath an hous,
> But he noot which the righte wey is thider,
> And to a dronke man the wey is slider.
> And certes, in this world so faren we;
> We seken faste after felicitee,
> But we goon wrong ful often, trewely. (1251–56, 1260–67)

Arcite's speech is drawn from the *Consolation* 3.p2, in which not Boethius but Philosophy speaks. Philosophy, rebuking human ignorance of ends and the vanity of human wishes, uses the image of the drunken man as a way of explaining how the human desire for "felicitee" is misguided. Here, however, the passage is presented as complaint, not consolation. Chaucer expands the image and puts it in the mouth of a suffering human, which greatly increases its poignancy. By shifting the context and emphasis of this speech, Chaucer achieves the opposite effect from that of the *Consolation*. Instead of a lesson about the folly of the desires that characterize the human condition, Chaucer focuses on what it feels like to be in that condition, on the *experience* of frustration and disorientation. Some scholars have interpreted Arcite's rhetorical "Why pleynen folk . . . ?" as a defense of Providence. Bernard Jefferson, for instance, using the *Consolation* as his standard for wisdom, reads this speech as evidence that Chaucer presents Arcite as more enlightened than Palamon, who blames the gods for fortune.[49] But Chaucer's adaptation of Boethius makes such a conclusion difficult to accept. What was a plausible defense in Lady Philosophy's mouth no longer holds for Arcite, who fails even to distinguish between "purveiaunce of God, or of Fortune." To Arcite, man's condition is so miserable and blind that he does not even know against whom to complain.

While Arcite rearticulates Boethian consolation in a way that questions Providence, Palamon does take the issue of suffering a step further by directly accusing "the cruel goddes that govern / This world" (1303–4). He questions whether the gods care about human beings, and is particularly troubled by the suffering of the innocent:

> What is mankynde moore unto you holde
> Than is the sheep that rouketh in the folde?
> For slayn is man right as another beest,
> And dwelleth eek in prison and arreest,
> And hath siknesse and greet adversitee,
> And ofte tymes gilteless, pardee. (1307–12)

Palamon's comparison of man to a helpless, will-less sheep links human experience to a Nature envisioned as at the mercy of an absolute power, which in this case is an indifferent heaven. Even more significant, Palamon's implication that human beings not only live but also die like animals can be seen to prefigure Theseus's later consolation that all must die: "He moot be deed, the kyng as shal a page" (3030). Whereas Theseus argues that death is part of a noble and natural cycle, Palamon suggests that one can as easily see mortality as bestial. His implicit retort to Theseus is, "He moot be deed, the kyng as shal a beest."

Like Arcite's, Palamon's complaint has its origins in the *Consolation of Philosophy*, but again one finds that Chaucer's portrait of the pagan gods has radically altered the context. In the *Consolation*, Boethius raises the problem of innocent suffering in a prayer to God. Boethius expresses his faith that the Creator is the source of order and that mankind does indeed have divine significance as a key part of that order:

O thou, what so evere thou be that knyttest alle boondes of thynges, loke on thise wrecchide erthes. We men, that ben noght a foul partie, but a fair partie of so greet a werk, we ben turmented in this see of fortune. (1.m5)

Boethius concludes with a reference to cosmic control provided by the fair chain of love (an element notably missing from Palamon's worldview), asking that God "fastne and ferme thise erthes stable with thilke bond by which thou governest the hevene that is so large." In this context of benevolent Providence, Palamon's complaint would indeed seem benighted, and perhaps at this point in *The Knight's Tale* one is meant to think so. But when Chaucer goes on to depict a heaven actually filled with "cruel goddes" indifferent to human happiness, he appears to confirm Palamon's worst suspicions.

By the time *The Knight's Tale* arrives at Theseus's crucial First Mover speech, the evidence, which culminates in the extensive description of Arcite's death, seems to be on the side of those who complain against heavenly justice. Theseus clearly has a great deal to justify, and he does so by explaining not the world as experienced by Palamon and Arcite, but essentially an entirely different one. That is, Theseus *reimagines* the world along more optimistic Boethian lines. Theseus argues that the First Mover "stable is and eterne" and that "every part dirryveth from his hool" (3004–6). As Jill Mann writes, the speech is meant to "[remind] us that there is a power beyond the planets, by which they are moved. They do not operate of their own volition; their power is only a secondary one."[50] Theseus imagines the planets as having no agency; the Prime Mover, which he identifies as Jupiter, is the only agent, and all else moves in harmony with divine directives. This is the familiar Boethian argument: what looks like chance is just a human misperception. But such a cosmology is patently false to the world Chaucer has created in *The Knight's Tale*. The Boethian explanation fails on the level of experience because the reader has seen that instead of the serene order imagined by Theseus, the *actual* cause of human fortune, in the observable world of the tale, is cosmic strife between the gods. And, contrary to Theseus's assertion, Jupiter is not the guiding force behind the planetary deities; his role has been usurped by Saturn, who can hardly be described as a beneficent and orderly First Mover. Instead of offering a picture of the gods that shows the order behind fortune, Chaucer essentially casts the gods in the image of fortune—capricious, callous, unpredictable. The pagan gods Chaucer introduces at the end of part 3 of *The Knight's Tale* embody all of Palamon and Arcite's fears and conjectures about divine malice. In short, Chaucer's changes to Boccaccio render Theseus's First Mover speech, *as an argument from experience*, inaccurate at best, and, at worst, specious to the level of parody.

The inadequacy of Theseus's description of the universe needs to be stressed because his identification of a First Mover behind the vicissitudes of fortune is so often taken to be a sign of his rationality and wisdom. Barbara Nolan, for instance, writes that Theseus's "rational intimations of divine order . . . enable his acts of amelioration in the *Tale*."[51] But in what sense are his intimations rational? In epistemological terms, the knowledge Theseus claims can only be a priori; he cannot infer the existence of divine order from observation of the world around him. It is therefore puzzling that Theseus should claim that his knowledge is empirical, "preeved by experience." On an empirical basis, Palamon and Arcite's cosmology makes much more sense than Theseus's. Their speeches about blind chance, cruel fortune, malign planetary influences, and vengeful deities provide a *logical* deduction from their experience of the world.

To defend Palamon and Arcite and to recognize the limitations of Theseus's First Mover argument is not to suggest that Theseus is fundamentally irrational or that readings of him as a strong and positive force in the poem are incorrect. My point is that the tension between conflicting ways of looking at the world, each with its own internal logic, enables Chaucer to leave open questions about love, fortune, fate, and Providence. While the dual perspective of *The Knight's Tale* is never fully resolved, Chaucer does suggest that there are better and worse ways to think about the world.

Although he never dismisses the authenticity of experience, Chaucer *does* privilege Theseus's philosophic voice at the conclusion of the poem. He does so not because Theseus's outlook is logical, but because it is imaginatively superior. Theseus offers an expanded vision of both capricious Fortune and tyrannous Cupid, subordinating the one to stable Providence and the other to the "faire cheyne of love" (2988). Because, as I have argued, Chaucer establishes love and fortune as manifestations of a single problem, reimagination of one necessarily includes a reimagination of the other.

Making Virtue of Necessitee: Theseus's Practical Wisdom

While Theseus fails as a theologian, he succeeds brilliantly as a politician. As rhetorically stirring as the First Mover speech is, Theseus realizes that suffering people cannot be consoled merely by being told to *think* differently about the world. Practical strategies are needed for coping. Scholars have noticed how over the course of the First Mover speech, "Theseus's reasoning descends to a practical sphere."[52] All human beings must find ways to continue living in the face of unpredictable phenomena, regardless of one's opinions about the origin of events. Whether human fortune comes from capricious gods or divine Providence is irrelevant at the level of immediate experience. This is the point of the generalizing of Theseus; his closing speech feels more like a working through of possibilities, incorporating both the transcendent optimism of Boethius and the world-weary pessimism of Egeus, than a unified philosophic creed. The observation made by both Theseus and Egeus, for instance, that death is common to all turns out to be not so much a consolation as a description of a universal problem in need of a practical response.

Rituals provide the means of coping in *The Knight's Tale*. The funeral of Arcite mediates between the pain of experience and the cerebral consolations of Boethius. It is in orchestrating this ceremony that Theseus reveals his true value as a leader: his beliefs about order may offer some intellectual consolation, but the practical aid he gives is ritualistic. J. A. Burrow expresses the importance of these closing rituals well:

Dead bodies cannot be left for the dogs, they must be cremated with the proper obsequies. Men cannot be left to fight in the woods like animals, they must settle their differences like gentlemen in the tourney. And sexual passion must eventually submit to "the bond that highte matrimoigne or mariage."[53]

Theseus's function, however, is not to control the powers that occasion "uncivilized" behavior, as Burrow and some other critics suggest, but to redirect them in the service of society. As Jill Mann puts it, "not denying or combating the role of chance, [Theseus] merely provides a civilized context within which it can operate."[54] The funeral is, broadly, the means for coping with the problem of Saturn, which is to say with the caprices of fortune that figure so prominently in the poem. The other closing ritual, the marriage of Palamon and Emelye, addresses the problem of Cupid by offering a context to mitigate the caprices of love. Palamon is no longer the passionate, burning lover when he weds Emelye. The death of Arcite leads to a sober and mature marriage that reflects an expanded understanding both of the cruelty of the world and of the possibilities for recovering and maintaining human dignity and even happiness. The marriage is also Chaucer's final comment on the parallel between love and fortune. Unlike the sudden fury of love at first sight or the unpredictable shifts of fortune, the marriage is not an accident but rather a carefully planned, ceremonious, social event designed for the purpose of communal healing. The tale's lessons about the uncertainty of fortune may, of course, make one hesitate to accept Theseus's confident pronouncement that the marriage will create "O partfit joye, lastynge everemo" (3072) or the Knight's "happily ever after" conclusion. But such optimism supports the tale's closing message about the need for human beings to move forward in the face of adversity. Chaucer ends *The Knight's Tale* with the reminder that Fortune's wheel is turning again, this time for the better. Marriage might not be a guarantee of happiness, but it does serve to mitigate the accidental nature of fortune and young love.

Theseus rightly emphasizes the practical when he points out that nothing is *gained* by railing against fortune. His age and maturity suggest that one must temper the instinct to complain about chance, just as one leaves the wildness of passion behind with youth. In *The Knight's Tale*, Chaucer undertakes what seems to be an impossible task: to confront the problem of evil squarely and yet to maintain an optimistic tone. Given the difficulty of this project, he succeeds surprisingly well. Theseus's emphasis on a practical, communal, ritualistic response to fortune—on a person's ability to *make* virtue of necessity and thereby to claim a measure of human agency in a world mostly beyond the reach of human control—establishes a patch of common ground for the advocates of the poem's conflicting worldviews.

Notes

I would like to thank A.C. Spearing, Jill Mann, and Elizabeth Bridgham for their valuable suggestions during the preparation of this essay.

1. Thomas Speght, ed., *The Works Of Our Ancient and learned English Poet Geffrey Chavcer, newly printed....* (London: Adam Islip, 1602).
2. Burrow, "The Canterbury Tales I: Romance," in *The Cambridge Chaucer Companion*, eds. Piero Boitani and Jill Mann (Cambridge: Cambridge University Press, 1986), 120.
3. Prologue *LGW* F 420–21. Chaucer quotations are from *The Riverside Chaucer*, 3rd ed., gen. ed. Larry D. Benson (Boston: Houghton Mifflin, 1987), hereafter

cited parenthetically by line number in the text. All references to *The Canterbury Tales* are to Fragment I unless otherwise indicated.
4. On medieval understandings of fortune in general, see Howard R. Patch, *The Goddess Fortuna in Mediaeval Literature* (1927; New York: Octagon Books, 1967); and F. P. Pickering, "Fortune," in *Literature and Art in the Middle Ages* (Coral Gables, FL: University of Miami Press, 1970), 168–222. On the significance of the Knight's fortune in drawing the first lot, see Jill Mann, "Chance and Destiny in *Troilus and Criseyde* and the *Knight's Tale*," in *The Cambridge Chaucer Companion*, 75–92; and Derek Pearsall, *The Canterbury Tales* (London: Allen & Unwin, 1985), 115.
5. Kaske, "Causality and Miracle: Philosophical Perspectives in the *Knight's Tale* and the *Man of Law's Tale*," in *Traditions and Innovations: Essays on British Literature of the Middle Ages and the Renaissance*, eds. David G. Allen and Robert A. White (Newark: University of Delaware Press, 1990), 12.
6. In this essay, I will generally not capitalize "fortune" unless I intend the meaning to encompass the personification of Lady Fortune, just as Love is only capitalized in reference to its incarnation in Cupid, the God of Love. I have tried to keep "love" and "fortune" both lowercase to underscore the parallel I am suggesting between them as abstract forces that affect the human condition. Chaucer's usage of these terms in *The Knight's Tale* is not entirely consistent; he generally does not treat fortune as a personification, though he several times refers to Cupid as the personification of love. This tendency to personify Love rather than fortune is in keeping with my assertion that Chaucer uses love as a way to make the operation of fortune more tangible.
7. Susan Crane marshals convincing evidence that "Chaucer and his contemporaries did attribute generic meaning to the term romaunce," but it remains notoriously difficult to apply the term with any precision. See Crane, *Gender and Romance in Chaucer's* Canterbury Tales (Princeton, NJ: Princeton University Press, 1994), 9. In considering poetic type and function, I am not interested in drawing boundaries, but rather in stressing an awareness on Chaucer's part of different poetic approaches to common themes. Even if Chaucer's ideas about genre do not necessarily match those of modern readers, he clearly has an understanding of how a poet's treatment of his subject matter depends on the type of poem he is writing. Perhaps the best example of this generic awareness comes at the end of *Troilus and Criseyde*. The setting of Chaucer's story, Troy during the Trojan War, is the material of epic, which Virgil, in the opening line of the *Aeneid*, tells us deals with feats of arms. Chaucer, however, has chosen to tell a story about love, and this choice dictates his emphasis in the poem:

> And if I hadde ytaken for to write
> The armes of this ilke worthi man [Troilus],
> Than wolde ich of his batailles endite;
> But for that I to writen first bigan
> Of his love, I have seyd as I kan— (V.1765–69)

Although Chaucer may not use genre as a formal template, he does identify himself here as a poet undertaking a specific type of project: a poem about love.
8. Bloomfield, "Episodic Motivation and Marvels in Epic and Romance," in *Essays and Explorations: Studies in Ideas, Language, and Literature* (Cambridge, MA: Harvard University Press, 1970), 123.

9. Crane, *Gender and Romance*, 165–69; Nolan, *Chaucer and the Tradition of the Roman Antique* (Cambridge: Cambridge University Press, 1992), 252.
10. Crane, *Gender and Romance*, chapter 5.
11. Mann, "Chance and Destiny," 87.
12. Nolan, *Chaucer and the Tradition of the* Roman Antique, 252, 353 n. 21.
13. Nolan, 252.
14. A. C. Spearing, Introduction, *The Knight's Tale*, ed. Spearing, rev. ed. (Cambridge: Cambridge University Press, 1996), 91–111. See also Spearing, "Classical Antiquity in Chaucer's Chivalric Romances," in *Chivalry, Knighthood and War in the Middle Ages*, ed. Susan Ridyard (Sewanee, TN: University of the South Press, 1999), 55.
15. Spearing, "Classical Antiquity," 54.
16. Patch, *The Goddess Fortuna in Mediaeval Literature*, 29, 90–98. For a discussion of the influence of Machaut on Chaucer's conception of fortune, see James I. Wimsatt, "Chaucer, Fortune, and Machaut's 'Il m'est avis,'" in *Chaucer Problems and Perspectives: Essays Presented to Paul E. Beichner, C.S.C.*, ed. Edward Vasta and Zacharias P. Thundy (Notre Dame: University of Notre Dame Press, 1979), 119–31.
17. The same correspondence sometimes occurs in Chaucer's earlier poetry. Compare the mourning knight's description of his first encounter with the group of beautiful ladies that includes his future wife in *The Book of the Duchess*: "Shal I clepe hyt hap other grace / That broght me there? Nay, but Fortune . . ." (810–11).
18. One does not have to accept A. J. Minnis's argument that Palamon, Arcite, and Emelye are themselves "young fatalists" to recognize the profoundly fatalistic tone of the language used to describe love. See Minnis, *Chaucer and Pagan Antiquity* (Woodbridge, Suffolk: Boydell & Brewer, 1982), 131–34.
19. W. A. Davenport, *Chaucer: Complaint and Narrative* (Cambridge: D. S. Brewer, 1988), 97.
20. In the *Roman de la Rose*, the character Ami presents himself in this capacity.
21. Readers who feel that the Boethian conclusion to *The Knight's Tale* adequately defends free will are sure to object to my characterization of necessity in the poem, asserting (rightly) that the main point of Theseus's First Mover speech is to reject fatalism. The concluding part of this essay suggests that Chaucer, *pace* Boethius, leaves the question of free will open; but at the moment I wish simply to point out how boldly Chaucer frames the problem. Whether or not Chaucer ultimately refutes determinism, the image of human beings at the mercy of forces they can neither understand nor control is absolutely central not only to Arcite's crucial speech but to *The Knight's Tale* as a whole.
22. Compare also Chaucer's description of Egeus as one "[t]hat knew this worldes transmutacioun, / As he hadde seyn it chaunge both up and doun" (2839–40).
23. "For man is cause of that schal falle . . . / And natheles yet som men wryte / And sein that fortune is to wyte" (Gower, *Confessio Amantis*, ed. G. C. Macaulay [Oxford: Clarendon, 1901], Prologue 528–30). See also Spearing, Introduction, *KT*, 90, 101.
24. Salter, *Chaucer: The Knight's Tale and the Clerk's Tale*, Studies in English Literature 5 (London: Edward Arnold; Great Neck, NY: Barron's Educational Series, 1962), 9, 11–12.
25. See J. A. Burrow, "Chaucer's Knight's Tale and the Three Ages of Man," in *Essays on Medieval Literature* (Oxford: Clarendon, 1984), 27–48.
26. In his envoi, Boccaccio claims that the *Teseida* is "the first to bid [the Muses]

sing in the vernacular of Latium what has never been seen thus before: the toils endured for Mars." But in the invocation to book 1, he calls on both Mars and Venus because, as he explains in the gloss, he "must treat both of battles and of love." Giovanni Boccaccio, *The Book of Theseus [Il Teseida delle Nozze d'Emilia]*, trans. Bernadette Marie McCoy (New York: Medieval Text Association, 1975).

27. Boccaccio, X.23–24.
28. *Troilus and Criseyde* offers much praise of "Benigne Love" (III.1261), particularly in the *Canticus Troili* that ends book 3. Pandarus, speaking typically about love in religious terms, tells Troilus that "Love, of his goodnesse, / Hath the converted out of wikkednesse" (I.998–99). Lest one think that Pandarus is not a reliable authority on love, the poet himself makes similar claims about love's ennobling and peacemaking effects. He argues that Cupid's irresistibility is ultimately for the best, since love "hath the cruel herte apesed, / And worthi folk maad worthier of name, / And causeth moost to dreden vice and shame" (I.250–52).
29. J. D. Burnley, *Chaucer's Language and the Philosophers' Tradition* (Cambridge: Brewer, 1979), 28.
30. James I. Wimsatt, "Reason, Machaut, and the Franklin," in *The Olde Daunce: Love, Friendship, Sex, and Marriage in the Medieval World*, ed. Robert R. Edwards and Stephen Spector (Albany, NY: SUNY Press, 1991), 201. For a recent analysis of the appropriation of Boethius in the *Remede de Fortune*, see Sylvia Huot, "Guillaume de Machaut and the Consolation of Poetry," *Modern Philology* 100.2 (2002): 169–95.
31. Davenport, *Complaint*, 8. Davenport's is the only book-length study of Chaucer's use of complaint, and is also the only one to emphasize the complaints embedded in Chaucer's narrative works. For relatively recent analyses of Chaucer's self-advertised Complaints to Venus, Mars, Pity, and His Lady, see Lee Patterson, "Writing Amorous Wrongs: Chaucer and the Order of Complaint," in *The Idea of Medieval Literature*, ed. James M. Dean and Christian K. Zacher (Newark: University of Delaware Press, 1992): 55–71; Carolynn Van Dyke, "'To Whom Shul We Compleyn?': The Poetics of Agency in Chaucer's Complaints," *Style* 31.3 (Fall 1997): 370–90.
32. Davenport, *Complaint*, 99.
33. Palamon, employing the term "aventure" (1288) instead of "cas," makes exactly the same connection between love and fortune in his lament (1281–1333).
34. Davenport, *Complaint*, 103.
35. This is an important point, because scholars so frequently talk about how Chaucer extends his themes from the particular to the general. Davenport, for example, emphasizes "the effect of Chaucer's staying away from Arcite and Palamon as individual actors, instead externalising the elements of their natures into symbolic figures [e.g., the gods] and buildings," and elsewhere comments on the "philosophical enlargement" that "forc[es] human weeping to dwindle into an instance of that very transitoriness which is its occasion" (*Complaint*, 117, 177). While it is important to stress this externalizing aspect of Chaucer's craft against arguments that Palamon and Arcite are somehow "characters" in the novelistic sense, it must be remembered that the externalization is meant to address questions posed at the level of individual experience. One can as easily suggest that instead of an extension of theme from individual humans to symbolic gods, *The Knight's Tale* presents the opposite—a distillation from the divine sphere to the earthly. This is perhaps just another

way of describing the same technique, but it serves to underscore Chaucer's own emphasis on human experience, his attempts to try to understand humanity by way of larger things. Instead of using "philosophical enlargement" to belittle human suffering, Chaucer places human experience within a larger framework to evoke empathy with the general human condition.

36. Boccaccio, V.75.
37. Boccaccio, IX.3.
38. Boccaccio, 257–58. (Glosses cited by page number.)
39. These questions have caused many critics to challenge Theseus's efficacy in ordering the concluding events of the tale. See, for example, Kathleen Blake, "Order and the Noble Life," *Modern Language Quarterly* 34 (1978): 3–19; Stewart Justman, "'Auctoritee' and The Knight's Tale," *Modern Language Quarterly* 39 (1978): 3–14; Bernhard D. Harder, "Fortune's Chain of Love: Chaucer's Irony in Theseus's Marriage Counselling," *University of Windsor Review* 18.1 (1984): 47–52.
40. Spearing, Introduction, *KT*, 107. This discrepancy in Theseus's interpretation of the heavens presents us with a problem in interpreting him. As Salter points out, "Our difficulty does not lie in reconciling the death of Arcite with a divinely ordained plan, but in reconciling the noble account of this plan with the ugly manifestation of divine motives and activities which Chaucer has allowed his poem to give" (*Chaucer*, 31).
41. See Alan T. Gaylord, "The Role of Saturn in the Knight's Tale," *The Chaucer Review* 8.3 (1974): 171–90, for a synopsis of the debate as of 1974. Thirty years have not brought us any closer to consensus.
42. Robertson, *A Preface to Chaucer: Studies in Medieval Perspectives* (Princeton, NJ: Princeton University Press, 1962), 262 (emphasis added).
43. Gaylord, "Role of Saturn," 184–85. Gaylord reads Saturn not as a grandly sinister force of mayhem but as "a sign of a dark destiny to which the willful passions of men commit them" (185).
44. Minnis, *Pagan Antiquity*, 141. See also Salter, who feels that the poem "insist[s] upon the pitiful state of man and the revengeful attitude of the gods who shape his destiny" (*Chaucer*, 28); and Spearing, Introduction, *KT*, 84.
45. Salter, *Chaucer*, 32.
46. See Minnis, *Pagan Antiquity*; Nolan, *Chaucer and the Tradition of the* Roman Antique, chapter 7; Spearing, Introduction, *KT*, 91–111; and Spearing, "Classical Antiquity." The notion of a dual imagination of the pagan world is consistent with F. Anne Payne's interpretation of *The Knight's Tale* as Menippean satire, a genre characterized by the presentation of opposing ideas or philosophies without reconciling them. Payne, *Chaucer and Menippean Satire* (Madison, WI: University of Wisconsin Press, 1981), 207–31, particularly 207–9.
47. The Wife asserts, "Experience, though noon auctoritee / Were in this world, is right ynogh for me / To speke of wo that is in mariage" (III.1–3). On the experience/authority debate in Chaucer's work, see Willi Erzgräber, "'Auctorite' and 'Experience' in Chaucer," in *Intellectuals and Writers in Fourteenth-Century Europe*, ed. Piero Boitani and Anna Torti (Tübingen: Gunter Narr Verlag; Cambridge: Brewer, 1984), 67–87; John Lawlor, *Chaucer* (New York: Harper & Row, 1969), *passim*.
48. This has been observed by Salter: "Some of the sentiments [expressed by Palamon and Arcite] clearly derive from the complaint of Boethius to God, and in its original context, this complaint receives brisk correction from the 'noryce, Philosophie'. In the present context, however, it has an almost uncanny accuracy and relevance" (*Chaucer*, 21).

49. See Bernard L. Jefferson, *Chaucer and the Consolation of Philosophy of Boethius* (1916; New York: Haskell House, 1965), 131; P. M. Kean, *Chaucer and the Making of English Poetry* (London: Routledge & Kegan Paul, 1972), 2:13.
50. Mann, "Chance and Destiny," 90.
51. Nolan, *Chaucer and the Tradition of the* Roman Antique, 279; see also Robert B. Burlin, *Chaucerian Fiction* (Princeton, NJ: Princeton University Press, 1977), 104; and Charles Muscatine, *Chaucer and the French Tradition* (Berkeley: University of California Press, 1957), 183–84.
52. Salter, *Chaucer*, 35; see also Spearing, Introduction, *KT*, 104–8.
53. Burrow, "Three Ages of Man," 47.
54. Mann, "Chance and Destiny," 88.

Clément Marot, the Roman de la Rose, *and Poetic Identity*

JENNIFER MONAHAN

The *Roman de la Rose* was unquestionably the most influential text of the French Middle Ages. It served as the predominant literary model for generations of writers, survived in some three hundred manuscripts, and was printed twenty-one times between 1480 and 1538. Its images became commonplace—the lyric of the fourteenth and fifteenth centuries is populated by Bel Acceuils, Dangers, and Faux Semblants—and the dream vision became a standard way of introducing allegorical discourse. Not only did it shape the literary expression of desire during the later Middle Ages, it informed viewpoints on an exceptionally wide variety of other subjects as well. It influenced discourse on monasticism and on women throughout the later medieval period, and became in many ways the founding text in the *querelle des femmes*. At the beginning of the sixteenth century, its prestige was such that Jean Molinet claimed the *Rose*'s *sententiae* had become proverbs and its contents were common intellectual property, on a level with the alphabet or the Lord's Prayer.[1]

Despite its monumental impact on late medieval French literature, the influence of the *Rose* during the early Renaissance has more or less gone unexamined, even though it was the canonical text par excellence at a time when literary norms were being redefined. I intend to look at one aspect of *Rose* reception during the watershed years of the early sixteenth century: Clément Marot's engagement with the *Rose* in his *Temple de Cupido*, written as the literary ethic of the Rhétoriqueurs began to shift and allegory began to be replaced by a more individualized representation of interiority.[2] Clément Marot is frequently recognized as a writer whose increased emphasis on poetic subjectivity marked a break with Rhétoriqueur practices and set the stage for the ethic of the Pléiade.[3] His first published work, the *Temple de Cupido* (1515), can be seen as a hybrid text in the way it spans the gap between medieval and Renaissance lyric conventions and between erotic and religious registers.

This article aims to show how the *Rose*, as a highly canonical text whose fragmentation and ambiguity enabled rewritings, functions in Marot's *Temple de Cupido* as a backdrop against which a poetic persona emerges.[4]

Medievalia et Humanistica, New Series, Number 31 (Paul Maurice Clogan, ed.), Rowman & Littlefield Publishers, Inc., 2005.

Marot does not merely recycle the topoi of the *Rose*, but uses the *Rose*'s multivalence and eroticism in order to take his distance from both. Marot's reworking of the *Rose* has repercussions not only for his elaboration of the figure of Ferme Amour, which has been identified as a central current in his work, but also for the attribution debate surrounding the 1526 edition of the *Roman de la Rose* and its moralizing prologue, which have sometimes been attributed to Clément Marot.[5] In the attribution debate, the interpretation of the *Rose* that is advanced in the 1526 edition has never been fully compared to Marot's engagement with the *Rose* in the *Temple de Cupido*, whose attribution is unquestioned. Not only does Marot's reworking of the *Rose* in the *Temple de Cupido* correspond to his evangelical leanings, it does not align with the 1526 prologue, further tipping the scales away from a plausible attribution of this edition to Marot. Comparison of the *Temple de Cupido* with the *Roman de la Rose* sheds light not only on Marot's articulation of a poetic identity, but also on the prominence of the *Roman de la Rose* in the early sixteenth century and its implication in the tension between erotic love lyric and the lyricism of religious devotion during this period.

The plot of the *Temple de Cupido* bears obvious similarities to the *Roman de la Rose*. Its motifs are instantly recognizable to anyone familiar with late medieval lyric: Cupid, contemplating his power over humanity, notices that the narrator's writings are frequently critical of love and punishes him by firing an arrow "of mortal wood, feathered with vengeance."[6] The languishing narrator, in an effort to cure himself of love for his "cruel mistress," sets out on a quest for Ferme Amour. Close to despair after a fruitless search throughout much of the world, he decides to seek Ferme Amour in the Temple Cupidique and joins a crowd of other pilgrims sowing mounds of roses on the path to the temple. The narrator is granted entrance to the temple by Bel Acceuil, who leads him along a narrow path into the "enclosed flowering garden" (synonymous with the temple).[7] After considering every aspect of the temple, the narrator describes his discouragement at finding only "lustful, burning Love" and "fickle love" (459, 466) instead of Ferme Amour, whose description has both political and religious overtones.[8] Suddenly, looking through a screen at the choir (*cueur*) of the temple, he sees Ferme Amour standing between a prince and a lady who are easily identifiable as François Ier and Claude de France. Bel Acceuil opens the screen, and the narrator enters the *cueur du temple* and the service of Ferme Amour. The poem ends with an evocation of the joys of serving such a mistress.

Marot's engagement with the *Rose* is also an engagement with Jean Lemaire de Belges: much of the imagery of the *Temple de Cupido* comes from the *Rose* by way of the *Concorde des deux langages*, written a mere four years earlier in 1511. The setting of an allegorical temple is Lemaire's invention, not Guillaume de Lorris's or Jean de Meun's, and the *Temple de Cupido* shares with its immediate predecessor an overt assimilation of

Catholic rites into a courtly context. (Marot's image of beds as altars [369–72], for instance, comes directly from *Concorde* 14, ll. 173–80.) The narrator's status as one of a crowd of lovers likewise has its precedent in the *Concorde*, as does his disillusionment with the initial object of his desire. This debt is unacknowledged, however: the *Temple de Cupido* does not mention its most recent and most conspicuous source, even though it names other sources whose influence is less pervasive ("Ovidius, maistre Alain Chartier, / Petrarche, aussi le Rommant de la Rose" [323–4] as well as Molinet's *Temple de Mars* [289]).

The notion that the love represented in the *Temple de Cupido* is intended to replace and supersede that described in the *Rose* is reinforced by a number of textual parallels between the two works. Allegories that initially appear merely to recycle the *Roman de la Rose* have in fact been reworked in thematically significant ways. In the *Rose*, it takes Amant more than 21,000 lines to enter the sanctuary in which he is at last granted access to the object of his desire. In Marot's poem, not only does the organizing metaphor of a temple evoke this sacred space, but the fact that the lover is granted almost instant access to it suggests that the *Temple de Cupido* picks up where the *Rose* leaves off. Moreover, the means of entry to each is described in very similar terms. In Jean de Meun's *Rose*, the Lover/Pilgrim describes the access to the sanctuary as a narrow path along which he was the first to pass (21604–42; 352).[9] The mention of an *estroit sentier* (albeit a well-traveled one) as Marot's narrator enters the temple of Cupid both recalls and desexualizes the final passage of the *Rose*. "Bel Acceuil the well-schooled, who took me by the right hand and by a very narrow path led me into the beautiful enclosure of which he was the first porter. . . . That path had several travelers, since Bel Acceuil guarded the gate."[10] Once inside the temple, the narrator describes the *Brandon de Venus* as a mere lamp; this is a marked reduction from its status in the *Rose*, where Venus's throwing of the torch allows the storming of the castle and Amant's subsequent conquest (21221–32). One of the ironies of Jean de Meun's text was the sheer amount of highly erudite text devoted to a simple seduction. Through Marot's comic deflation, the desire so elaborately enshrined in the *Roman de la Rose* is reinscribed at the bottom of a spiritual hierarchy, functioning not as the goal of arduous effort but instead as a point of departure that is quickly superseded.

This reduction of the *Rose*'s imagery is repeated when the narrator finds the object of his desires, Ferme Amour. Marot's narrator first glimpses Ferme Amour through a screen ("the door made of flowers and green shrubs";[11] this image has a clear source in the final passage of the *Rose*, where Amant's progress toward the sanctuary is impeded by a barrier (21581–611). When the narrator of the *Temple de Cupido* is finally granted access to Ferme Amour, the description of this climactic moment conflates the imagery of the plucking of the Rose in Jean de Meun's text (21640–701; 352–3) with that of the evocation of the *parc de l'aignelet* in

Genius's speech (19990lff.; 328ff.): "then Bel Acceuil opened for me the heart of the Temple, which is a green meadow."¹²

Marot's use of the *Rose* in this context lends added weight to the *Temple*. The religious resonances of the pilgrim's approach to the sanctuary in the *Rose* tie in well to the religious current of Marot's poem, with its overt evocation of Christian charity. At the same time, the obscene connotations of this moment in the *Rose* are conspicuously absent in the *Temple de Cupido*.¹³ Echoes of the divine in evocation of love have an incontrovertible precedent in the *Rose*: part of what made the *Rose* scandalous was its use of religious imagery in apparent reference to sexuality.¹⁴ This use of Catholic imagery to represent the carnal had been reiterated a mere four years earlier by the appearance of the *Concorde des deux langages,* with its cynical representation of the ritualization of desire. Both of these texts provide a precedent for the playfulness of Marot's *Temple*. However, if Marot is to adopt the same image of a temple, he needs to take his distance from these works and specify that the image of a temple does in fact refer to the divine rather than the carnal. In so doing, he reinscribes the religious imagery of the *Rose* and the *Concorde* within a moral framework. These specific references to Jean de Meun's portion of the *Rose* demonstrate that the allegory of Ferme Amour takes on added cogency if it is read in light of its source text. If Ferme Amour is indeed the unifying thread for Marot's work, as Defaux claims, then it takes part of its force from a use of Jean de Meun's religious imagery while denying the possibility of an obscene interpretation.

A particularly influential reading of the *Temple de Cupido* has been advanced by Gérard Defaux, who argues that the figure of Ferme Amour in the *Temple de Cupido* constitutes the first manifestation of what will be the defining current of Marot's poetic identity: a systematic project of replacing the glorification of worldly love with that of charity and inscribing religious lyricism within poetic forms associated with the expression of erotic desire. In the intellectual ferment of the early Reformation, his works helped set the trend of neoplatonic and overtly Christian themes in poetry. A group of minor poets, Dolet, Saint-Gelais, and others—whose works likewise celebrated *anteros*—congregated around Marot and Marguerite de Navarre. Both within and outside this group, the theme of Ferme Amour was associated with Marot's name.

Defaux presents extensive evidence for Marot's critique of the courtly and Petrarchan traditions and his efforts to overwrite them with a lyric celebrating the soul's love for Christ. In this reading, Defaux relies heavily on the *Temple de Cupido* and presents the image of Ferme Amour as the outgrowth not of Italian neoplatonism but of the *Rose* and the *querelle*.¹⁵ Although Defaux's reading has much to recommend it, it does not fully explore the complexity of either the *Roman de la Rose* or the *querelle*. The representation of Ferme Amour as an emblem of Pauline charity and therefore an expression of evangelical ideals is linked by Defaux to Raison's speech in the *Rose*.[16] While Ferme Amour may have overtones of Pauline charity, the figure of Raison is more complex. Raison does indeed criticize the limitations of erotic love and invoke charity, but her pronouncements are too compromised by the context in which they appear to be read as a straightforward endorsement of charity.[17] Although some critics have contended that Raison's condemnation of *fol'amour* and evocation of charity make her speech the moral center of the poem, the bulk of critical opinion views Raison as merely one compromised voice among many.[18] The speeches of most of Jean de Meun's characters are marked by ironic contradiction, and Raison is no exception. Her praise of charity immediately precedes one of the best-known passages in the work, Raison's description of the castration of Saturn. Her evocation of the fall from the Golden Age is characterized by an absence of euphemism: not only does she use the word *coilles* (balls), but she rhymes it with *andoilles* (sausages) (5607–8; 113). When the scandalized Lover objects, she proclaims that if, when she chose names for the created world, she had called testicles "relics" and relics "balls," the lover would object to her use of the word "relics" (7079–85; 135). The passage culminates with Raison's insistence that her words are to be read allegorically rather than at face value (7123–38; 136). Raison's speech makes explicit the equivalence between genitalia and relics that generates much of the tension between erotic and spiritual registers and makes the religious language of the *Rose*'s final section so scandalous. To posit Jean de Meun's Raison as a source for Marot's Ferme Amour strictly on the basis of Raison's endorsement of charity and condemnation of *fol'amour* is to overlook the linguistic aspect of her discourse, where an apparent endorsement of plain speech is coupled with an injunction to read allegorically. The equivalence drawn between the erotic and the divine in allegorical language also informs Marot's *Temple de Cupido*. Whereas the *Rose* uses religious imagery in an erotic context, Marot uses similar allegory to insist on the subordination of erotic desire to longing for the divine.

The overall pattern of medieval *Rose* reception makes it more plausible that Marot is drawing on the *Rose*'s conflation of erotic desire and religious worship rather than on Raison's problematic equation of Amor with charity. The view of Raison as the moral center of the poem is a modern one, given its most extended treatment by John Fleming; nowhere in medieval *Rose* reception is such an interpretation advanced. Although Defaux maintains that Marot's engagement with the *Rose* was shaped by the *querelle*, the manuscript and print history of the *querelle* suggests that its impact was not very widespread. All of the manuscripts that contain Christine de Pizan's contribution to the *querelle* date from the early fifteenth century. Only in one manuscript (BN fr. 1563) do the *querelle* documents appear with the *Roman de la Rose*, but in a version that is distinctly unflattering to Christine de Pizan's viewpoint.[19] Jean Molinet, writing in 1500, seems unaware of her participation.[20] The *Epistre au Dieu d'Amours* was still in circulation, but was printed without any mention of Christine's name or of the other *querelle* documents. Although Gerson's treatise seems to have fared better, appearing in manuscripts through the end of the fifteenth century, it never appeared with the *Roman de la Rose*, and only once with the *Testament Jean de Meun*. The limited reception of the *querelle*, especially compared to the monumental impact of the *Rose*, makes it more likely that Marot is drawing directly on the *Rose*.

Moreover, the endorsement of mature love and marital harmony in the *Temple de Cupido*, which is as prominent as the evocation of charity (504–16), can likewise be traced to the *Rose* tradition. Marot's representation of Ferme Amour next to François Ier and Claude de France can be partially explained as glorification of a patron, but takes on a much greater richness of meaning if it is read in light of the *Rose* and its cynical treatment of marriage. Praise of a ruler's moral rectitude—a well-worn medieval trope—situates the *Temple de Cupido* in the tension between occasional poetry and personal lyric that characterizes the transition between the Rhétoriqueur period and a more modern notion of poetic subjectivity. The glorification of marriage seems not to have its roots in any Reformation polemics, since this section of Marot's poem was not significantly revised between 1515 and 1538. However, in Jean de Meun's portion of the *Roman de la Rose*, marriage is represented in strongly negative terms in the speeches of La Vieille and the Mari Jaloux, and it is conspicuously not mentioned at all in Genius's enthusiastic recommendation of procreative sexuality.[21] The image of Ferme Amour in the company of a recently married couple therefore emphasizes the difference between the *Rose*'s negative portrayal of matrimony and Marot's own inscription of desire within a moral framework.

It is generally acknowledged that Marot's representation of interiority, and particularly his insistence on sincerity of expression, constitute a significant innovation. However, as Defaux reminds us, this insistence on authentic representation of the self is itself a literary posture and therefore contains an element of fiction.[22] François Rigolot agrees that Marot's affirmations of singularity and autonomy set him apart from earlier writers. Like Defaux, he stresses that this endeavor is not free from literary artifice, and points to a tension between the desire to communicate plainly the essence of the divine word and the necessity of using rhetorical tropes to do so.[23] But if individuality and clarity are such paramount goals for Marot, why does he rely so heavily on the *Rose*, a highly canonical and notoriously ambiguous text?

Hope Glidden argues that the *Rose*'s injunction toward plain speech as the mode of expression best suited to the communication of spiritual truths struck a chord with Marot's evangelical convictions.[24] Although Jean de Meun's attitude toward plain speech is a matter of critical disagreement, the *Rose*'s genre (allegory), its centrifugal structure, and its sheer size (22,000 lines) are sharply at odds with an endorsement of direct speech. Moreover, issues of reading are foregrounded too insistently for Jean's text to be a coded plea for clarity.[25]

The aspect of the *Rose* that enabled Marot's rewriting is not something expressed in a specific passage (be it Raison's opposition of *fol'amour* and charity or any other), but precisely the centrifugal nature of Jean de Meun's text and the possibility of multiple readings. A text that presents itself simultaneously as courtly narrative of seduction and as repository of erudition, and that maintains the tension between literal and figurative registers, offers an extraordinarily rich nexus of meanings. Jean de Meun's text uses courtly motifs as a means of approach to questions of epistemology, and it does so in a way that forces individual interpretation. This aspect of the *Rose* may well have appealed most to Marot's evangelical leanings. Paradoxically, Marot draws on the *Rose*'s adaptability to multiple readings in order to take his distance not only from its eroticism but also from its ambiguity.

Not only does Marot's use of the *Rose* in the *Temple de Cupido* shed light on the tension between erotic and religious lyric in his work, it constitutes an important element in the evolution of his poetic persona over the course of his career. It used to be standard to treat Marot's use of medieval materials as a mere point of reference for his literary debut, an influence he transformed rather than rejected but nevertheless ultimately outgrew.[26] However, the revisions Marot made to the *Temple de Cupido* for its republication in the *Adolescence Clementine* (1532) and the 1538 edition of his *Oeuvres* (published under his close supervision) demonstrate that the influence of the *Roman de la Rose* on Marot's elaboration of a poetic persona can be traced far beyond the early stages of his career. Although many of the revisions are simply aesthetic—reorganizing stanzas, changing rhymes, and so forth—a significant number of them involve the writing in of more overt textual parallels to the *Rose*. The version of the *Temple de Cupido* that appears in the 1538 edition of Marot's works relies more heavily on the *Roman de la Rose* than does the 1515 *princeps* edition.[27] In some cases, only individual words have been changed, but these changes consistently evoke the *Rose*. For instance, the fifteen lines that describe the beginning of the narrator's journey to the *Temple de Cupido* contain one reference to *pelerins* in 1515; by 1532, this passage mentions *pelerins* three times (ll. 95–110).[28] At the moment when the narrator first glimpses Ferme Amour, a reference to flowers (498) replaces the initial reference to "the god Pan." Elsewhere, Marot changes the names of his allegorical figures to align them more closely with those of the *Rose*: "Honor the archpriest" becomes "Genius the archpriest" (366) and "the handsome god Pharete" is transformed into "the god of Love" (112).[29] The latter revision (which dates from 1538 rather than 1532) illustrates particularly well the movement toward a medieval source, since a classical reference is replaced with an allusion to the *Rose*.

In other instances, these changes operate at the level of stanzas. In the *princeps* edition, Bel Acceuil is mentioned in two successive stanzas; even if his name did not clarify his function, the context makes this clear. The addition in 1532 of a full stanza describing his function does not therefore clarify the passage; the expansion of his role was presumably intended to heighten the parallel between the *Temple de Cupido* and the *Rose*.[30] The expanded description of the God of Love's arrows follows a similar pattern:

(1515) "One is of gold, the other of silver. The gold one gives many people ease in Love, and the silver brings unhappiness."

(1532 and 1538) "The one tipped with shining gold causes love's attraction. The other, most exceedingly dangerous, has an ill-attached tip of lead with a flattened point, and extinguishes love in the heart."[31]

In this case, Marot may be referring more to the tradition that grew out of this passage of the *Rose* (ll. 921–78 from Guillaume de Lorris's section) rather than to the *Rose* itself; in either case, reliance on medieval topoi is increased from one edition to the next. Nor is this increased intertextuality limited to the *Rose*: the later editions also make explicit a reference to Molinet's *Temple de Mars* (l. 289) and contain passages that echo Lemaire's *Concorde des deux langages* more closely than in 1515.

That a teenaged Marot writing in the opening years of the century would make use of the *Rose* is hardly surprising; that the *Rose* should assume greater importance when Marot the mature poet prepares an edition of his complete works initially seems incongruous. How then can we account for this appearance of increased reliance on medieval paradigms? These revisions are consistent with a pattern that has already been observed in Marot's poetry: he presents his work in a way that creates the illusion of an evolution away from medieval forms. All of his *rondeaux* and *ballades* are included in the *Adolescence Clémentine*, even when this involves backdating them to make their composition appear anterior to 1526. The ideological implications of the title *Adolescence* and its presentation of the works contained therein as "youthful works" and "first efforts" ("*coups d'essay*") are readily apparent.[32] The *Temple de Cupido* (placed second in the *Adolescence*, between a translation of the first eclogue from Virgil's *Bucolics* and Marot's *Jugement de Minos*, also a translation) is therefore presented with implicit criticism. This reshuffling of texts in order to create the impression of a movement toward more modern forms is widespread in Marot's work: he likewise rebaptizes a number of *huitains* and *dizains* as *epigrammes* in order to make them appear more recent.[33] However, until now, the revisions to the *Temple de Cupido* have not attracted critical attention, even though they fit in admirably well with this current in Marot's work. In light of Marot's self-conscious presentation of his works, it seems likely that the 1538 revisions to the *Temple de Cupido* are an attempt to rewrite the early part of his career in light of an easily recognizable medieval model. The *Rose* was not simply an influence that Marot left behind (as he would apparently have us believe), but a model that continued to inform his public presentation of his early career. Marot's engagement with the *Rose* over the course of his career proves that in the early part of the sixteenth century, the *Rose* was both a well-known text whose influence was readily acknowledged and an emblem of that from which one takes one's distance.

Marot's reorientation of Jean de Meun's imagery in the articulation of evangelical ideals has implications beyond the study of Marot's own works. His use of the *Roman de la Rose* in his *Temple de Cupido* can also be brought to bear on the question of attribution of the 1526 "moralized" edition of the *Rose*. No discussion of the 1526 edition has compared the interpretations of the *Rose*'s imagery in this edition's prologue (known as the *Exposition moralle sur le Rommant de la Rose*) with the *Temple de Cupido*, where Marot's reorientation of the topoi of the *Rose* is indeed consistent with what is known of his religious convictions.

This edition, first printed in 1526 (reprintings appeared in 1529, 1531, and 1538) is surrounded by several misconceptions. It is true that this edition updates the language of the *Rose*, providing a "correction as much of the poor and overly old language, showing its ancient beginning and origin of language, as of the imperfect meters, almost all corrupted."[34] However, such an undertaking is less innovative than is commonly supposed, since each of the printed editions to precede this one had also included a modernization of the language and meter, affecting virtually every other line (Bourdillon 150). The reworking contained in the 1526 edition, although more extensive than the other verse editions, is by no means unprecedented. Other updates to the work had also preceded the 1526 modernization: "nota" in the margins are extremely common in the manuscript tradition, and the verse titles, which function as chapter headings to divide the work into sections, are also found in all of the earlier printed editions.[35]

Labeling the work as a moralization is also misleading. In contrast to works like the fourteenth-century *Ovide Moralisé* or Jean Molinet's 1500 moralization of the *Roman de la rose*, both of which contain almost as much gloss as text, the interpretive apparatus of the 1526 edition is quite scant. The marginal glosses are so timid that they would be more accurately characterized as rubrics. Hardly ever do they offer an interpretation of the text; instead they call attention to events in the plot, to mentions of *auctores*, and to well-known passages. Only very rarely do the glosses propose an interpretation; when they do, the author could hardly be said to be going out on an interpretive limb. For instance, the whole dialogue between Reason and the Lover over the word "couilles" is glossed mainly with "nota" or "note on the works of Nature"; the most specific gloss tells us only that "Reason gave names to natural things" without ever addressing the question of language use central to the passage.[36]

The *Exposition moralle*, not the glosses, provides the only real interpretive apparatus, but the range of interpretations it proposes by is quite limited.[37] The prologue tells us that the Rose itself can be read as referring to the papal rose, or the state of grace, or the state of wisdom, or the Virgin Mary.[38] The glosses proposed not only fail to account for the rest of the narrative, but are problematic from a doctrinal standpoint. To claim that the Rose represents the state of wisdom is to overlook the lover's rejection of Reason in his quest for the Rose, since Jean de Meun specifically claims that the pursuit of love is contrary to reason. (While wisdom could be said to supercede reason, an opposition between the two would be difficult to establish, and certainly the prologue makes no attempt to do so.) Reference to the papal rose seems gratuitous except as a declaration of the writer's religious convictions. Arguing that the Rose stands for the state of grace is at odds with the narrative of the *Roman* in two ways. First, the assertion that grace is "difficult to obtain, not because of him who gives it" implies no hesitation on the part of those in whose power it is to accord or deny the Rose, thereby shifting full responsibility to the lover for all the delays in his quest. The original narrative of the *Roman* is full of outside obstacles, but such a stance refuses to admit them. Furthermore, grace by its very definition is bestowed without having been earned by the one who receives it; this contradicts the narrative of the *Roman*, in which the Lover's pursuit finally earns him the object of his desire. Likewise, the third gloss, according to which the Rose represents the Virgin Mary, is also doctrinally questionable and at odds with the narrative of the *Roman*. Although a Catholic defense of the Virgin is hardly surprising given the time period, the author of the defense takes an extreme stance in positing Mary (rather than a member of the Trinity) as the ultimate object of spiritual longing.

The *Exposition moralle* is further limited by the fact that it proposes glosses for the figure of the Rose, but offers no indications as to how we are to interpret the other elements of the narrative. Interpreting the Rose as object of spiritual rather than carnal desire is far less difficult than finding a moralizing reading for episodes such as the discourses of Le Jaloux or La Vieille, but for the more controversial passages no uplifting meanings are offered. As Rosemond Tuve dryly comments, "[the interpretation offered by the *Exposition moralle*] might do very well if we had lost the work itself."[39]

Attribution of the 1526 edition to Clément Marot remains questionable. Discussions in favor of attribution to Marot (K. Sneyders de Vogel, Sylvio Baridon) or against it (Philip August Becker, Bernard Weinberg, Gérard Defaux) all rely on the same set of facts.[40] The basis for a claim of authorship by Marot relies entirely on two pieces of evidence: the attribution made by Pasquier in the late sixteenth century and the notation in one surviving copy "Clément Marot gave me this book."[41] However, Marot's name and *devise* appear nowhere in the edition or the *Exposition moralle*. While some of his shorter works circulated anonymously, nothing of this length was printed without Marot's name attached to it. For Baridon, the anonymity of the text can be explained by Marot's imprisonment during the spring of 1526. This explanation overlooks the anonymity of the three reprintings, which cannot be explained by events in Marot's life and does not align with Marot's consistent supervision of the printing of his works. Baridon's argument appears tenuous.

Those who challenge attribution claim stylistic differences between Marot's generally lively prose and the cumbersome phrasing of the *Exposition moralle*. Less subjectively, the preface to Marot's edition of Villon indicates editorial precepts quite different from those set forth in the *Exposition moralle*, since it discusses the establishment of a correct text without addressing questions of hermeneutics.[42] Finally, the heavy-handed Catholicism of the *Exposition moralle*—which claims that the Rose can be understood as "the papal rose" and "The glorious Virgin Mary . . . which heretics cannot easily obtain" (Baridon, ed., vol. 1, 90–91)—is difficult to reconcile with what is known of Marot's beliefs. Indeed, these are the two phrases to which Defaux objects most strenuously when he denies the attribution of the *Exposition moralle* to Marot: "Marot, in 1526, would never have spoken such words, he who was about to be accused of being a 'lutherist' and a 'heretic' . . . The *Exposition moralle* did not come from his pen. And the edition of the *Roman* is no doubt not his work."[43]

Hope Glidden points to several instances in the 1526 edition where the text has been changed in ways that attenuate the eroticism of the original and that hint at a reorientation of conventional courtly ideology. She argues that Marot has changed the text of the *Rose* to make it more palatable to an evangelical audience. However, the variants she points to are minor—a word here, a line there—and concern neither well-known passages nor the passages generally viewed as obscene. The changes are so subtle that they could easily escape the notice of even an attentive reader. Moreover, Glidden's analysis is based on a comparison of two modern editions, Lecoy's edition of the *Rose* and Baridon's edition of the 1526 text. A comparison of Baridon's edition with the 1493 printing of the *Rose* by Jehan du Pré (identified by Baridon as the source for the 1526 modernization) reveals that, for five of the eight passages under analysis, the changes were already present in 1493 and therefore cannot possibly be attributed to Marot.

In this attribution debate, the role of Marot's *Temple de Cupido* has received virtually no attention. Although the *Temple de Cupido* has been held up as proof that Marot was familiar with the *Roman de la Rose*, no discussion of the 1526 edition has taken into account that the *Temple de Cupido* does not simply reuse the *Rose*'s imagery, but reworks it in ways that are consistent with what is known of Marot's religious convictions. Marot engages with the *Rose* in a work whose attribution is unquestionable. In the *Temple de Cupido*, not only does Marot's treatment of the thematics of the *Rose* correspond to his evangelical leanings, it does not align with the interpretations proposed in the *Exposition moralle*. In the *Temple de Cupido*,

Marot uses the imagery of the *Rose* to figure an interior space for devotion, not to represent "the state of wisdom" or "the state of grace," let alone "the papal rose" or "the glorious Virgin Mary." Although the disjunction between Marot's use of the *Rose* in the *Temple de Cupido* and the tone of the *Exposition moralle* does not definitively resolve the problem of attribution, it is a neglected piece of evidence that further tips the scales away from a plausible attribution of the edition to Marot.

Marot's use of the *Roman de la Rose* and the 1526 edition both constitute key elements in the study of *Rose* reception in the early Renaissance. Jean de Meun's text, with its multivalence and fusion of contrasting registers, formed a model that was easily adaptable for Marot's project of working within the conventions of love poetry while asserting a *plus hault sens* for his work. For Marot, the *Rose* functions as a backdrop, almost as an archetype, in relation to which he articulates a poetic persona. The mere fact that the *Temple de Cupido* can be linked to several different aspects of the *Rose* tradition is likewise proof of the enormous influence of Guillaume de Lorris and Jean de Meun's text at the turn of the sixteenth century. However, if it is consciously used to archaize a work in 1538, then its influence had clearly waned. The 1526 edition, whose prologue announces the need to modernize and explicate the text, likewise demonstrates that the work was beginning to be perceived as a cultural artifact rather than as a text whose relevance was immediately apparent. The reprintings of this edition (in 1529, 1531, and 1538) also attest to a decline in its influence, since the quality of both paper and proofing went steadily downhill. While the larger history of *Rose* reception in the sixteenth century deserves more extensive study, an examination of Marot's use of it makes clear that while the *Rose* had clearly lost much of its cultural prestige by midcentury, it nevertheless played a key role in the cultural shifts of the early Renaissance. Having shaped literary discourse on love for more than two centuries, its influence did not simply evaporate overnight, but rather continued to inform lyric practice in these pivotal years.

Notes

1. "Le dit rommant a esté ourdy tant subtilement et tuissu de si bonne main / et est l'ouvrage tant incorporé en la memoire des hommes que de le coucher en autre stille ne sera moindre nouvelleté que de forgier ung nouvel a.b.c. Car les sentences . . . sont desja contournees en prouverbes communs. . . . chascun cognoist l'industrie d'amours et que le *Romant de la Rose* nous en demonstre si cler enseignement que ce nous est commune patenostre. . . . ["The said romance was so subtly crafted and woven by such a deft hand, and the work is so incorporated into the memory of men that changing it into another style will be no less novel than forging a new alphabet. For its sententiae . . . have already become common proverbs. Everyone knows the work of love and the *Roman de la Rose* demonstrates such clear teaching of it that it is a common Our

Father."] Jean Molinet, *C'est le rommant de la Rose moralisé* . . . (Lyon: Guillaume Balsarin, 1503), f. v v°.
2. Hope Glidden, "Marot's *Le Roman de la Rose* and Evangelical Poetics," in *Translation and the Transmission of Culture: 1300–1600*, ed. Jeanette Beer and Kenneth Lloyd-Jones (Kalamazoo, MI: Medieval Institute Publications, 1995), 142–74, 144.
3. The much-maligned Rhétoriqueur style marked the triumph of form over subjectivity—or rather the expression of subjectivity only through minute manipulations of form. *Formes fixes* like the *ballade* and *rondeau* limited generic flexibility, while the conditions of court patronage circumscribed the range of available subjects and forced poets to demonstrate their mastery of their craft. Innovation took place almost solely through wordplay, with the result that elaborate imagery and verbal pyrotechnics took precedence over the expression of individual emotion. Appreciation of the Rhétoriqueur ethic is fairly recent; Paul Zumthor's *Le masque et la lumière* (Paris: Seuil, 1977) was key in this critical reappraisal.
4. All text references and line numbers are from Defaux's edition of the *Oeuvres poétiques*, vol. 1 (Clément Marot, *Oeuvres poétiques*, ed. Gérard Defaux, 2 vols. [Paris: Dunod-Bordas, 1990–93]). All translations are mine.
5. For a discussion of the importance of Ferme Amour both in Marot's work and elsewhere in early-sixteenth-century lyric, see Gérard Defaux, "Les Deux Amours de Clément Marot," *Rivista de Letterature Moderne e Comparate* 46.1 (1993): 1–30.
6. "de bois mortel, empenné de vengeance" (29).
7. "clos flory verger" (143).
8. "Amour venerique, et ardant" and "amour muable" (459, 466).

> . . . la Dame tant illustre
> Celle de qui jadis le trescler lustre
> Souloit chasser toute obscure souffrance
> Faisant regner Paix divine soubz France:
> Celle pour vray (sanz le blasme d'aulcun)
> Qui de deux cueurs maintesfois ne faict qu'un:
> Celle par qui Christ, qui souffrit moleste,
> Laissa jadis le hault throsne celeste,
> Et habita ceste basse vallée,
> Pour retirer nature maculée
> De la prison infernale & obscure. (485–95)

["The most illustrious lady, she whose bright radiance used to drive away all suffering, making divine Peace reign over France, she who often (without anyone's criticism) truly makes two hearts into one: She through whom Christ, who suffered torment, left his high celestial throne and lived in this low valley to save soiled Nature from the dark infernal prison."]
9. Guillaume de Lorris and Jean de Meun, *Le Roman de la Rose*, ed. Felix Lecoy, 3 vols. (Paris: Champion, 1965–70). All line numbers are from this edition. Page numbers refer to Charles Dahlberg's translation, *The Romance of the Rose* (Princeton, NJ: Princeton University Press, 1995). This passage is immediately preceded by a comparison of old and young women in which the metaphor of wide and narrow paths functions as an equivalent to the description of the pilgrim's staff, scrip, and hammers (*Rose* 21370ff.). A sexual interpretation is difficult to avoid.

10.
> . . . Bel Acceuil le bien apris
> Qui de sa main dextre m'a pris,
> Et par ung fort estroict sentier
> Me feist entrer au beau pourpris
> Dont il estoit premier Portier . . .
> Celluy chemin tindrent plusieurs passans,
> Car Bel Acceuil en gardoit la barriere. (*Temple* 178–88)

11. ". . . la porte / Faicte de fleurs et d'arbrisseaulx tous verds" (*Temple* 488–9). Another reference to narrow paths in 480–1 immediately precedes this passage.
12. "Lors Bel Acceuil m'a le buisson ouvert / Du cueur du Temple, estant un pré tout verd" (517–18). The *parc de l'aignelet*, whose Biblical resonances are extremely rich, is likewise accessible only by "une estroite sante serie / qui toute est herbue et florie / tant est po marchiee et battue" (*Rose* 19912–14) ["the narrow calm path that is so little traveled and beaten down that it is covered with flowers and grass" (328)].
13. *Rose* 21553–700; 352–4.
14. In discussing the tension between the carnal and the divine inherent in Jean de Meun's text, Sylvia Huot comments that "part of what troubled the critics of the *Rose* was its reversal of the normal system of allegory. A sensual language used for spiritual allegory would not have been surprising; this, after all, can be found in the Bible itself, in the Song of Songs. But in the *Rose*, spiritual language carries an erotic sense" (*The* Romance of the Rose *and Its Medieval Readers: Interpretations, Reception, Manuscript Tradition* [Cambridge: Cambridge University Press, 1993], 300).
15. Defaux, "Les Deux Amours," 13–14.
16. Ibid., n. 44.
17.
> Tu peuz amer generaumant
> touz ceus du monde leaumant.
> Aime les touz touz autant conme un,
> Au mains de l'amour dou conmun.
> Fei tant que tels envers tous soies
> Con tous envers toi les voudroies;
> ne fei vers nul ne pourchace
> for ce que tu vieuz qu'en te face.;
> et s'ainsinc voloies amer,
> l'en t'en devroit quite clamer;
> et ceste iés tu tenuz a sivre
> sans ceste ne doit nus hom vivre. (*Rose* 5417–28)

[You can lawfully love all those of the world in a general way: love them all as much as one, at least with the love of what is common to all. Act in such a way that you may be toward all as you would wish them all to be toward you. Neither act nor pursue a course of action toward any man except that course that you want men to take toward you. If you want to love in this way, men should proclaim you free from any blame for it. You are bound to pursue this love; no man should live without it (111).]

18. The view that Raison's speech provides the key to understanding the *Rose* has

been given its most extended treatment by John Fleming, *The* Roman de la Rose*: A Study in Allegory and Iconography* (Princeton, NJ: Princeton University Press, 1969), and *Reason and the Lover* (Princeton, NJ: Princeton University Press, 1984). Most recent critical assessments of the *Rose* focus on the emergence of meaning from the tension between various discourses. For a discussion of problems of signification in Jean de Meun's portion of the *Rose*, see David Hult, "Language and Dismemberment: Abelard, Origen and the *Romance of the Rose*," in *Rethinking the* Roman de la Rose, ed. K. Brownlee and S. Huot (Philadelphia: University of Pennsylvania Press, 1992), 101–30; Nancy Regalado, "'Des contraires choses': la fonction poétique de la citation et des exemples dans le *Roman de la Rose* de Jean de Meun," *Littérature* 41 (1981): 62–81.

19. For a complete discussion of the manuscript history of the *querelle*, see the introduction to Hicks, ed., *Le Débat sur le Roman de la Rose* (Paris: Champion, 1977).
20. "Verité est que maistre Jehan Jarson fort auctorisé en theologie et de tresclere renommé a la requeste faveur d'aucunes notables dames composa ung petit livre intitulé la reprobacion du Romant de la Rose . . ." [" It is true that master Jean Gerson, who was very well-versed in theology and of a brilliant reputation, at the request of several notable women composed a treatise entitled the Reprobation of the Romance of the Rose"] (Molinet cli r°; translation mine).
21. Hicks, ed., *Le Débat*, 61–2; 143.
22. Defaux, "Clément Marot: poésie, autobiographie et roman," in *Writing the Renaissance: Essays on Sixteenth-Century Literature in Honor of Floyd Gray*, ed. Raymond La Charité (Lexington, KY: French Forum, 1992).
23. Rigolot, "Clément Marot et l'émergence de la conscience littéraire à la Renaissance," in *La Génération Marot*, ed. G. Defaux (Paris: Champion, 1997), 21–34, 29–33.
24. Glidden, "Marot's *Le Roman de la Rose*," 159–61.
25. See n. 19.
26. Robert Griffin, *Clément Marot and the Inflections of Poetic Voice* (Berkeley: University of California Press, 1974), chapter 1; Annette Tomarken, "Clément Marot and the Grands Rhétoriqueurs," *Symposium* 32 (1978): 41–55; and John McLelland, "La Poésie à l'époque de l'humanisme: Molinet, Lemaire de Belges et Marot," in *L'Humanisme français au début de la Renaissance: Colloque International de Tours* (1973), 313–14. Work on Marot done since the rehabilitation of the Rhétoriqueurs presents a more nuanced view of Marot's use of the traditions available to him. See Defaux, "Les Deux Amours"; Glidden, "Marot's *Le Roman de la Rose*"; Rigolot, "Clément Marot et l'émergence"; Cynthia Skenazi, "Eutopie et Utopie dans *Le Temple de Cupido* de Marot," *French Studies* 49.1 (1995): 17–28; Timothy Hampton, "Vergers des Lettres: L'Allegorie politique et morale de l'Enfer," in *Clément Marot, "Prince des poëtes françois," 1496-1996: Actes du Colloque International de Cahors en Quercy*, ed. Defaux and Simonin (Paris: Champion, 1997), 237–48.
27. For a discussion of the authority of this edition, see the introduction to Defaux's edition (vol. 1, clxxv–clxxxvi). This edition also provides a complete list of variants (417–26), allowing an easy reconstruction of the 1515 text.
28. Line numbers are from Defaux's edition and therefore correspond to the 1538 text.
29. "le Dieu Pan"; "honneur l'archiprestre," and "Genius l'archiprestre" (*Temple* 366); "le beau dieu Pharete" and "le Dieu d'Amour" (112).

30. The influence of the *Concorde des deux langages* is also visible, since Bel Acceuil works in tandem with Faulx Dangier, whose task it is to chase pilgrims out the back gate of the garden (*Temple* 189–92). Compare to *Concorde* 21, ll. 333–45; 43, ll. 120–62. Jean Lemaire de Belges, *La Concorde des deux langages*, ed. Jean Frappier (Paris: Droz, 1947).
31.
> (1515) . . . lung est dor / laultre dargent
> Cil qui est dor / a mainte gent
> En Amors done guarison
> Et celuy dargent marisson
> . . . l'ung ferré d'or tresluisant
> Cause les amoureux attraictz
> L'autre dangereux plus que [traictz]
> Porte ung fer de plomb mal couché
> Par la pointe tout rebouché
> Et rend l'amour des cueurs estaincte. (155–62)

32. Defaux's edition contains a discussion of the ideological importance of the preface to the *Adolescence*; Rigolot characterizes it as the "birth certificate of a writer still unsure of his talent" ("l'acte de naissance d'un écrivain encore peu sûr de son talent") ("Clément Marot et l'émergence," 28).
33. Griffin, 33.
34. "correction tant du mauvais et trop ancien langaige sentant son invétéré commencement et origine de parler que de l'imparfaicte quantité des mettres, tous quasi corrompuz" (Baridon, ed., vol. 1, 89–90). All translations from the *Exposition morale* are mine.
35. F. W. Bourdillon, "The Early Editions of the *Roman de la Rose*," in Huot, *Medieval Readers* (London: Bibliographical Society, 1906), chapter 1.
36. "Nota des oeuvres de Nature," "Raison a baillé les noms aux choses naturelles."
37. Silvio F. Baridon, ed., *Le Roman de la Rose dans la version attribuée à Clément Marot* (Milan: Instituto Editoriale Cisalpino, 1954). In the 1526 printing, this section was entitled the *Preambule du livre*; the title was changed to *Exposition moralle du Rommant de la Rose*. Other than a change in the explicit, Baridon does not specify whether the text was modified between printings (vol. 1, 69).
38. "Je dis doncques premierement que par la rose qui tant est appettée de l'amant est entendu l'estat de sapience bien et justement a la rose conforme pour les valeurs doulceurs et odeurs qui en elle sont . . . Et en ceste maniere d'exposer sera la Rose figurée par la rose papalle . . . Secondement on peult entendre par la Rose l'estat de grace qui semblablement est a avoir difficile, non pas de la part de celluy qui la donne, car c'est Dieu le tout puissant, mais de la partie du pécheur qui toujours est empesché et eslongné du collateur d'icelle . . . Tiercement nous pouvons entendre par la rose la glorieuse vierge Marie pour ses bontez doulceurs et parfections de grace, desquelles je me tais pour le présent. Et sachez que ceste virginalle rose n'est aux héreticques facile d'avoir et n'y eust seullement que Malle Bouche qui les empesche d'approcher de sa bonté, car ilz ont mal d'elle parlé, voulans maculer et denigrer son naturel bon honneur en disant qu'il ne la fault saluer et appeler mere de pitié et miséricorde . . . Quartement nous pouvons par la rose comprendre le souverain bien infiny et la gloire d'éternelle béatitude . . ." (Baridon, ed., vol. 1, 90–91). ["I therefore say first that by the Rose which the Lover so desires we can under-

stand the state of wisdom which well and justly corresponds to the Rose because of the values, sweetness and smells within it . . . By this manner of exposition the Rose is a figure for the papal rose . . . Secondly we can understand by the Rose the state of grace which is likewise difficult to obtain, not because of him who gives it, for that is God the all-powerful, but because of the sinner who is always distant from the giver. Thirdly we can understand by the Rose the glorious virgin Mary for her goodness, sweetness and perfections of grace, of which I will not speak at present. And know that this virginal rose is not easy for heretics to have, if only because Malle Bouche keeps them from approaching her goodness, for they have spoken ill of her, trying to stain and denigrate her natural good honor by saying that we cannot hail her and call her mother of pity and mercy. Fourthly we can understand by the Rose the infinite sovereign good and the glory of eternal beatitude."]

39. Rosemond Tuve, *Allegorical Imagery: Some Medieval Books and Their Posterity* (Princeton, NJ: Princeton University Press, 1966), 234.
40. My information on the views of Becker, Sneyders de Vogel, and Weinberg comes from Baridon's introduction (vol. 1, 56–63).
41. "Clément Marot m'a donné ce livre" (Baridon, ed., vol. 1, 60, 70).
42. For a comparison of the two prefaces, see David Hult, "La fortune du *Roman de la rose* à l'époque de Clément Marot," in *Clément Marot, "Prince des poëtes françois": Actes du colloque international de Cahors en Quercy 21–25 mai 1996*, Ed. Defaux and Simonin (Paris: Champion, 1997), 143–56; and Stephen J. Nichols, "Marot, Villon, and the *Roman de la Rose*: A Study in the Language of Creation and Re-creation," *Studies in Philology* 63 (1966): 135–43; 64 (1967): 25–43. Nichols demonstrates that the same editorial precepts are used to establish the text of both editions. However, he sidesteps both the attribution debate and the question of why, if editorial precepts are discussed so prominently in Marot's edition of Villon, they are conspicuously absent in the preface to the 1526 *Rose*.
43. "Jamais Marot, en 1526, n'eût pu parler un tel langage, lui qui allait bientôt être accusé d'être "lutheriste" et "heretique" . . . Cette *Exposition moralle* n'est pas sortie de sa plume. Et l'édition du *Roman* n'est sans doute pas son fait" (*Oeuvres poétiques*, vol. 2, 1360).

Atrocities and the Executions of Peasant Rebel Leaders in Late Medieval and Early Modern Europe

PAUL FREEDMAN

In the spring and summer of 1514, peasants in Hungary launched a revolt against the rulers of the kingdom. A crusade preached against the Turks by the cardinal-archbishop of Esztergom turned into a holy war against the Hungarian nobles whom the peasants accused of betraying the Christian cause by continuing their exploitative lordship and refusing to make any effort to defend the realm. After two months the rebellion was put down by Janos Zápolya, the governor (*voivod*) of Transylvania, who defeated the peasant army near Temesvár (modern Timosoara in Romania). The peasant commander, a member of the minor nobility known alternatively as György Dózsa or Georg Zeckel, was captured and about ten days thereafter (on or near July 25) executed in a manner so stunningly barbarous that across Europe contemporaries, inured though they were to gruesome public spectacles, took notice. Dózsa was placed on an iron throne that was then heated while a red-hot iron circlet was placed on his head in a mock coronation ceremony. Still alive, the partially roasted Dózsa was then removed from the throne and his followers, who had been starved for this purpose, were forced to eat his flesh. Two who demurred were immediately dispatched. Dózsa's remains were then quartered and sent around Hungary for display.[1]

In a letter dated July 31, 1514, the Bamberg cathedral canon Lorenz Beheim wrote to the Nuremberg humanist Willibald Pirckheimer condemning the tortures and executions meted out to peasants, which, he said, would have been more justly applied to robber barons of Franconia.[2] Even those who denounced the violence and defiance of the Hungarian rebels felt uneasy about the savagery of the repression. Giovanni Vitale, an Italian living in central Europe, wrote to a Roman friend later in 1514, describing Dózsa's end as frightful (*atrox*) but ultimately merited.[3] Zápolya himself is reputed to have felt guilt over this deed and legend has it that he was unable ever again to see the elevated host at mass.

The execution of Dózsa was long remembered, if not with complete accuracy. Michel de Montaigne, writing seventy years later, used this incident (which he located in Poland), as an example of officially sanctioned cruelty.[4] In *The Tragedy of Hoffman*, an English play performed at the beginning of the seventeenth century, the protagonist avenges the torture and execution of his father by the "duke of Luninberge" by killing the duke's son Otho by means of a burning crown.[5]

The denouement to the Hungarian uprising is a startling example of ludic, carnivalesque inversion, not in the hands of the lower orders mocking their superiors but as a dramatization of seigneurial domination. In what follows I will discuss the implications of this quasi-official atrocity and point to some similar if not quite so spectacular incidents with different sorts of perpetrators and victims.

As is well known, late medieval and early modern Europe saw frequent and elaborate public acts of torture and execution. Often these were stiffly choreographed events whose solemnity and meticulous preparation made the infliction of mutilation and death more horrifyingly impressive. The auto da fe of the Spanish Inquisition or the guillotine of the French Revolution were punctilious and ritualized, but the dignity of the official ceremonial was accompanied by humiliating clothes, the tumbril, or other expressions of contempt for the condemned. While exceptional individuals might merit a certain paradoxical deference at execution (condemned royal officials in fifteenth-century France being garbed in their robes of state on the way to the scaffold, for example[6]), it was more often thought necessary to dramatize the abjectness of the condemned whose evil deeds had separated him from the world of the living even before undergoing the final punishment.[7]

At Temesvár there was plenty of ceremony, but the emphasis was on mock seriousness and grotesquely festive reversal. The first surviving report of the execution is in a rather cheerful letter from the normally melancholic king of Hungary and Bohemia, Vladislav II. Writing to the imperial legate, Vladislav says that this Zeckel (as he calls him) was apprehended on the Feast of the Division of the Apostles (July 15). He describes the details of the execution and adds that it was quite appropriate that Zeckel's entourage, whom the rebel leader used to refer to affectionately as his "beasts," should have been forced to eat him. The violence is implicitly justified by the resulting dispersion of the peasants without further bloodshed.[8] A contemporary German account reports that while the execution scene was being set up, pipes and violins played and as Dózsa was roasted, dancing monks sang a Te Deum.[9] The illustrated title page to this pamphlet shows in rather schematic form Dózsa crowned and on the throne, one man biting his upper arm. The tableau is flanked by two musicians, one playing a wind and another a stringed instrument (figure 1). The

Die auffrur so geschehen ist im Vngerlandt, mit den Creützern, Vnnd auch darbey wie man der Creützer Haubtman hat gefangen vnnd getödt Zeckel Jorg.

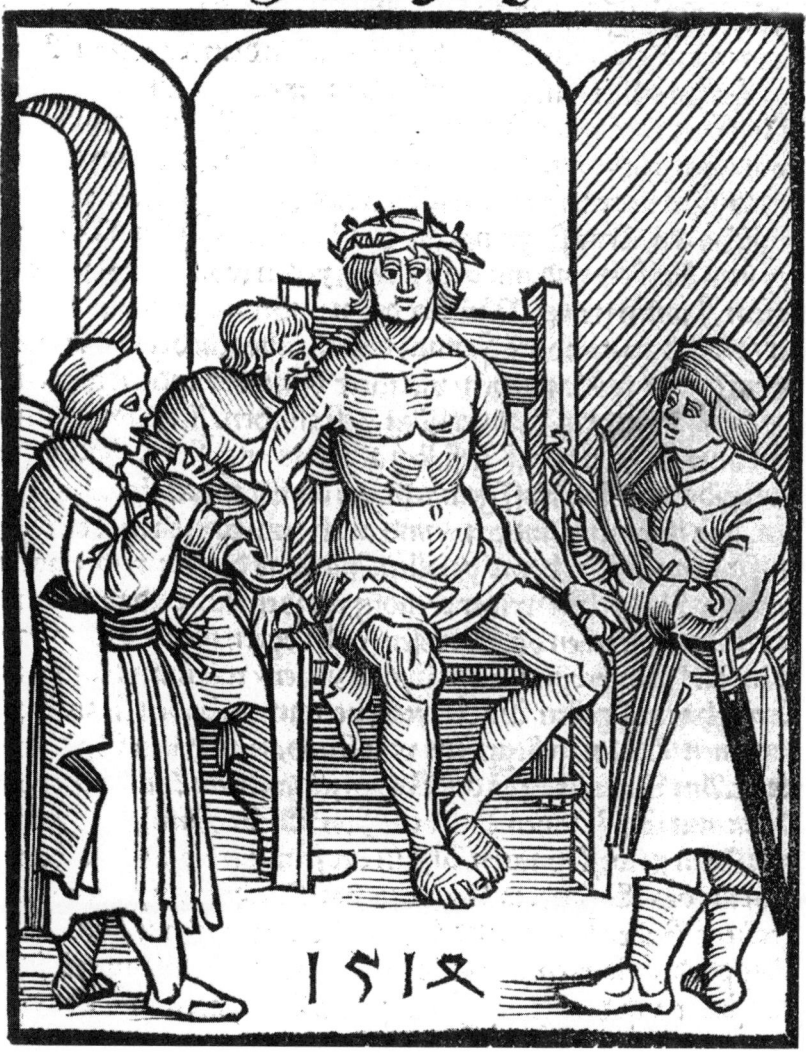

Figure 1.

scene is surprisingly static, even tranquil. The woodcut appears to have circulated independently and its implications contradict the rather hostile text of the pamphlet. Without the gestures and actions of the accompanying three figures, Dózsa could easily be confused with Christ as the Man of Sorrows. In late medieval representations Christ is seated while being mocked, tormented, and crowned with thorns by his executioners.[10] Indeed, Dózsa would come to be regarded as a martyr especially among Franciscans and in popular legend, and a chapel in his honor was eventually constructed on the site of his execution, the marketplace at Temesvár.

A more chaotic scene is depicted in another illustration dating from five years after the event (figure 2). Here as trumpets play, crowds of figures bite or torment the agonized Dózsa. In the background three men are impaled on standing poles, while another lies skewered on the ground at Dózsa's feet preparatory to being raised up as well. Mockery and carnivalesque inversion set an especially horrifying example or indicate martyrdom, two opposed but in some sense complementary uses and implications of cruelty. Stories of Christian martyrdom included not only endless torture but humiliation. Nowhere was this more detailed or frequently repeated than in fifteenth- and sixteenth-century depictions of the crucifixion.[11]

What is particularly interesting is that the complicated iconography of Dózsa's execution was more a pastiche of already-established elements of savagery, reversal, and mockery than a ceremony invented for the occasion. Punishing rebels against royal authority by means of iron thrones or crowns, coerced cannibalism, and the allusion to both martyrdom and just punishment all had fairly well-established precedents in 1514 and some subsequent history as well. This is not to say that Zápolya and his associates ransacked available chronicles for ideas before deciding on the method of dispatching their captive but quite the reverse: that as the exercise was supposed to serve as a memorable example to discourage other would-be rebels, it had to correspond to a recognizable symbolic language.

There was an obvious logic to including a humiliating mock crowning in the punishment meted out to rebels and traitors. The Biblical crown of thorns or the paper crown placed on the head of the captured Duke of York in Shakespeare's *Henry VI, Part 3* are famous examples. To go a step further and make the crown the actual instrument of death might have struck those performing the execution as peculiarly appropriate. In 1197, over three hundred years before the Hungarian rebellion, the emperor Henry VI suppressed an uprising of Sicilian nobles and ordered that a red-hot crown be nailed to the head of the ringleader who had claimed the title of king of Sicily.[12] Later the mock coronation/execution was deemed even more appropriate to inflict on lower-class rebels who dared usurp powers that belonged to the royal authority. Jacques Calle, one of the leaders of the French Jacquerie of 1358, was captured by the king of Navarre and placed nude on a hot piece of iron while his head was

Atrocities and the Executions of Peasant Rebel Leaders 105

Figure 2.

crowned by a burning iron circlet. "Thus," according to the *Anonimalle Chronicle*, "he finished his evil life as an example to others."[13]

The suppression of a peasant uprising that spread across parts of Croatia and Slovenia in 1573 included putting to death a rebel leader, a certain Matija Gubec, by means of the hot iron crown (without any sort of throne in this case). George Draskovic, archbishop of Zagreb and imperial *ban* of the region, wrote to the emperor Maximilian II asking for permission to put this punishment into effect. In his letter he refers to the rebel leader derisively as "Gubecz Bey," the use of a Turkish honorific implying apostasy in addition to treason. The punishment, once again, is stated as intended to serve as an example to others.[14] Here the claim is made that Gubec declared himself king, an unlikely event unsupported in any other source, but an assertion that legitimated the mock coronation. The punishment is another carnivalesque inversion in which impudent pretense is savagely but comically (and, in the eyes of the executioners, appropriately) repressed.

In at least one instance the same manner of killing was performed by peasants against an unfortunate random member of the upper classes (or at least a plausible story was circulated to that effect). Peasant bands known as "Tuchins" in Artois and Picardy revolted in 1384. Among their supposed atrocities was the execution of a hapless Scottish squire named (somewhat generically) John Patrick. He had the misfortune to be caught by the rebels who had determined to kill anyone they came across who possessed courtly or urban speech, manners, or affect. As a practical test, those whose hands were not calloused by manual labor were to be executed. Failing that test, John Patrick was dispatched by being "crowned" with a burning tripod.[15]

Peasant atrocities, or more accurately *stories* of peasant atrocities, tended to involve a frenzied inversion of authority in which a generally chaotic expression of supposed bestial violence was dramatized by a savage symbolism. Rape, murder, cannibalism, roasting are all topoi of peasant rebellion as described by literate contemporaries. Hungarian peasants in 1514 were labeled in one alarmed account *crucifixores* (crucifiers) who call themselves *cruciferos* (crusaders, those bearing the cross): perpetrators of terrible atrocities posing as defenders of Christ. This letter, by four provincial governors to a fifth, warns of the "rage" and "furor" of the peasants that will, if unchecked, not only lead to the extermination of the noble leaders but the barbarous rape and murder of their families.[16] The peasants' rage is a species of natural force or innate savagery that has now, according to this letter, "boiled over" (*efferbuit*). Similarly Giovanni Vitale says that although the movement began as a sincere crusade, it degenerated into wild and random violence, especially rape and torture, which are emblematic peasant atrocities. Vitale specifically mentions impaling nobles before the eyes of their wives and children, or raping the wives while their husbands were forced to watch. These are not landlords killed by their tenants but, as with the account of Tuchin violence, unfortunate members of a hated class who have fallen into the hands of the rebels.[17]

The French Jacquerie of 1358 is probably the *locus classicus* for medieval stories of peasant atrocities. According to the account of the chronicler Jean le Bel, a knight was murdered by peasants who then forced his wife and children to watch as he was roasted. After raping the wife, the rebels then forced her to eat the knight's flesh, and then she too was killed.[18] The story was repeated by Froissart, whose chronicles would of course become known throughout Europe. Writing at some distance from the event, Froissart embellished slightly on Jean le Bel's account, adding to the story of the roasted knight, for example, the detail that he was turned on a spit.[19] The atrocious execution of Dózsa at Temesvár, therefore, mocked the pretensions to rule by means of a ghastly coronation, and mimicked what were regarded as canonical peasant atrocities, namely roasting and enforced cannibalism.

Whether or not such peasant atrocities really took place is unlikely to be demonstrated, these were what nobles believed peasants in rebellion customarily did. And yet there are other precedents for this aspect of the horrific drama. In 1456 a crusade was led by Hunyadi to relieve the Turkish siege of Belgrade. This anticipates the 1514 crusade in that here too peasant soldiers denounced the nobility for shirking their military and Christian obligations and continuing to levy exactions to enrich themselves rather than contributing to the crusade.[20] Also during this campaign, a conspiracy to betray the army to the Turks was discovered and the ringleader was burned at the stake, after which his associates were forced to eat his charred remains.[21]

For the most part the atrocities I've described have a somewhat stereotypic post–Black Death aura. But the background to at least one of the symbolic atrocities goes back further to accounts of Christian martyrdom, reminding us, as with the iconography of Dózsa, that one side's exemplary punishment is another side's exemplary resistance. The execution of a number of saints included the imposition of a red-hot metal crown.[22] This is especially true of the St. Christopher legend. Christopher is best known for carrying the increasingly heavy Christ child across a river, hence his status as the protector of travelers until he was recently decommissioned by the Church. Often in the Eastern churches, and less commonly in the West, he was a dog-headed saint whose quasi-human status exhibited the care of God for even the most distant and unpromising peoples.

Christopher is one of those saints whose martyrdom was long and drawn out because tortures that kill normal people left him untouched. Among these torments was that he was placed on a glowing-hot iron stool or gridiron or covered with a glowing iron mantle, and, especially in Western iconography, his head was covered with a similarly heated helmet.[23] This is not necessarily a mock coronation, it should be noted, because Christopher's attributed crime was not a claim to any sort of political authority. His was a martyrdom that imitated Christ's sacrificial humiliation, so the association with the derisive crown of thorns was logical.

An early text describing this aspect of Christopher's passion is a fragment of a martyrdom account contained in the Anglo-Saxon manuscript, BL Cotton Vitellius A.xv, which also has the unique copy of *Beowulf* and the collection of exotica known as *The Wonders of the East*. In this incomplete saint's life, Christopher is tortured over several days and only dies on the third day by decapitation. The fragment in Cotton Vitellius begins with his torture, but in other early English accounts he begins as a dog-headed semi-human who is miraculously transformed by his conversion and martyrdom. On the first day of his torture he is enthroned on an iron seat set over a massive fire and crowned with a burning helm, but this has no effect.[24] In *The Golden Legend*, which would enshrine hagiographic images for future learned and popular culture, Christopher first is crowned with an iron helmet and then placed in an iron chair above a raging fire fed by pitch, again to no avail.[25] While artistic depictions of St. Christopher usually show him carrying the Christ child, the details of his martyrdom were also occasionally presented. A Romanesque painted altar frontal from twelfth-century Catalonia shows Christopher's torture and death in panels surrounding a central representation of Christopher carrying Christ. In the lower left-hand section, he is half-lying on the ground, surrounded by flames as an iron cap is placed over his head at the order of the emperor while the hand of God protects him (figure 3).[26]

We've seen that various elements of the multi-atrocity execution of Dózsa had separate precedents or afterlife: the iron crown, the throne, roasting, and cannibalism. These were mingled with other horrible reputed deeds (such as rape) in earlier instances. All the incidents, both official and spontaneous, were in the nature of public spectacles, the public including not only those who were supposed to take home an indelible lesson from the performance, but a smaller humiliated "participating" audience (family, followers) who had to witness the atrocious cruelty or take part in it, or be similarly victimized in sequence. These events were not simply outbreaks of frenzied peasant violence (although chroniclers of peasant wars portray them this way), nor were they solely theatrical demonstrations of established power on the order of the ceremonial penances and executions already mentioned. The elements of atrocity were borrowed and traveled back and forth between lower-class rebels and upper-class enforcers of state authority and so were mutually referential.

The common people did not have a monopoly on the carnivalesque ceremonies of social reversal. We have learned from Bakhtin and of course from historians such as Natalie Davis and Robert Darnton about the complex symbolic order and representation inscribed in what were once dismissed as merely excesses of bizarre, lower-class frenzy.[27] The public infliction of torture and mutilation, whether at the hands of a mob or the

Figure 3.

state, fulfills in a disturbing but apposite manner the ludic qualities of the Carnival and its association with the all-too-malleable body.

What is perhaps more disturbing is the pleasure taken by the modern public in the ritualized mutilation, murder, and/or humiliation of victims of officially sanctioned mob violence. The recent examples of Rwanda and Bosnia demonstrate this. Lynchings in the early-twentieth-century American South were family entertainment. Far from being secret atrocities, they spun off postcards and other memorabilia.[28] The 1938 *Anschluss* was marked in Vienna by forcing elderly Jews to scrub the sidewalks on their hands and knees. Daniel Goldhagen's book, although flawed in its interpretations and conclusions, nevertheless presents evidence of the picnic-like atmosphere surrounding the burning of villages, the hunt for Jews, and their murder reported casually by perpetrators to those back home.[29] The "terrible secret" of the Holocaust, as Walter Laqueur termed it, and the industrialized extermination of the camps existed alongside a hideously theatricalized world of atrocities and a not-so-secret world of public or informally publicized spectacle in which the supposed arrogance or social claims made by those considered subordinate were obsessively—symbolically as well as physically—extirpated.[30]

The atrocity of 1514 is fairly isolated and limited in its impact compared with modern instances of persecution and genocide, but it shows the ability of the political authorities to participate in or imitate popular carnivalesque rites of misrule and indicates that these rites were composed of multiple elements with a complicated symbolic past.

Notes

1. Documents concerning the Hungarian Peasants' War are collected in *Monumenta rusticorum in Hungaria rebellium*, ed. Antonius Fekete Nagy et al. (Budapest: Akadémiai Kiadó, 1979). Most of the secondary literature is in Hungarian, but see Gábor Barta, "Der ungarische Bauernkrieg vom Jahre 1514," in *Aus der Geschichte der ostmitteleuropäische Bauernbewegungen im XVI–XVII Jahrhundert*, ed. Gusztáv Heckenast (Budapest: Akadémiai Kiadó, 1977), 63–69; Peter Gunst, "Der ungarische Bauernaufstand von 1514," in *Revolte und Revolution in Europa*, ed. Peter Blickle (Munich: Oldenbourg, 1975), 62–83; Norman Housely, "Crusading as Social Revolt: The Hungarian Peasant Uprising of 1514," *Journal of Ecclesiastical History* 49 (1998): 1–28; Paul Freedman, "The Hungarian Peasant Revolt of 1514," in *Grafenauerjev Zbornik* (Ljubljana: SAZU, 1996), 431–46.
2. Siegfried Hoyer, "Der ungarische Bauernkrieg in deutschen Flugschriften und Chroniken," in *Ostmitteleuropäische Bauernbewegungen*, 464.
3. *Monumenta rusticorum*, no. 200, p. 245. A similar conclusion was reached by the Italian historian of Hungary, Gian Michele Bruto, in the later sixteenth century: Brutus János Mihály, *Magyar Históriája, 1490–1552*, ed. Ferencz Toldy, Monumenta Hungariae Historia XII, vol. 1 (Pest: Ferdinánd Eggenberger, 1863), 372–76.

4. László Báti, "Montaignes Aufzeichnung über György Dózsas Tod," in *Ostmitteleuropäische Bauernbewegungen*, 457–60.
5. Henry Chettle, *The Tragedy of Hoffman, or A Revenge for a Father* (London: I.N. for Hugh Perry, 1631; repr. Oxford: Malone Society, 1951), lines 152–234. I am grateful to Sara Lipton for pointing this out to me.
6. Examples in Johann Huizinga, *The Waning of the Middle Ages* (New York: Doubleday, 1954), 11–12.
7. On the symbolism and meaning of public torture and execution, see Mitchell B. Merback, *The Thief, the Cross and the Wheel: Pain and the Spectacle of Punishment in Medieval and Renaissance Europe* (Chicago: University of Chicago Press, 1999). On notions of cruelty, see Daniel Baraz, *Medieval Cruelty: Changing Perception, Late Antiquity to the Early Modern Period* (Ithaca, NY: Cornell University Press, 2003).
8. Letter of Vladislav II to Nicolai Székely de Kövend in *Monumenta rusticorum*, no. 142, pp. 175–76: "Qui quidem Georgius Zekel ignito primum ferro coronatus est, deinde nudo corpore ligatus ad pedes a suis militibus, quos haydones Hungra lingua vocant, quorum opera tot tantaque mala perpetraverat et quos tam ioco quam serio bestias vocitare consueverat vivus dentibus discerptus et devoratus est. Postremo cadaver in quatuor partes dissectum patibulo suspensum est. Hoc genere mortis et vitam et crudelitatem suam terminavit. Et hoc pacto tota illa rusticorum turba sub Themeswar absque sanguinis effusione dissipata est et tumultus sedata."
9. *Die auffrur so geschehen ist im Ungerlandt mit den Creutzern, vund auch darbey wie man den Creutzer Haubtman hat gefangen unnd getödt* (Nuremberg, 1514). Copies of this rare pamphlet are in Budapest, Magyar Tudományos Akadémia Könyvtára, RM IV 88; Budapest, Széchényi Library, Röp; 18b (photocopy); Wolfenbüttel, Herzog August Bibliothek (described in *Ungarische Drucke und Hungarica 1480–1720, Katalog der Herzog August Bibliothek Wolfenbüttel*, ed. S. Katalin Németh, vol. 1 [Munich, 1993], 23).
10. Mariana D. Birnbaum, "A Mock Calvary in 1514? The Dózsa Passion," in *European Iconography East and West: Selected Papers of the Szeged International Conference, June 9–12, 1993*, ed. György E. Szonyi (Leiden: E. J. Brill, 1996), figure 2 and her commentary, 97–98. A cycle of paintings by Giovanni Canavesio at the church of Notre-Dame de Fontaines at La Brigue (Provence) presents Christ in tableaux similar to the woodcut of Dósza's torment. Canavesio based his representation of Christ being tortured and crowned with thorns on a painting (c. 1480) of the crowning by Israhel van Meckenem now in the National Gallery in Washington. See Véronique Plesch, "Not Only Against the Jews: Antisemitic Iconography and Its Functions at La Brigue," *Studies in Iconography* 23 (2002): 144–50.
11. Merback, *The Thief, the Cross and the Wheel*, especially 11–100.
12. David Abulafia, *Frederick II, a Medieval Emperor* (London: Allen Lane, 1988), 85.
13. *The Anonimalle Chronicle*, ed. V. H. Galbraith (Manchester, 1927), 42. "Et le dit Jak pristrent et mistrent a sa penaunce pur sa mauveite et luy fierent sere tite new sour une treschaude et ardaunt tresde de ferre; et une autre chaude et ardaunt tresde mystrent sur sount test en lieu de coroune, et issint finyst sa mauveys vie a ensample des autres."
14. In Fr. Rački, "Hrvatsko-Slovenska seljačka buna," *Starina* 7 (1875): 212: "Quendam ex ipsis, Gubecz Begum vocatum et noviter regem nominatum, ferrea eaque candenti corona, si Maiestatis V. S. voluntas accesserit, in aliorum

exemplum coronabimus." I am grateful to Oto Luthar for this reference and to Jane Miles for translating portions of Bogo Grafenauer, *Boj za staro pravdo na slovenskem 15. in 16 stoletju* (The Struggle for the Old Right in Fifteenth- and Sixteenth-Century Slovenia) (Ljubljana: Drzaza zal Slovenije, 1974), and Ignacij Voje, *Nemirno Balkan: zgodovinski pregled od 6. do 18. stoletja* (Balkan Unrest: Historical Overview from the Sixth to the Eighteenth Century) (Ljubljana: Drzaza zal Slovenije, 1994), 224–27.

15. *Chronique du religieux de Saint-Denys*, ed. M. L. Bellaguet, vol. 1 (Paris: L'Imprimerie de Crapelet, 1839), 308–10: "Exequturum facinorosum edictum [i.e., that those with uncalloused hands be killed] omnes jurant; et quamvis inde multos peremerint, quorum nomina non tenentur, tamen a fide dignis comperii, quod quemdam insignem armigerum, Scotum nacione, ad regem Arragonie destinatum, Johannem Patricii nomine, ceperunt, durante rabie, quem cum tripode ardenti coronantes nequiter interfecerunt." On this revolt see Vincent Challet, "La révolte des Tuchins: banditisme social ou sociabilité villageoise?" *Médiévales* 34 (1986): 101–12.

16. Letter of the counts of Nógrád, Hont, Pest, and Heves to the count of Abaúj, *Monumenta rusticorum*, no. 73, p. 116: "Quot homicidia, quot stupra et adulteria quotque cedes et incendia per maledictos sceleratissimosque cruxifixores illos, que se se cruciferos appellabant, sed crucis pocius Christi persecutores fuerant . . ."

17. *Monumenta rusticorum*, no. 200, p. 244: "Evocati interdum quotquot nobilium vi apprehendere possunt, eorum corpora acutissimis studibus transfodiunt ante uxorum et liberorum oculos; neque hoc satis videtur vindictae, sed coram maritis miseras uxores stupro violant omnisque exercitus . . ."

18. In Marie-Thérèse de Medeiros, *Jacques et chroniqueurs: une étude comparée de récits contemporains relatant la Jacquerie de 1358* (Paris: H. Champion, 1979), 186: "Je n'oseroie escrire ne raconter les horribles faiz ne les inconveniens que faisoeient aux dames; mais, entre les aultres deshonnestes faiz, ils touerent ung chevalier et le mirent en hast et le rostirent, voyant la dame et les enfans. Aprez ce que X ou XII eurent enforcié la dame, il luy en voulurent fair mengier par force, puis ilz le firent morir de mal mort."

19. Ibid., 189.

20. The events of this crusade were observed by Giovanni de Tagliacozzo, whose letters are collected in Ludwig von Thallóczy and Antal Áldásy, eds., *Magyarország melléktartomáyainak oklevéltára*, vol. 2 (Budapest, 1907). On the anger against the nobles, see Tagliacozzo's account in Luke Wadding, ed., *Annales Minorum seu trium ordinum a S. Francisco institutorum*, vol. 12, part 3 (Quaracchi: Tipografia Barbera, Alfani e Venturi, 1932), 793.

21. Birnbaum, "A Mock Calvary," 95.

22. Hippolyte Delehaye, *Les passions des martyrs et les genres littéraires* (Brussels: Société des Bollandistes, 1921), 282–87.

23. *Lexikon der Christlichen Ikonographie* 5:506; Hans-Friedrich Rosenfeld, "Der Heilige Christophorus: Seine Verehrung und seine Legende," *Acta Academiae Aboensis, Humaniora* 10 (part 3) (1937): 358.

24. Joyce Tally Lionarons, "The Old English Legend of Saint Christopher," in *Marvels, Monsters and Miracles: Studies in the Medieval and Early Modern Imaginations*, ed. Timothy S. Jones and David A. Sprunger (Kalamazoo, MI: Medieval Institute Press, 2002), 180. See also the edition of an eighth-century passion of St. Christopher based on a Würzburg (Universitätsbibliothek) manuscript in Rosenfeld, "Der Heilige Christophorus," 526, which also refers to an iron helmet (*cassidis*).

25. Jacobus de Voragine, *The Golden Legend*, trans. William Granger Ryan, vol. 2 (Princeton, NJ: Princeton University Press, 1993), 14.
26. Barcelona, Museu Nacional d'Art de Catalunya, MNAC/MAC 4370, Taula de Sant Cristòfol. I am grateful to Montserrat Pages Paretas for this information.
27. Mikhail Bahktin, *Rabelais and His World*, trans. Hélène Iswolski (Cambridge, MA: MIT Press, 1968); Natalie Zemon Davis, *Society and Culture in Early Modern France* (Stanford, CA: Stanford University Press, 1975); Robert Darnton, *The Great Cat Massacre and Other Episodes in French Cultural History* (New York: Vintage Books, 1984).
28. *Without Sanctuary: Lynching Photography in America*, ed. James Allen et al. (Santa Fe, NM: Twin Palms, 2000).
29. Daniel Jonah Goldhagen, *Hitler's Willing Executioners: Ordinary Germans and the Holocaust* (New York: Alfred A. Knopf, 1996).
30. Walter Laqueur, *The Terrible Secret: An Investigation into the Suppression of Information about Hitler's "Final Solution"* (Boston: Little, Brown, 1980); Inga Clendinnen, *Reading the Holocaust* (Cambridge: Cambridge University Press, 1999).

Two New Dictionaries of Old French

SUZANNE KOCHER

Algirdas Julien Greimas. *Dictionnaire de l'ancien français*. 3rd edition. Paris: Larousse-Bordas/HER, 2001. Pp. xx + 630. 3 charts.

Frédéric Godefroy. *Lexique de l'ancien français*. Edited and condensed by Jean Bonnard and Amédée Salmon. Introduction by Jean Dufournet. Paris: Honoré Champion, 2003. Pp. v + 637.

There is good news for all those who could use a one-volume dictionary of Old French with definitions in modern French. Algirdas Greimas offers medievalists a welcome third edition of his *Dictionnaire de l'ancien français*. Meanwhile the paperback *Lexique de l'ancien français* has been revised and a new introduction added to this lexicon that Jean Bonnard and Amédée Salmon extracted from Frédéric Godefroy's venerable ten-volume *Dictionnaire de l'ancienne langue française* a century ago. Because of their common sources, the two new volumes define many of the same words, yet it is difficult to imagine how their organization, format, and function could differ more.

The more erudite dictionary is Greimas's. This attractive hardcover represents the dialects of French as they were written from 1080 to 1350. Some of its entries come from recently compiled glossaries, but most come from the magisterial dictionaries of Godefroy and of Tobler-Lommatzsch. The resulting volume defines an impressive 80 percent of the words amassed by Godefroy, yet is much easier to read and quicker to handle than Godefroy's original ten enormous tomes or their digital counterparts. Readers will appreciate its straightforward preface, as well as the necessary lists of abbreviations. Also helpful are charts that detail the forms of Old French articles (*li, les* . . .), demonstratives (*cil, cel* . . .), and possessives (*mes, mi* . . .). New improvements to its layout make this dictionary even more delightful to use than its previous edition, and visually far clearer than any other Old French lexicon available. The entry words stand out nicely in dark bold type with sufficient white space around each entry. At the upper left and lower right corner of each opening, guide words are printed in legible italics; these guide words appear in their entirety, which makes them more useful than if they were incomplete. This hardcover volume is pleasing to the eye and to the hand, with crisp high-quality print on fine smooth paper, and a well-sewn durable binding that conveniently lies flat when open. In all, the production team at Larousse has done beautiful work.

The entries offer all that one could wish for. Greimas lists variant spellings, parts of speech, and the source of a term's first known written use, with an approximate date. Sometimes a brief etymology follows. Next appears a comprehensive list of definitions, offering a valuable and generous range of near synonyms. Entries include medieval words whose spellings have been preserved in modern French while their meanings have changed. Likewise Greimas helpfully defines many phrases and idiomatic expressions. His definitions are efficient and so accessible that Francophone readers will rarely need to reach for a modern French dictionary. Another excellent feature is that Greimas illustrates some definitions with authentic quotations that illuminate terms' connotations or usage. Because they are not translated, the examples will especially help users who already read Old French comfortably.

The new third edition corrects the few typographic errors present in the previous version, though its revision does not seem to take into account the questions that Claude Régnier raised when he reviewed the first edition in *L'information littéraire* 22 (1970): 235–36. Nor does it repair the sexist and heterosexist bias that mars certain entries. For instance, Greimas elliptically defines the noun *bon* as "le plaisir que procure une femme" ("the pleasure that a woman gives"), whereas in medieval texts it can equally well refer to pleasure that a man gives to a lover of either gender. Similarly, is the verb *gesir* really best defined as "Coucher (avec une personne d'un autre sexe)" ("To lie [with a person of another sex]")? Here Greimas is following Godefroy, but he could do better, and I hope a future edition of this invaluable dictionary will replace the sexist and heterosexist euphemisms with more accurate definitions that bring readers closer to the Old French.

A significant and compelling strength of Greimas's dictionary is its principle of organizing entries by families. Each main entry compiles the word's derivates in all parts of speech. The advantage of this structure is that one can easily read the whole entry as a single "story" and thus gain a much fuller sense of a word's range of connotations than if one looked up only a single form. As a result, the lexicon's organization is partly etymological and only secondarily alphabetic. This may not bother specialists, but for less confident readers of Old French it compounds the inherent difficulty posed by variant spellings.

To attenuate such difficulty, Greimas offers two kinds of help. First, for some common alternate spellings he gives one-line cross-references enhanced by a brief definition. Second, he simplifies searches by reducing orthographic variation in entry words: here the dictionary uses F instead of PH, C or QU instead of K, and G instead of W, and it leaves out H where this letter was not pronounced before a vowel. The author assumes we have enough experience and patience to search by the remaining permutations that are possible in Old French dialects, by interchanging G and J as needed, O and U, U and L, I and Y, I and E, C and QU, C and S, S and Z, double consonants and single ones, and so on. In short, one can locate words most easily if one already knows their range of medieval spellings and recognizes their etymologies and parts of speech. For example, to find definitions for the noun *companage* ("food eaten with bread"), one must look among the derivates of *compaignon*. Some cross-references send the user on wild goose chases: if you look up the verb *recueudre* ("take, receive, collect"), you find a cross-reference to *cueudre*, but frustratingly the latter spelling is not listed anywhere; therefore you will need the presence of mind to look again under *cueillir*. The successful search requires a willingness to search both upstream and downstream in the alphabet. Sometimes even a trained reader of Old French simply has to scan the pages that correspond to the letter(s) that a word's main entry might start with.

How lucky, then, that in 2003 the user-friendly *Lexique de l'ancien français* was revised and newly typeset in greatly superior format than previously. Frédéric Godefroy is justly credited as its author although he was not alive to see its first edition in 1901, when Jean Bonnard and Amédée Salmon distilled the *Lexique* from Godefroy's vast *Dictionnaire de l'ancienne langue française*. Since that date, the *Lexique* has merited a century's worth of reprintings, and now has reached both its most readable and most portable form as an almost pocket-sized paperback. Its organization is straightforwardly alphabetical: each term is defined in a separate entry, consisting of the part of speech and a very succinct definition, often only a one-word equivalent. This lexicon expressly applies the principle of brevity in all things. It offers no etymologies, dates, or examples. Nor does it even give a key to its abbreviations. Its pages are dedicated to listing as many separate Old French lexical items as possible, and in this the *Lexique* far surpasses its rival. Despite the impressive number of entries in the *Lexique* (perhaps 60,000 individual forms), countless common spellings do not appear and cross-references are few. Thus the reader will often need to make multiple searches. These are slightly impeded by the lexicon's visual format. Instead of a full guide word, only the guide word's first three letters label each page, so, for instance, one finds seventeen consecutive pages all labeled only "DES." Also, the new layout is dense, in small typeface, but far more legible than the previous edition.

The one-volume dictionaries of Old French are most useful in conjunction with one another and with the older reference books from which most of their entries are compiled. Sometimes the *Lexique* provides the quickest means to a synonym; alternately, or afterward, one can find a much fuller range of denotations in Greimas. To explore more varied examples of medieval usage, one turns to Godefroy's ten-volume *Dictionnaire* and *Com-*

plément (online or in print), and to Tobler and Lommatzsch's *Altfranzösisches Wörterbuch* (printed in German, or as an expensive CD or DVD). No single dictionary can satisfy readers' contradictory desiderata: that it be comprehensive as well as legible, affordable, and convenient to use. Happily, Greimas's excellent *Dictionnaire* is now better than ever and remains indispensable for the experienced reader of Old French. Newcomers to the language will want to begin instead with the paperback *Lexique*, then later reward their progress with a copy of Greimas. Cheaper than the average textbook, the two dictionaries are excellent values, and everyone who reads Old French deserves to own them both.

Suzanne Kocher, University of Louisiana at Lafayette

Review Notices

John Aberth. *A Knight at the Movies: Medieval History on Film.* New York and London: Routledge, 2003. Pp. 332. Illustrations.

This readable, clearly presented, and enthusiastic study of films about the medieval period is to be welcomed. Many more people acquire their images of the Middle Ages from the screen than from the page, so it is worth analyzing what we are getting from historical film. Aberth describes the purpose of his book as being "to illustrate the complex relationship between modern and medieval history, for how we choose to remember the past reveals much about how we live at the present." One cannot disagree with that.

The book is organized thematically—Arthurian films, crusading films, and so forth. Each chapter contains a long section describing the relevant historical reality (the length of these historical sections may be too great for professional academics but is probably right for the wider reading public the book aims at). This is then followed by a section analyzing films in the category. Certain classics get extensive treatment, the twenty-eight pages dedicated to Bergman's *Seventh Seal* leading all the rest. *El Cid* (twenty-two pages), *Alexander Nevsky* (thirteen pages), and *La Passion de Jeanne d'Arc* (twelve pages) are not unexpected. The Egyptian epic *Saladin* (fifteen pages) is more of a surprise and inclusion of such less familiar titles is a strength of the book.

An analysis of the chronological distribution of the films discussed shows a clear peak in the 1950s and 1960s, with a predominance of the '60s (despite the long section dedicated to *The Seventh Seal* of 1957). It may be significant that the author was in his teens in the 1970s, when all these films would have been shown on TV. The 1990s are relatively thinly represented and the 1940s virtually invisible. Those who teach courses on medieval films will recognize this gap in the 1940s (despite Olivier's memorable *Henry V* of 1946). Perhaps World War II diverted interest. Immediately preceding this barren decade, there are the two spectacular and spectacularly different medieval films of 1938, *Alexander Nevsky* and *The Adventures of Robin Hood.*

In his preface the author avows, "I try to more than simply pass judgement on whether a particular film is historically accurate or not." Yet the question of historical accuracy does loom large. Sometimes there are matters of simple fact: in *Alfred the Great* (1969), Ealhswith, Alfred's wife, becomes the lover of the Viking chief Guthrum; in *El Cid* (1961) the corpse of the Spanish hero is fastened to his horse, in order to lead his troops in a victorious sortie from the walls of Valencia; Cecil B. DeMille's *The Crusades* of 1935 shows an encounter between the Holy Roman Emperor, Frederick Barbarossa (d. 1190), and the Muslim leader Saladin during the siege of Acre in the Third Crusade (1191). It is unlikely these events took place as depicted. Because the author skimps movies of the 1990s, however, the sitting duck in this field, *Braveheart* (1995), escapes detailed analysis. Hence the absence of a bridge at the Battle of Stirling Bridge (1297), the government's prohibition of bagpipes (shifted from the eighteenth century to the thirteenth), and the fathering of the future Edward III by William Wallace (d. 1305) on Isabella of France (arrived in Britain 1308) are either not discussed or given only cursory mention.

Many films with a medieval setting are based not on historical events but on literary works or legends from the Middle Ages. King Arthur and Robin Hood are the great examples. Here it is more difficult to ask questions about "accuracy" or "authenticity," and Aberth often runs into dead-end questions about the faithfulness of film Arthurs and Robins to the medieval literary traditions. As devotees of Harry Potter or *Lord of the Rings* know, closeness to the adapted text is not the only criterion for artistic success in the movies.

In any case, does historical accuracy matter? Aberth acknowledges that historical film may require a certain streamlining of reality in the interest of narrative drive or visual impact. Who can doubt, for instance, that the sibling rivalry of the young princes Alfonso and Sancho in *El Cid* would have only been complicated by the presence of their historically attested brother Garcia? More important than such individual inaccuracies as the removal or fusion of characters, the changing of names, or the introduction of impossible encounters is the overall ideological coloring of the film. This may be revealed by deviations from historical reality but is also more pervasive than that. Aberth is acutely aware (perhaps too much so) of the resonances of contemporary politics in the films he discusses. Errol Flynn's *Adventures of Robin Hood* radiates "elemental democracy" and "conservative socialism," with "Maid Marian leaving the outlaw camp . . . a convinced New Dealer"; "the threat from traitors within the realm" in *The Black Knight* of 1954 is clearly a counterpart to the "red scares" of McCarthyism; the portrayal of Alfred the Great in the 1969 film of the same name as a "would-be monk who'd rather pray than fight fits perfectly with the counterculture in America and Britain during the 1960s."

The author makes his own ideological preferences quite clear. He is opposed to Fascism, finding Franco's Spain a "subtext" in *El Cid* ("the Cid of the film . . . is a Fascist vision of what this medieval hero should have been like"); he is opposed to Stalinism and has interesting reflections on the way Eisenstein's reputation has not suffered from his association with Stalin as Leni Riefenstahl's has from her association with Hitler; and he regards the application of Marxist theory to the Middle Ages as a "joke." And while not characterized by an explicit feminism, he is sensitive to the limitations to the portrayal of women in the Egyptian film *Saladin*. The film is "in fact deeply conservative and chauvinistic in its overall treatment of the fair sex." Understandably, the fair sex might be cross about this.

In addition to locating the films in their contemporary political climate in this way, Aberth analyzes the fads and fashions of medieval historians, who sometimes (but not so often) influence the making of movies. However, the relation he seeks to establish between these trends in historiography and cinematic vision is not always convincing. A case in point is the description of *Erik the Viking*, where Tim Robbins (in an unusual piece of casting) plays a Viking not very good at rape ("I actually prefer that there's some sort of mutual feeling between two people"). Aberth comments that this "embodies the revisionism of Viking history that had been taking place for three decades before the film came out," a revisionism insisting that Vikings were not simply mindless predators. This surely misses the point completely. The film is aiming at comic effect, and one premise of the comic effect is that the audience will think of Vikings as looters, pillagers, and rapists. As in *Monty Python and the Holy Grail*, which also involved Terry Jones, director of *Erik the Viking*, it is absolutely necessary for parody that a strong stereotype is already in place.

With a subject in which personal judgment is so important, there will be plenty of room for disagreements. Aberth, himself author of a book on the Black Death, deems it "anachronistic" to apply modern medical knowledge to our interpretation of medieval disease. But surely we do know more about the epidemics of the past than the men and women of the past did. Whatever one thinks of Milla Jovovich's Joan of Arc in *The Messenger* (1999), to call her "a hyperkinetic, crazed psychotic on speed" is dismissive of a genuine attempt to render the oddity and charisma of a peasant girl who led armies of knights to victory. The judgment on the earlier *Jeanne la Pucelle* (1994), that the final cry at the stake is bitter and full of anger and pain, thus making the Maid "all too human" and not "the sacrificial Christ-like Joan who has gone to meet her Maker," contains enormous assumptions about the state of mind in which the historical Joan experienced her agonizing death. Abused and killed by her enemies, abandoned by her king, with a botched attempt at surrender behind her, perhaps she was bitter.

The book thus stimulates disagreement as well as admiration. On balance, however, it is a valuable addition to the literature on the subject that can be strongly recommended. It is well produced, has a useful guide to further reading (to which one should add Stuart Airlie, "Strange Eventful Histories: The Middle Ages in the Cinema," in *The Medieval World*, ed. Peter Linehan and Janet L. Nelson [London, 2001]), and an excellent index.

Robert Bartlett
University of St. Andrews

Peter Hunter Blair. *An Introduction to Anglo-Saxon England.* 3rd edition with a new introduction by Simon Keynes. Cambridge: Cambridge University Press, 2003. Pp. xxxv, 384. 32 illustrations.

For a long time there have been two essential surveys of the history and culture of Anglo-Saxon England—Sir Frank Stenton's *Anglo-Saxon England*, first published by Oxford University Press in 1943, and Peter Hunter Blair's *An Introduction to Anglo-Saxon England*, first published by Cambridge University Press in 1956. Generations of Anglo-Saxonists have used both to get the lay of the land, as it were, as a prelude to specialized study in the period's history, literature, art, or material culture. Stenton's book is the longer—more detailed in its treatment of the period's history and extending a couple of decades into early Norman England. Hunter Blair's, though shorter, pays more attention to art, literature, and culture and, if intangibles can be weighed, is the easier read. Oxford issued a third edition of Stenton's book posthumously in the late 1960s, while Cambridge answered with a second edition of Hunter Blair's in 1977. Oxford reissued Stenton's third edition in 1989 as a paperback and subsequently reissued it in paperback in 1998 "in new covers," as the back of the title page proudly proclaims. Hunter Blair, who died in 1982, did not live to revise his book, but Cambridge has reissued it in 2003 as a third edition (though an exact reprint of the second), with a new introduction by Simon Keynes. If there is some rivalry here, it is a justified and productive one, for the two books support and complement each other; graduate students in the various disciplines that comprise Anglo-Saxon studies need to read both, and professionals could do worse than come back to them every few years to keep from getting overspecialized. If the reissues remind us to do this, they are well justified.

Keynes's introduction to the third edition of Hunter Blair's book is subtitled "Changing Perceptions of Anglo-Saxon History." It is a fairly comprehensive overview of how the various subfields pursued by Anglo-Saxonists have developed since the book's earlier appearances. It should be no surprise to us that much has been done in the past twenty-seven years. Using a delicate old topos of which medieval writers were quite fond, Keynes explains,

Historians active in the first decade of the twenty-first century like to imagine, of course, that they know more about Anglo-Saxon England than was possible in the 1940s or in the 1950s [when Stenton's and Hunter Blair's books first appeared]. If they are right, it is largely because they have the advantage of being able to stand on the broad shoulders of their predecessors; yet it is also because they have some additional evidence, better editions and advanced understandings of primary sources, research tools more powerful than a card-index, and the insights of all those working in adjacent disciplines. (xxii–xxxiii)

As Keynes points out, advances in archaeology, literary analysis of Anglo-Saxon texts, and interpretation of charters, law-codes, and coins have particularly been important in the last several decades. Perhaps more important, historians and—I would add—literary critics, translators, and art historians have "question[ed] the assumptions which helped in the past to determine the received view of events" (xxviii). One could list specific work—new editions of texts, the latest archaeological campaign at Sutton Hoo, and so forth—that does not factor into this third edition of Hunter Blair's book and thus needs to be consulted as a corrective to it.

But that would, I fear, miss the point. Hunter Blair's still admirable book fulfills its role as an "Introduction" to its subject. It is fast paced yet comprehensive, touching on just about every important aspect of Anglo-Saxon history and culture. Those interested in poetry, numismatics, sculpture, runes, Germanic paganism, Benedictine monasticism, and agricultural economics can find a start here. As a literary scholar I of course found myself thinking about recent discussions over things like the dating of *Beowulf*, the relationship between orality and literacy, and gendered poetics while rereading Hunter Blair's survey of Old English literature. But the absence of these topics does not diminish the book's usefulness. There always is more to say about anything, so the issue is how well Hunter Blair can serve as a starting point for further study. There were no errors or misleading discussions in this section, the one I am most qualified to judge. Though I will have to enumerate for the next group of graduate students who will read the book at my suggestion the various topics it does not treat, what the book has to offer will enable them to see the recent specialist discussions in broad context. That is a very good thing. On a recent automobile trip, I was guided by a ten-year-old edition of Rand McNally's *Road Atlas*. There were a couple of surprises—a few new roads, maybe a shortcut that could have saved ten minutes. But I got to my destination safely and in good time and saw plenty of interesting scenery along the way. It was a good trip.

Robert Boenig
Texas A&M University

Paul Brand. *Kings, Barons and Justices: The Making and Enforcement of Legislation in Thirteenth-Century England.* Cambridge: Cambridge University Press, 2003. Pp. 508.

Paul Brand's new book is an extraordinary work of completely original scholarship, an historical and intellectual tour de force. At its center lies the legislation known to historians as the Provisions of Westminster. This was promulgated by King Henry III in October 1259, while under the control of a baronial council. In the following years it was revised and reissued by the king himself or his magnate opponents, depending on who was in control of the realm. Finally, in 1267, the king, now restored completely to power, proclaimed a definitive version in the Statute of Marlborough. In their scope and detail the Provisions of Westminster have no real precedent in English legislative history, and are the precursors of the great statutes issued in the 1270s and 1280s by King Edward I.

Although Brand's book has its origins in his unpublished doctoral thesis completed in 1974, it is essentially a new work. The thesis has been reorganized and expanded and a vast amount of new research undertaken. Brand's essential aim is to investigate how the legislation evolved between 1258 and 1267, why it was thought necessary, and how far it was actually implemented—implemented, that is, both between 1259 and 1267 itself and then subsequently between 1267 and 1307. The study of the evolution of the legislation is based on a detailed examination of the surviving drafts, the various versions of the legislation (definitive texts and translations are given in an appendix), and the first schedule of grievances drawn up in 1258 and known as the Petition of the Barons. Since the legislation was essentially concerned to reform criminal law procedure and offer new remedies in the field of civil litigation, the investigation of how far it was implemented has required a comprehensive examination of all the surviving rolls of the eyre in the localities, the common bench at Westminster, and the king's bench traveling with the king, as well as the Year Books that recorded the arguments of the judges and lawyers. Brand's knowledge of this material, gigantic in size and mostly unprinted, is completely unique. His footnotes with reference after reference to hitherto unknown lawsuits are truly awesome. No other scholar could have come anywhere near writing this book. Brand has also had to work more or less alone. When situating his book historiographically in the introduction, he goes back to the works of Jacob, Treharne, and Plucknett, all written in the first half of the last century and none of them based on any kind of thorough study of the unprinted legal material. Brand makes little or no reference to the large amount written about the politics, society, and economy of thirteenth-century England in recent years. It is simply not helpful or relevant to his purpose.

What then does Brand teach us? We can now see, thanks to his comparison of the different preambles, how the king came to claim ownership of the legislation, eliminating statements that it was conceived by "the common counsel of the realm" and instead stressing his own initiative. We also have a far clearer idea of why the reforms were thought necessary. On the criminal side Brand shows how the practices of the king's judges and sheriffs had created a range of grievances with which the legislation sought to deal. (This is, incidentally, one of the few areas where Brand has been helped by the work of a previous scholar, the late C. A. F. Meekings.) On the civil side, Brand shows that the first three chapters of the Provisions of Westminster, which sought to restrict the obligation of tenants to attend the private courts of their lords, were a response to "the new aggressiveness of lords" who were trying to enforce attendance ("suit") as an incident of tenure even though it had never been performed previously and was not mentioned as an obligation in any charter of enfeoffment. In all these areas, Brand has no doubt that the legislation was responding to very real grievances. But, and here we come to a major theme of the book, Brand is also very clear that the legislation was not always as innovatory or significant as it seems. Some of it did little more than reiterate and duplicate existing rules, for example when it laid down that lords should not take distraints from outside their fees. Some of it was a response not to generalized problems but to particular cases. The chapter, newly introduced into the Statute of Marlborough protecting a lord's rights of wardship, was prompted not by widespread attempts at evasion of such rights, but by a case that had recently come before the common bench where the complaining lord was the king's chancellor, Walter of Merton!

The picture of how far the legislation was implemented and what difference it made is similarly nuanced. A new chapter introduced into the 1263 version of the Provisions of Westminster, for example, was highly successful in extending the scope of the writ of entry and making it available to a much greater number of litigants. Likewise, the chapter in the 1259 Provisions which required briefer adjournments in actions of dower meant that these now passed through the legal system at twice the speed of most other litigation, greatly benefiting widows. Peasants, however, were less lucky. They had been the real beneficiaries from the chapters in the Provisions of Westminster that prevented the king's justices from levying the *murdrum* fine in cases of misadventure and unnecessarily amercing villages for failing to attend inquests. The first of these, although it remained in force, proved of little benefit in alleviating the financial burdens of the *murdrum* fine. The second was effectively repealed by the Statute of Marlborough in 1267, thus protecting the revenues of the crown. On the civil side, the legal action introduced to implement the chapters on attendance at private courts, the jewel in the crown of the 1259 legislation, was in regular but not common use after 1267. A new clause introduced in 1267 which specified that tenants were not in future to perform suit of court or any other service in addition to that specified in their charters of enfeoffment was robbed of all practical effect by the very restrictive way it was interpreted by the courts. Most tenants seem to have preferred to pursue the issue of court attendance through the existing action of replevin, in which they sought the recovery of what had been seized by the lord to enforce the suit. Some other parts of the legislation fared even worse, with no writs being devised to initiate legal actions under their terms, or, if writs were devised, with very few people bothering to obtain them.

At the end of Brand's book one cannot help but sense a paradox, perhaps an inevitable one. The best legal minds of the period clearly poured effort and ingenuity into drafting the legislation and devising the writs to put at least some of it into effect. Yet those same legal minds were also devising a labyrinth of legal argument and procedure that made it very difficult for plaintiffs to win their cases. By far the most common outcome of the pleaded cases under suit of court legislation was for them to disappear from the rolls without any recorded verdict. On some occasions this may have been the result of some satisfactory out-of-court settlement, but it is impossible to be certain. Again and again those who did benefit from the legislation promulgated between 1259 and 1267 were the rich and powerful. Whereas the peasant communities of fourteen Bedfordshire villages failed in the action they brought against two royal bailiffs for demanding a "beaupleder" fine contrary to the Statute of Marlborough, the great earl of Gloucester exploited the legislation from its start in 1259, withdrawing the money his tenants had previously paid to the sheriff of Dorset. Likewise, the legislation restricting attendance at the sheriff's tourn was chiefly enforced in favor of exchequer officials; the writ enabling lords to bring actions to secure accounts from their stewards was only available to those who enjoyed special royal favor. The only plaintiff to win a clear-cut victory in the little-used action devised to safeguard a lord's rights of wardship was none other than Thomas of Weyland, at the time the chief justice of the common bench, the court where the case was being heard! The law, it seems, was run by and for lawyers. Brand's book ends on a positive note: "the legislation as a whole made a significant and lasting contribution to the continuing development of the medieval common law." But he is equally clear that the legislation was not all it seemed, and it was one thing to commence a legal action, quite another to bring it through to a conclusion.

Brand has therefore placed a great edifice across the length of the thirteenth century. The challenge to other historians, as perhaps to Brand himself, is to consider how that edifice relates to the wider politics and society of the period. The immediate political background to the development of the legislation in 1258–59 is indeed one of the few areas where Brand's interpretation can be questioned. The most striking aspect of the reforms of 1259 was the way, in such matters as suit of court, they upheld the interests of tenants against their lords, thus apparently cutting across the interests of the leading reformers, who were all, of course, of magnate status. Why was this? Brand's explanation appears, at least in part, to turn on the revival of the power of the king, who sought to win popularity and defend his own rights by curbing the abuses of the magnates. I am very doubtful, however, as to whether the king, in this early period of the reform movement, had the power to influence legislation in any major way. Rather, the explanation for the antimagnate chapters may lie in the willingness, indeed the determination, of the reformers themselves to promulgate them.

A key piece of evidence in all this is provided by the so-called "Ordinances of the Magnates." Brand describes these as a document issued by the king in February 1259 "giving his side of things, pointing out how he had made various concessions but that it was only now that the magnates were beginning to make their own parallel ones." The document of February 1259, however, was not issued by the king at all. It was a charter of the leading reformers, the ruling council of fifteen and the twelve representing the community at parliaments. In the charter they promised to submit themselves and their officials to the same reforms as those accepted by the king. But everyone knew that the king had not accepted those reforms willingly. They had been imposed upon him. The determination of the leading reformers, despite opposition from more conservative elements, to cleanse their own stables is revealed in the well-known quarrel, almost certainly over the Ordinances of the Magnates, in which Simon de Montfort upbraided the earl of Gloucester for backsliding over the reforms. Graphically and convincingly described by Matthew Paris, this surprisingly does not feature in Brand's account. It was almost certainly such opposition that led to the Ordinances of the Magnates, although drawn up on February 22, only being publicly proclaimed on March 28. They were proclaimed in letters patent of the king, but these were simply letters issued by the reformers in the king's name.

There were essentially two reasons why the more radical magnates were prepared to push on with the reforms even at their own cost. One was idealism. Reading Brand's book, one has sometimes to remind oneself that this was as much the age of the friars as that of the lawyers. If the two worlds met it may well have been in the way the reforms of 1259 dealt with the grievances of wide sections of society from the unfree peasantry upward. The "religion and virtue" of Simon de Montfort, described in John Maddicott's biography, another brilliant work of thirteenth-century scholarship, provides an understanding of the reforms of 1259 very much complementary to Paul Brand's own. A second reason was more calculating. The reformers, having coerced the king, were embarked on a dangerous enterprise and needed wide support. They were also under pressure from below. That some of the reforms were shaped by the grievances revealed by the inquiries of the four knights set up in each county in 1258 is suggested by Brand. But he could perhaps have pressed this line of thought further. He does not refer, another surprising omission, to the famous protest made by "the community of the bachelry of England" at the October 1259 Westminster parliament, as described by the Burton abbey annalist. This body, representing broadly the interests of the county gentry, complained that so far the magnates had simply looked after their own interests and done nothing for the common good. The protest did not produce the Provisions of Westminster, for these already existed in draft, but it may well have ensured, as the Burton annalist indicates, their immediate promulgation. It certainly reveals the kinds of pressures the magnates were under.

It is easy to argue the toss over such matters, and doubtless Brand could formulate replies to some of the points made here. It is much more difficult to relate his findings to the structures of English society and the whole question of what was going on in the localities. It seems clear from the legislation and related litigation that this was a period when lords and tenants were, as Brand says, "often in dispute" over the lord's entitlement to a range of services, including suit of court. The use of distraint to enforce contentious services was constantly challenged by tenants. Indeed the surviving litigation may only be the tip of the iceberg since many actions of replevin took place in county courts, the records of which hardly survive. Brand provides a brief (two-page) social analysis of the litigants in suit of court cases, but many of the plaintiffs and defendants who people his pages are mere names. Who were the "newly aggressive lords"? Were they encouraged by the laxity of Henry III's personal rule (as I have argued)? Did they become far more overbearing during the 1258–67 period of reform and rebellion, as the first chapter of the Statute of Marlborough states? Who were the victims, knights and gentry, free tenants between the gentry and the peasantry, peasants? Were the tensions related to wider social and economic changes like "the crisis of the knightly class," postulated by Peter Coss, or the transition from "feudalism" to "bastard feudalism"? These are not easy questions to answer. Perhaps one way forward will be through regional studies that set Brand's litigants and litigation in their local social and economic context. That Brand himself does not approach such wider issues is no criticism of his work. *Ars longa vita brevis*. As it is he has written a book that will always be definitive in its own terms and will constantly challenge the terms of everyone else who writes about England in the thirteenth century.

David Carpenter
King's College, London

Julia Boffey and A. S. G. Edwards, eds. *Medieval Manuscripts in the Norlin Library and the Department of Fine Arts at the University of Colorado at Boulder: A Summary Catalogue.* Fairview, NC: Pegasus Press, 2002. Pp. 93. 15 illustrations.

This catalogue of medieval manuscripts at the University of Colorado at Boulder was prepared by Professor A. S. G. Edwards (University of Victoria) and Julia Boffey (Reader, University of London) and by eleven students of the University of Colorado. The catalogue describes all the medieval manuscripts, Latin and vernacular, at the university. And then follow four indexes, noticing manuscripts by author or work, by date, by country, and by provenance. Finally, there are fifteen plates.

The descriptions of manuscripts are arranged in sections according to the different collections: Miscellaneous (forty-three items), Otto Ege Collection (forty-five items), James Hayes Collection (fifty-two items), S. Harrison Thomson Collection (forty-four items), and the holdings of the Fine Arts Department of the university (seven items).

A severely brief set of remarks introduces each section, disclosing that Ege (1888–1951) was a biblioclast, Hayes (1907–1993) was a calligrapher, and Thomson (1895–1975) was a professor at the university and an outstanding paleographer. Each description of a manuscript is concise and indicates, wherever applicable, author and/or work, place, date, size of leaf, material, number of leaves and columns, size of text area, number of lines, ruling and bounding, prickings, size and color of initials, collation, provenance, catchwords and signatures, and subjects of historiated initials.

The catalogue reveals the medieval manuscript holdings at the university. As one might expect, there is a large number of Bibles and liturgical works among the 191 items, including thirty-nine Bibles, twenty-nine Books of Hours, twelve breviaries and twelve missals, and fourteen psalters. But several classical pagan writers are represented: Cicero by two manuscripts, and Horace, Livy, Terence, and Virgil by one manuscript each. And there are a few manuscripts of Christian authors. Besides two items for both Augustine and Jerome and three items for Gregory the Great, there is one item each for Pseudo-Augustine, Prosper, Eriugena, Peter Damian, Peter Lombard, Peter Riga, and Thomas Aquinas. Only one of the manuscripts (MS 355) is noticed in the catalogue as being as early as the ninth century. There are no tenth-century manuscripts at the university, but five are said to be of the eleventh century, and fifteen are claimed to be of the twelfth century.

The descriptions are not free of inconsistencies, omissions, and outright errors. There is a mixture of English and Latin titles. Thus, the very first entry (p. 19) has *Meditations, Soliloquies*, as well as *Manuale . . . de verbo domini* and *De fide ad Petrum*, and while MS 321 is headed *Commentary on Galatians*, MS 333 is headed *In Iohannis Evangelium*. Sometimes dates appear as "s. xiii^2" (e.g., pp. 24, 78) and sometimes as "second half of s. xii" or "second half of s. xiii" (e.g., pp. 40, 30). Jerome in the catalogue merits to be called "St." (Ege 35 and Thomson 11), but not Augustine (e.g., 333 OS), Gregory the Great (e.g., Ege 41), Bede (Thomson 23), Peter Damian (Thomson 14), or Thomas Aquinas (Ege 40)! Sometimes editions of texts are reported (e.g., MS 333 OS) and frequently not (e.g., Ege 7, Ege 41, Hayes 68 Oversize 1)—anyway, the more recent editions in Corpus Christianorum should be cited for MSS Hayes 135 Oversize 1 and Thomson 23, instead of the old editions in Patrologia Latina. The portions of text are recorded for manuscripts of Virgil and Cicero (Hayes 12 and 13 and

Thomson 31) but not for Livy (Ege 39), Terence (Hayes 9), Peter Riga (Ege 7), or others. Sometimes we are told how leaves were ruled and bounded (e.g., Ege 29 and 33) and frequently not (e.g., MSS Ege 12, Ege 17, Ege 32). Sometimes prices paid for manuscripts are noticed (e.g., MS 314) and frequently not (e.g., MS 356).

Indeed there are many omissions in the catalogue. Thirteen unidentified works are listed, often without any indication of subject matter, and twenty-six works are noticed with a question mark, and it would be helpful to have one or more samples of the text in all these cases to aid readers in trying to make an identification. It seems amazing too that in such instances as "Religious Text (?)" (Thomson 7), "Legal Text (?)" (Thomson 18), and "Philosophical Text (?)" (Thomson 42), the general category, however vague, could not be determined. Likewise, about eleven manuscripts have a question after the proposed date, and one feels that a careful examination of plates with dated specimens would make a more assured dating possible. Also, for many manuscripts (e.g., Hayes 28, Thomson 10 and 14) there is no breakdown into the part of a century that the manuscript was written, and here again reproductions of dated specimens should aid.

The absence of information gives rise to many reasonable questions. For example, who was Norlin, after whom the library was named, and when was it founded? How is it that no records seem to have been kept about the acquisition of manuscripts before the late 1980s (p. 19) and why does no one know when the collection of such a luminary of the university as S. Harrison Thomson was acquired? Manuscript Thomson 38 is an unidentified text with references to Justinus, Bede, Isidore, and Hugh of St. Victor: is Thomson 41 the same as Thomson 38, with virtually the same heading in the catalogue? What is the evidence for such specific dates as 1210–1220 (MS 316), 1450 (Hayes 5), and 1400 (Hayes 32)? It would indeed be very unusual for Hayes 5 and 32 to bear a date if the texts are truly from Books of Hours.

Also, what are the documents about in 352, in Hayes 41 and 119 Oversize 2, and in Thomson 34 and 36? Is the civil law text in Thomson 21 from the corpus of Justinian, and if so, from what work? Thomson 15 is headed "Gratian (?), Decretum (?)," but it should be possible to decide rather easily whether the work is the *Decretum*, especially with the concordance of T. Reuter and G. Silagi (5 vols., Munich, 1990). Similarly, the question raised in the catalogue (p. 41) about whether two leaves at Columbia University are from the same manuscript as Ege 5 should be easily answered, as well as the question (p. 38) whether all Ege's portfolios of "Fifty Original Leaves" were compiled from the same group of manuscripts—why not find out, since pages 37–38 of the catalogue trace thirty-nine other sets? What is the evidence that MS 1 was written in Venice or that Ege 1 was written in Switzerland? How does it come that an English private letter concerning an English manor was written in France?—can that be right in the case of MS 348? What colors appear in the "painted initials" of Ege 20 and 35? What is the identification or description of the coats of arms in MS 313? What became of the missing manuscript leaves (items 25, 30, 47, 48, and 50) in the Ege collection? We are told (p. xii) that a local collector, John Feldman, "gave or sold more than thirty manuscripts or leaves to UCB." Why, then, does the index on provenance list only twenty-one items for Feldman?

Furthermore, there are some clear errors in the descriptions. Cicero's work is not *Paradoxica Stoicorum* (pp. 61 and 84) but *Paradoxa Stoicorum*. Another wrong title is *Martyrum* (pp. 61 and 85). "Martyrum" can only be the genitive plural of "martyr" (perhaps "Martyrology" is meant). "Calendar page" (p. 74) should be "Calendar leaf," since both recto and verso are indicated for the "page." The initial with a dragon noticed on page 25 is properly not a historiated initial but a decorative initial. Normally a midcentury text is dated with "mid." as in "mid. s. xiii" (Ege 13), but the period after "mid" is incorrect. The reporting of an important inscription on page 23 contains errors, as is mostly evident by comparison with the transcription in Sotheby's catalogue for 6 December 1988, page 37, lot 31: "frater" (not in Sotheby's catalogue) should grammatically be "fratri"; also, "theologa" should be "theologia"; and "de genetricis" ought to be "dei genitricis." Furthermore, the date of the manuscript of Peter Riga's *Aurora* (Ege 7) should be moved from the early thirteenth century to the second half of the twelfth: I have seen leaves of the text, which have caudate *e*. By an odd mistake, more than two lines of the description of MS 313 are repeated.

Just as the descriptions have flaws, so too do the indexes. The General Index should have a heading "Unidentified Texts," since there are as many as thirteen items that fall into this category. "Psalter (?)" before the entire list of psalters is misleading because only some of the psalters are indicated in the descriptions as unsure. On the other hand, the descriptions have for Hayes 63 "Lectionary (?)," but the "(?)" is ignored in the General Index. The descriptions have for Hayes 37 and 38 "Antiphonal (?) or gradual (?)" but these two items are indexed only as "Antiphonal" with the "(?)" accompanying only Hayes 38. MS 80 appears among the descriptions with the heading "Distinctiones evangeliorum," but this heading does not stand in the index, where MS 80 is listed as "Anonymi sermones de tempore" and as "Definitiones vitiorum et virtutum"; yet nothing is said in the description about sermons or about virtues. Thomson 38 is headed "Unidentified Text" among the descriptions, but this same manuscript is listed in the index as "Chronicle (?)"; yet nothing about the possibility of a chronicle is mentioned in the description.

Even the plates have their share of weaknesses. Some photographs are so tiny that one cannot derive much of an impression of the script (see plates 1–3, 6, 8, 12, 14, and 15). In the third photograph of plate 1, the initial appears as a smudge and without any accompanying writing in the rest of the page. The important interrogation-sign that appears beside "Cambridge" for Ege 6 and beside "Oxford" for Ege 13 is dropped in plates 8 and 10 respectively. The caption for the first photograph in plate 9 reads "Book of Hours, Gigantibus," but what is "Gigantibus" doing here? Nothing in the photograph or in the description of Hayes 8 explains "Gigantibus." More serious perhaps is incorrect labeling: the captions for the first and third pictures of plate 7 should be switched; the captions for the two pictures of plate 12 should be interchanged; and the labels for the two pictures of plate 13 should be switched. Unfortunately, no photograph is provided for the ninth-century manuscript (MS 355), the oldest manuscript described in the catalogue.

In discerning weaknesses in the catalogue, one should not ignore favorable features. The crisp, concise descriptions make the catalogue very readable. The effort to identify and locate leaves and fragments from the same manuscript is laudable. One can learn, for example, that the Terence manuscript (Hayes 9) once had 103 leaves but that now about 25 leaves are known. And it is interesting to see the range of prices paid for manuscripts, something rarely divulged by institutions. For example, an undecorated thirteenth-century Bible leaf cost $150 in 1993 (p. 27), whereas a thirteenth-century leaf with a picture of Job and a decorative initial cost $5,000 in 1991 (p. 26).

Still, after the weak and strong features of the book are weighed, it is evident that the catalogue could strongly benefit from a careful revision.

Marvin L. Colker
University of Virginia

Joanna Cannon and André Vauchez. *Margherita of Cortona and the Lorenzetti: Sienese Art and the Cult of a Holy Woman in Medieval Tuscany*. University Park: Pennsylvania State University Press, 1999. Pp. xiv, 275. 26 color plates and 204 black-and-white illustrations.

An illiterate peasant and unwed mother, Margherita of Cortona made an unlikely saint and civic patron. She wasn't even from the Tuscan hill town of Cortona whose name she bears, but rather from the village of Laviano, in the marshy Valdichiana. Her beauty gave her a ticket out of this bleak existence. She caught the eye of a young nobleman and ran off to live with him in the nearby city of Montepulciano. Marriage was out of the question for two persons of such different social standing, but their relationship lasted some nine years and produced a son. It came to an abrupt and brutal end, however, with the murder of Margherita's lover. Fearing that her life, too, was in danger, Margherita fled with her young son, first to her father's home and then, when he turned her away, to Cortona. There she spent the second half of her life trying to atone for the sins of the first half: throwing herself into bodily austerities and works of charity, affiliating herself with the Franciscan Order of Penitents, and eventually withdrawing to a cell perched high above the city, next to the semiruined church of San Basilio, where she spent the last decade of her life in intense spiritual colloquies with her beloved Jesus. When she died in 1297, the city immediately took possession of her remains, entrusting them to Badia, the rector of San Basilio. They immediately became a focal point of local devotion, and over the course of the fourteenth century, the tiny chapel of San Basilio that housed them grew into a large and lavishly decorated church known in local usage as Santa Margherita. This irregular situation—civic authorities controlling the relics of a Franciscan holy woman, which lay in a church dedicated to an uncanonized saint—took centuries to sort out, but the resolution is hardly surprising. In 1392, after a brief tenure by the Benedictine monks of Monte Oliveto, the church of San Basilio/Santa Margherita and the body it housed passed into the hands of the Franciscan order. The combined pressure of the Franciscan order and the city of Cortona eventually won for Margherita papal beatification in 1623 and canonization in 1728. At last, after 450 years, her church could officially bear her name.

Joanna Cannon and André Vauchez do not attempt to resolve the question of *why* any of this should have happened: why Margherita went to Cortona, why the Franciscans accepted a woman of her character, why she distanced herself from them in the last decade of her life, and why the city of Cortona adopted her as a civic patron. They fix their attention firmly on the *what* and *how* of her cult: what images of her were presented to the faithful, how those images promoted reverence for her, and for what reasons. The result is the most elaborate, sophisticated, and original treatment to date of the role of art in the promotion of a civic cult.

André Vauchez contributed the first two chapters, on Cortona in the time of Margherita and on her life and cult, as well as a brief afterword. The leading expert in late medieval sainthood, with a special interest in female penitents and an unsurpassed mastery of papal canonization proceedings, Vauchez here remakes himself as a local historian. He draws on the *Legenda* written by Margherita's confessor, the Franciscan friar Giunta Bevegnati; the documents collected and published by Fra Giunta's great eighteenth-century editor, Lodovico da Pelago; and the recent work of Anna Benvenuti, Franco Cardini, and others to craft a masterful narrative, deftly sketching the features of both the city and its saint. As thorough and exact as he is concise, Vauchez effectively sums up the current state of our knowledge. Any further advances will have to come from the unearthing of new sources, whether textual or pictorial. And even if Cortona's still largely untouched civic and ecclesiastical archives yield no fresh documentation of the shadowy Margherita of Cortona, they can certainly enrich our understanding of the Cortona of Margherita.

The visual sources are brought fully into play by Joanna Cannon, the art historian who is the chief author of this book. Three major representations of Margherita were produced in the century after her death, in three different formats: a large panel painting presenting a frontal image of the saint surrounded by nine smaller scenes from her life; the marble funerary monument, with a recumbent figure of Margherita flanked by angels surmounting four relief panels depicting scenes from her life and two showing postmortem miracles; and the mural paintings of Margherita's life and miracles that once adorned the chapel and nave of the new church raised in her honor. Each of these presents special problems of interpretation. The panel painting has suffered severe abrasion and undergone several restorations. The tomb monument has been variously dated to c. 1315 and 1362. Most problematic of all, the mural paintings are no longer extant, having been destroyed in subsequent remodelings of the church, and so are known only through the seventeenth-century watercolor copies of them submitted as part of the canonization dossier. Cannon's ingenious solutions to these problems, and especially her detailed reconstruction of the lost mural cycle, both clarify the meanings ascribed to Margherita by the promoters of her cult and offer an object lesson in art historical method.

The earliest visual representation of Margherita, the panel now in the Museo Diocesano of Cortona, was painted in the years immediately after her death, at the same time that Fra Giunta was composing his *Legenda*. Rather than deriving from that text, the panel thus constitutes "a parallel to the text, reflecting the views and memories of Margherita that seemed, after her death in 1297, most crucial and vivid to those who had known her and tended her cult" (163). It portrays Margherita as an absolved penitent, highlighting her private spiritual journey rather than her affiliation with the Franciscan order, and calling attention to her eucharistic devotion and her special relation with the Christ rather than her postmortem miracles. Five of the six panels on the funerary monument (which Cannon places toward the earlier end of the chronological window, tentatively suggesting a date around 1325) resemble scenes on the panel painting; however, eliminating some of the episodes from Margherita's life and adding images of supplicants at her tomb shifts the focus to the saint as a source of miraculous help. In short, "The concentration on Margherita's private pilgrimage of penance and prayer, so vivid to her spiritual supervisors Giunta and Badia, is here overtaken by a vision of her relation to and importance for others" (173).

Cannon's greatest challenge and most significant contribution is her reconstruction of the lost mural paintings of the church of Santa Margherita. On the basis of the few surviving fragments of painting, she argues that the nave was decorated with a cycle of scenes from Genesis and from the New Testament—in particular, an elaborate Way to Calvary that she links with a version in Assisi that Pietro Lorenzetti completed in 1320, or soon thereafter. She admits, however, that the links between the two cycles concern design rather than execution, making it at least as plausible that the Cortona work was painted not by Pietro Lorenzetti, but by someone familiar with his work, such as his brother Ambrogio.

It was to Ambrogio Lorenzetti that Giorgio Vasari, in the second edition of his *Vite* (1568), ascribed the fresco decoration of Santa Margherita. This attribution is not independently confirmed by any written source and has been dismissed out of hand by some other scholars. At best, it must be viewed with the same skepticism due all of Vasari's remarks on Trecento art, which are often confusing or erroneous: in the case of Santa Margherita, for example, he credits the design of the new church to Nicola Pisano, who died more than a decade before its construction began, and ascribes its decoration to Barna of Siena as well as to Lorenzetti.

Cannon mounts the most thorough defense yet—perhaps the most thorough possible—of Lorenzetti's authorship of the lost mural paintings of Santa Margherita. She carefully traces parallels between known works of the Lorenzetti brothers throughout central Italy and the lost paintings of Santa Margherita as transmitted through the watercolor copies. This is the only approach available, but one fraught with difficulties nonetheless. Portions of the mural paintings had already deteriorated and been partially repainted by the time the watercolors were executed, as evidenced by blank areas and anachronistic clothing styles in the watercolors. Even if the artist responsible for the watercolors tried to reproduce the images faithfully, to the point of imitating a by then antiquated manner, no evaluation of the brushwork is possible and any assessment of the style rests on shaky ground. Comparing the surviving tomb monument with its watercolor copy calls to mind those games that ask children to spot the differences between two drawings, though in this case the variants are too numerous to list. The watercolor is faithful to the basic iconography, but not to the details of drapery, pose, scale, or architecture. Under these circumstances, Vasari's ascription of the frescoes to Lorenzetti (or Barna), like Cannon's acceptance of it, must be viewed with extreme caution—particularly when we have documentation of another artist working at Santa Margherita.

In 1990, I published records of payments made in 1370 and 1371 by the church of Santa Margherita to a local Cortonese artist named Giovanni di Ristoro "because he painted the miracles of Santa Margherita in the large chapel of the said church."[1] This poses obvious problems for Cannon, who rejects the attribution of the frescoes to Giovanni di Ristoro without offering a convincing explanation of what else the payments might have been for. She points out (as I had) that the amounts paid to Giovanni di Ristoro were quite small for a major mural cycle, and argues that "the finest scenes in the cycle were indeed works of originality and imaginative quality, which employed a range of reference likely to have been beyond the reach of a modestly paid, local artist and occasional odd-job man" (115).

The project as Cannon reconstructs it was indeed an ambitious one. The fourteenth-century church was a single-nave basilica consisting of three bays, with a large chapel at liturgical east, where the altar would have stood. The north wall of the chapel was covered with five scenes from Margherita's life, ending with her funeral; facing them, on the south wall of the chapel, were images of five miracles she performed. Next to these, in the first bay, nine more scenes showed additional episodes of the life and miracles of the saint, closing with Cardinal Napoleone Orsini's visit to her tomb. Great prominence is given to Margherita's role as an active force for good, responding to supplicants and intervening in the lives of the people of Cortona in manifold ways: distributing bread to the poor, calming the sea, curing the ill, preventing a suicide, and reviving the dead. The shift already apparent in the passage from the panel painting of the penitent sinner to the tomb monument's bas reliefs of the wonder-working saint is here carried still further, in sharp contract to the image of the saint conveyed in Fra Giunta's *Legenda*. "While the *Legenda* provides a guide to the inner life of asceticism, penance, mysticism, and reclusion, the frescoes propose the outward life of a good citizen and member of the Third Order, assisting members of many parts of the community in life—and after death" (212).

I find Cannon's reconstruction of the decorative program completely convincing, as is her careful delineation of the several messages propounded by the various visual and literary sources. None of this, of course, depends in any way on her attribution of the frescoes to Ambrogio Lorenzetti. The frescoes would mean what they mean, in the same way and for the same public, whether they were painted by Ambrogio Lorenzetti or Giovanni di Ristoro. It is hard not to succumb to the lure of the label, however, especially in the world of art: when the commercial value of a work depends so much on the name of the artist attached to it, one easily falls into thinking of artistic value in the same way and assuming that an important work must have been done by an important artist. The fetish of the name seems to inspire at least some of the tenacity with which Cannon clings to her conviction that Lorenzetti was responsible for the mural decoration of Santa Margherita, despite the contrary evidence of the payments to Giovanni di Ristoro.

It may be that we are both right. Cannon astutely points out that the mural scenes in the first bay of the nave seem to complement those of the chapel. In her reconstruction, the chapel presented a complete tale, with scenes from the saint's life on one wall facing scenes of her miracles on the other. The paintings in the nave mingle life and miracles without any clear order, though care is taken not to repeat any events depicted in the chapel. What is more, the scenes in the chapel present some anomalies.

The handling of the architectural setting in one scene on the south wall of the chapel is less subtle than that in the Giottesque Assisi Adoration with which Cannon compares it (133); the scene of a boat threatened by a storm (also on the south wall) shows more similarities to paintings from later in the fourteenth century, including one dated 1370, than to works from the 1330s (144 n. 35); and so on. Perhaps we should see two (if not three) distinct phases in this decorative program, and at least two sets of hands at work—as, for that matter, Vasari suggested. The payments to Giovanni di Ristoro make no mention of the nave. They refer to work done in the *capella grande* of the church, and specify that he painted there the miracles of Margherita, a description that applies to the scenes found on the south wall of the chapel, in Cannon's reconstruction, but not to the scenes from Margherita's life on the facing wall. If Giovanni di Ristoro was responsible for only a portion of the mural decoration, the modest scale of his payments would not be so out of line; and a church struggling with the miserable economic conditions of the 1370s might well have sought to save money by employing local talent. If Giovanni's work occasionally showed the influence of Lorenzetti's, it wasn't because he had traveled to Assisi to study it. All he had to do was look over his shoulder, at the frescoes of the life of Margherita.

Daniel Bornstein,
Texas A&M University

Notes

1. Daniel Bornstein, "Pittori sconosciuti e pitture perdute nella Cortona tardomedioevale," *Rivista d'Arte* 42 (1990): 227–44; the document quoted is published on page 239.

Jane Chance, ed. *Tolkien and the Invention of Myth: A Reader*. Lexington: University of Kentucky Press, 2004. Pp. xx, 340.

The mainstream success of director Peter Jackson's *Lord of the Rings* film trilogy (2001–2003) has had its academic counterpart: a resurgence in the visibility of Tolkien studies both inside and outside of the university. Classics of Tolkien scholarship (like Tom Shippey's *Road to Middle-earth*, Verlyn Flieger's *Splintered Light*, and Paul Kocher's *Master of Middle-earth*) have been reprinted and can be purchased at one's local chain bookstore. Meanwhile, the organization Tolkien at Kalamazoo has been impressively successful in its efforts to increase Tolkien's visibility at the annual International Congress on Medieval Studies: over the last five years (including the upcoming 2005 Congress), the group has sponsored or cosponsored some twenty-five sessions. Editor Jane Chance has gathered together eleven of the papers from those sessions (primarily those at the 2002 and 2003 Congresses) to serve as the core of the book under review, *Tolkien and the Invention of Myth: A Reader*. She has also included two essays presented in other forums as well as four previously printed in scholarly journals. Add in what appears to be an essay written specifically for inclusion in the volume, and you have an impressive total of eighteen papers on Tolkien.

Chance has organized this plethora of material into five sections, one devoted to methodology and four examining Tolkien's debts to (and modifications of) Classical, Old Norse, Old English, and Finnish mythology. As she notes in her introduction, Tolkien's mythmaking practice owed much to the medieval principle of *inventio* (not just "invention," but also "discovery"). She states that the purpose of *Tolkien and the Invention of Myth* is "to demonstrate how some of these 'inventions' happened—how particular mythological features crept into his fiction and how they were reworked and adapted to Tolkien's different purpose" (4). Previous scholars have individually explored Tolkien's debts to specific medieval myths, but "no one volume has attempted to deconstruct these touch points to understand the vertical and horizontal genealogies of influence in his mythology" (5). The broad scope of Chance's anthology is certainly a substantial step in that direction.

Michaela Baltasar opens the methodology section with an essay reading Tolkien's aesthetically focused approach to myth and folklore as a reaction against competing approaches exemplified by Max Müller (myth as allegory) and Andrew Lang (myth as anthropology). Catherine Madsen argues against attempts to define Tolkien's work as essentially Christian, claiming instead that the spiritual ethos pervading a book like *The Lord of the Rings* is more akin to natural religion. Mary E. Zimmer takes a different approach to religion: she finds a Christian-Neoplatonic "verbal magic" (50) at work in *The Lord of the Rings*, a magic in which the characters subcreatively alter their reality through their use of language. In the final essay of this section, David Lyle Jeffrey locates the allegory of *The Lord of the Rings* not in the reductive interpretations that Tolkien openly despised but in Tolkien's dedication to philology and "the recovery made possible by the meaning of *names*" (68).

The Classical section of the book begins with Gerely Nagy's comparative reading of Plato's and Tolkien's attitudes toward myth-making: both authors seem concerned to save myth by transferring it from tradition to new discursive contexts. Looking at late Roman accounts of mixed marriages between Romans and barbarians, Sandra Ballif Straubhaar not only finds a historical model for Tolkien's depictions of unions between Gondorians and Northmen—she also puts together a powerful counterargument to simplistic assertions of Tolkien's racism. Jen Stevens identifies key points of contact between Ovid's *Metamorphoses* story of Pyramus and Thisbe and Tolkien's *Silmarillion* account of Beren and Lúthien while simultaneously stressing Tolkien's revision of Ovidian narrative to downplay the necessity of tragedy. Kathleen E. Dubs closes out the section with a Boethian interpretation of Tolkien's *Lord of the Rings* interest in fate and chance, a reading that clarifies Tolkien's stance on providence via comparison with *The Consolation of Philosophy*.

Tom Shippey argues at the start of the Old Norse section that Tolkien used Snorri Sturluson's *Prose Edda* and Elias Lönnrot's *Kalevala*, "both the product of Christians looking back at but still in touch with pagan imaginations" (159), as templates for his own practice in providing his legendarium with a quality of "rootedness" (145). Marjorie J. Burns follows up with an essay that demonstrates how Tolkien transformed the unruly and rude pantheon of Norse deities into the more consistent and decorous Valar of *The Silmarillion*. Andy Dimond suggests that we see Old Norse accounts of Ragnarök (filtered through the sensibilities of their Christian recorders) as a basis for Tolkien's own apocalyptic vision in *The Return of the King*. Andrew Lazo steps outside the Middle Ages proper, ending this section of the anthology with an account of the Kolbítar, the Old Norse reading group that brought Tolkien and C. S. Lewis together for the first time. Lazo sees the two men's membership in the club as more than a means of providing them with mythic raw material: their shared membership also established the creative dynamic under which each writer influenced the other.

Michael D. C. Drout's essay, the first in the Old English section, uncovers Tolkien's attempts to provide England with a mythology by generating speculative connections between his fictional legends and otherwise obscure details of Anglo-Saxon prehistory: Tolkien retroactively erased these connections in his published work, but Drout shows how they form a key substratum of *The Lord of the Rings*. John R. Holmes looks at the oath-centered culture of the Anglo-Saxons (and a variety of specific Anglo-Saxon speech acts) to find a source for Tolkien's emphasis on oath-breaking (good and bad) in his fiction. This shorter section finishes with Alexandra Bolintineanu's exploration of the use of inset narratives in both *Beowulf* and *The Lord of the Rings*: Bolintineanu concentrates on the content of these narratives, stories in which past history becomes the basis for present action.

The final section of Chance's anthology, the Finnish section, is also the shortest: the three papers included here remain close to their conference roots. The first paper, Verlyn Flieger's, finds a compelling model for Tolkien's own authorial self-image in the practice of Elias Lönnrot, compiler of the *Kalevala* and provider of a Finnish national epic. Richard C. West looks closely at Tolkien's early encounters with the *Kalevala* and provides an account of the ways in which Tolkien transforms the Finnish story of

Kullervo into his own narrative of Túrin. The final essay of the section (and the anthology) is David Elton Gay's location of a source for Tom Bombadil and Treebeard in the *Kalevala*'s tales of the aged yet ageless singer Väinämöinen.

If we consider it as a work of Tolkien scholarship aimed at other Tolkien scholars, *Tolkien and the Invention of Myth* occasionally feels a bit too basic in its readings. The strongest essays—those by Baltasar, Madsen, Nagy, Straubhaar, Shippey, Lazo, Drout, Holmes, and Gay—go beyond the close reading of parallels and analogs to offer provocative new frameworks for understanding Tolkien. The other essays make interesting connections but either continue to stick largely to the conventions of the conference paper (narrow analysis of a single point, synopsis of texts specialists would know well, etc.) or end up repeating one another (this is particularly a problem with the Finnish material: Shippey's essay essentially scoops both Flieger's and West's). However, Chance's preface stresses that the anthology is "an introduction to the complex subject of Tolkien's mythmaking" (xiii), and this is indeed where the book shines. I would not hesitate to recommend it to those new to Tolkien studies or to those Tolkien scholars (professional or fannish) who have yet to turn their attention to Tolkien's debts to his medieval predecessors. *Tolkien and the Invention of Myth* is a strong foundation for further research into the mythic genealogies informing Middle-earth.

Robert Barrett
University of Illinois

Philomena Connolly. *Medieval Record Sources*. Dublin: Four Courts Press, 2002. Pp. 71. Map. 4 illustrations.

This slim volume, one of the Maynooth Research Guides for Irish Local History, is an enormously valuable resource for historians interested in medieval Ireland. The book provides a practical introduction to the manuscript and printed sources for Irish history from the twelfth century to the end of the Middle Ages. Many historians working on Irish medieval history over the last twenty years have benefited from Connolly's unparalleled knowledge of the record sources for Irish history, and her premature death in 2002 deprived the Irish historical world of one of its most generous scholars.

This book not only provides details about surviving records, but also sets those records in their context and explains the reasons behind the many losses of Irish medieval records. Connolly goes beyond printed records and records to be found in Irish repositories to look too at the collections in the Public Record Office in London and also at Vatican archive material. Her first three chapters deal with records of central and local government, ecclesiastical records, and private records. The fourth chapter, entitled "Substitute Material," covers the many collections of extracts from records now lost made between the late sixteenth and early twentieth centuries. This is particularly valuable in the light of the disastrous fire in June 1922 that destroyed the Public Record Office of Ireland's record store in the Four Courts.

This Maynooth series of research guides is particularly concerned to provide those interested in local history with practical information regarding the consultation of specific collections of historical material. Connolly provides valuable advice of this sort in her final two chapters. Chapter 5, "Access to Medieval Records," offers the researcher advice about the preliminary detective work needed to find archival material relevant to one's medieval research subject. Attention is directed to the guides to manuscript sources, and direction is also given about how to gain physical access to the various records. Further practical advice is provided in the final chapter, entitled "The Interpretation of Medieval Records," which discusses coping with medieval Latin, the problems of palaeography, dating issues, medieval currency, and identification of place names. These practical chapters, encapsulating the advice Connolly used to give research students, will be an essential starting point for anyone wishing to get to grips with the sources for Irish medieval history. Indeed, this final chapter is recommended to anyone new to archival research since it is relevant to a broader audience than those simply interested in medieval Irish history.

This is a slim volume, a mere seventy pages. Between its covers, however, is packed an enormous amount of knowledge. Connolly has distilled her own extensive archival knowledge into a work that will find a place on the shelves of all Irish historians and will be an essential starting place for those beginning work on any aspect of Irish medieval history.

Virginia Davis
Queen Mary, University of London

Philomena Connolly, ed. *Statute Rolls of the Irish Parliament: Richard III–Henry VIII*. Dublin: Four Courts Press for The National Archives of Ireland, 2002. Pp. 363.

The publication of the fifth volume of *Statute Rolls of the Irish Parliament* marks the conclusion of a project that was begun nearly two hundred years ago in 1811 when the newly constituted Irish Record Commission announced their intention to publish the enactments of the medieval Irish parliaments. In fact, no volumes emerged until the early twentieth century, when three were published under the aegis of the Public Record Office of Ireland before the disastrous Four Courts fire of 1922, which destroyed many Irish public records. This fire resulted in the loss of the bulk of those original statute rolls that had survived until the twentieth century, although in an appendix in this volume discussing the fate of the Irish statute rolls in the period covered by the volume (1484–1543), Connolly shows that many of the rolls for this period had already disappeared by the early seventeenth century. Some, in fact, were damaged within a short time of being compiled, as was the case of that for 1516, which four years later in 1520 was found to be mutilated, while that of 1499 was embezzled before 1527 by opponents of the Earl of Kildare. Record Commission transcripts of the statute rolls for 1 and 2–3 Richard III and 8 Henry VII survived the 1922 fire and these, plus the text of the only surviving roll, that for 28–29 Henry VIII, which had never been published in full, have provided the basis of this fifth and final volume. In addition it includes the Record Commissioners' translations of exemplifications of statutes for the reign of Edward IV. The completion of this work emphasizes the fact that Philomena Connolly was one of a distinguished list of Irish archivists who have done much to make Irish archive material accessible to the historian.

The proceedings of the Irish parliament were enrolled on a single series of rolls beginning in 1427, with no distinction between parliament rolls and statute rolls as was the practice in contemporary England. The Irish Parliament Rolls thus contain a considerable variety of material, including much administrative material relating to named individuals and institutions. Until 1495 the usual language of the rolls was Norman French, and the edition here matches the Norman French with a facing page containing an English translation. From 1495 the enactments were recorded in English. Connolly's introduction to this material provides a brief but very clear account of the compilation and nature of the rolls and of the parliamentary procedure and records in Ireland during this period.

The contents of the rolls, as one might expect, shed considerable light on the political affairs of late medieval Ireland, with the overwhelming dominance of the eighth earl of Kildare clear in the records of the two parliaments of Richard III, with, among other things, help for building works on Kildare's new castle at Castledermot and a license to found a family chantry in Dundalk being granted. The next surviving roll, that for 1493, shows, however, that many of those active in this parliament were seeking redress for what they considered past abuses by the Kildare administration. What we have in this collection of Irish parliament rolls is a series of snapshots of Irish public affairs because the final roll, that for 1536–37, forty-three years later, shows a radically changed situation in political, religious, and procedural terms. Politically, with the attainder of those involved in the rebellion of Silken Thomas, son of the ninth earl of Kildare, the Kildare supremacy was firmly at an end; in religious terms, this was the parliament that has come to be known as the Reformation parliament because much of its work was concerned with the theoretical and practical implementation of replacing the pope by the king as supreme head of the church in Ireland. This required an extensive series of acts to regulate church affairs in Ireland. There were also procedural changes. As noted above, the language has changed; the terminology of the rolls suggests a change in the way in which the king was perceived, and many of the acts are either directly taken from those of the English parliament or very closely based upon them. The making accessible of this previously unpublished original statute roll for 28–29 Henry VIII is one of the particular benefits of this volume.

Beyond the public and political dimension, this volume casts light on diverse aspects of life in late medieval Ireland: the coinage is reformed, dwellers on the Poddle river in Dublin are required to clean up their tenements to prevent flooding, the mayor and bailiffs of Waterford are licensed to make a pilgrimage to St. James of Compostela, a new fishing harbor is constructed at Skerries outside Dublin. Overall the completion of this long-running project by the publication of this impeccably edited final volume deserves to be celebrated. It is, however, a celebration tinged with sadness because of the unexpected and premature death of Philomena Connolly just after the publication of this volume. It is a testament to her scholarship and a reminder—to all those who knew her—of what a generous and talented scholar she was.

Virginia Davis
Queen Mary, University of London

Olivia Remie Constable. *Housing the Stranger in the Mediterranean World: Lodging, Trade, and Travel in Late Antiquity and the Middle Ages.* Cambridge: Cambridge University Press, 2003. Pp. xii, 428. 12 illustrations, 4 maps.

The author, associate professor of history at the University of Notre Dame and an authority on Muslim Spain (*Trade and Traders in Muslim Spain: The Commercial Realignment of the Iberian Peninsula, 900–1500* [Cambridge, 1994]), presents an exhaustive overview of the location, construction, use, and persistence of the Greek *pandocheion*, the Arabic *funduq*, and the Latin *fundicum*, and their evolution in Christian control as the *fondaco*. More than a survey of commercial buildings scattered from Spain to the Middle

East, the book recounts the ubiquity of these structures, used not only for lodging and storage but also as trade centers, pious institutions (the *waqf*), places for religious worship and for collecting taxes, settings for taverns, markets, and brothels, and much more. Their similarity to and difference from the *khan* and *caravanserai* are examined. The words and their variants, the travel patterns of their temporary inhabitants and roles of their permanent managers and owners, the evolving nature of the institutions they body forth, and the evidence they offer for cross-cultural relations likewise are carefully presented.

The book rests on a wealth of documents examined, sources sifted (there is a forty-two-page bibliography), and commercial and cultural implications followed out. An example of the physical fabric of the institution of the *funduq* itself is likely known already to travelers to such places as Granada with its Corral del Carbon, or *funduq al-jadid*, an excellently preserved example. And awareness of the existence of such places comes as well from the parable of the Good Samaritan, who lodges the assaulted traveler on the Jericho road in a *pandocheion* (Luke 10:30ff.). This was often of course a perfectly respectable place, but Luke uses *katalyma* to refer to the Bethlehem establishment that had no room for Joseph and Mary. But behind such picturesque buildings lies a wealth of history and dynamic similarities and differences that this book meticulously sets forth in great detail.

Beginning with the eastern Roman empire, the first chapter presents a cross-cultural institution, different from the *stabulum* and the *hospitium*, each with its own nuanced overtones, in Roman Syria and points beyond. The shift in the fourth century from commercial revenues as support for the institution to charitable and religious support as the lodgings are increasingly tied to monasteries, shrines, churches, and the like is assessed. The second chapter recounts what happened when the Byzantine cities of the Near East came under Muslim rule and much of the infrastructure of their cities and institutions was absorbed into the new Muslim context. The word *funduq* begins to appear in Arabic texts from the ninth century, a new word, but the Greek model persisted.

The third chapter assesses the roles of commerce, charity, and a community from the tenth, eleventh, and twelfth centuries increasingly penetrated by growing numbers of European merchants, fundamentally "other" than indigenous traders. The fourth chapter, "Colonies before Colonialism: Western Christian Trade and the Evolution of the *Fondaco*," brings us with much else to the establishment of the familiar loggia as a place of trade.

The fifth chapter, as well as the sixth, concentrates on Iberia with reference also to Sicily and the Crusader states, all converting the Muslim *funduq* to their own purposes as conquest of these regions went forward at roughly the same time.

Concluding chapters build on the details earlier presented to illustrate the changing patterns of Muslim commercial space in the later Middle Ages and the solidification of the *fondaco* system for Christian commerce, with its ensuing ubiquity in Mediterranean Europe, for example the Fondaco dei Turchi and the Fondaco dei Tedeschi in Venice. Finally, as the world rapidly changed in the early modern period, this institution that had flourished for well over a thousand years increasingly became irrelevant. Other institutions evolved to meet new social and commercial needs, institutions such as the ghetto. Though not mentioned, it is illuminating to note that the Fondaco dei Tedeschi in Venice is its main post office, and the Fondaco dei Turchi its museum of natural history. This book provides much insight into a large region of the Mediterranean world's commerce, communications, and cultures. It should prove definitive of the subject for a long time.

Charles Witke
University of Michigan

Carolyn Dinshaw and David Wallace, eds. *The Cambridge Companion to Medieval Women's Writing*. Cambridge: Cambridge University Press, 2003. Pp. xix + 289. 1 illustration.

This collection of newly commissioned essays explores the forms of women's involvement with textual culture, concentrating mainly on England in the later Middle Ages but also venturing into the wider European context (Heloise, continental mystics, Christine de Pizan, Joan of Arc). It contrives an exciting combination of the familiar and the new, offering plenty of reference to a predictable list of women-centered texts, but managing at the same time to whet the appetite with pointers to less familiar material. It deploys a range of critical discourses, exploring the variety of results that can be generated by theorized readings of different kinds, but does so without abandoning a commitment to scholarship and learning: Foucault, Freud, Lacan, and Nietzsche comfortably rub shoulders with a host of medieval authorities from Peter the Venerable to the enticingly named Christina the Astonishing.

The striking features of this volume are the extent of its coverage and its subtle organization. In considering the full range of women's involvement in textual culture it eschews spurious division into sections of "fact" and "fiction" or "authors" and "subjects," and divides itself instead into "Estates of Women," "Texts and Other Spaces," and "Medieval Women." The usual suspects are here (lives and texts that will figure on many reading lists: Christine de Pizan, Margery Kempe, *The Book of the Knight of the Tower*, Christina of Markyate), but arrestingly recontextualized. The chapters of the "Estates" section are especially carefully pitched: Dyan Elliott's discussion of marriage combines scrupulously detailed discussion of medieval law with analysis of various *Canterbury Tales* and with records of a case heard by an ecclesiastical court in which a woman's voice figures with particular poignancy. The other essays here purvey information on the states of childhood and widowhood alongside exciting speculation about virginity and relationships of various kinds between women.

The section called "Texts and Other Spaces" examines, again in sources of different kinds, those features of medieval women's lives that are hardest to recover or comprehend: their access to writing; the nature of their subjection to the institutional power of the church; their domestic situations and household concerns; the forms of selfhood nurtured by enclosure; and the implications of these for communities at large. I would like to have seen Sarah McNamer's essay on lyrics and romances (currently located among the third group of essays) in this section. It concentrates on anonymous writers, on readers, and on women as subjects in narratives and lyrics about love, thus naturally building on the points made in Jennifer Summit's admirable "Women and Authorship," extending Sarah Salih's consideration of women's environments and occupations (not least because so many lyrics and romances were gathered together in books for household consumption), and inviting comparison with the observations about space and selfhood that inform Christopher Cannon's discussion of enclosure.

"Lyrics and Romances" apart, the final section is a series of explorations of individual oeuvres, and of the means by which particular women's histories or writings have been constructed, that confirms the wisdom of the organizing principles which structure this collection. Since the earlier sections have allowed for the airing of issues central to many of these individual accounts (virginity, enclosure, literacy, and negotiations of ecclesiastical hegemony, to name just a few), the authors here have the space to do justice to complex subjects and to signal topics not covered elsewhere in the volume, such as "the interplay of written texts and lived lives" (a phrase used in Carolyn Dinshaw's discussion of Margery Kempe [230]). They offer consistently fresh and authoritative accounts, combining up-to-date and comprehensive scholarship with intriguing suggestions about modern possibilities for remaking medieval women's stories. Overall, this is a richly informative and stimulating volume for readers of all kinds. It demonstrates not just that women's involvement with and in medieval literature was dynamic and powerful, but illustrates in a general and perhaps even more significant way the value of studying textual culture through aspects of its relationship with the society in which it is produced.

Julia Boffey
University of London

Albert Derolez. *The Palaeography of Gothic Manuscript Books from the Twelfth to the Early Sixteenth Century*. Cambridge: Cambridge University Press, 2003. Pp. xxi + 203. 160 illustrations.

Albert Derolez is curator emeritus of special collections in the University Library of Ghent and professor emeritus of paleography and codicology at the Free University of Brussels. He is the author of the much-consulted *Codicologie des manuscrits en écriture humanistique sur parchemin* (1984) and has now published an important study of Gothic script.

In his new work, Derolez examines closely Late Carolingian and Gothic script from about 1100 to about 1530. He provides, particularly, a classification of the different Gothic handwriting styles: Derolez disavows the over-simple classification of Georges Despey, who sees only a twofold division, namely between book script and documentary script, and Derolez rejects the frequent practice of labeling a Gothic script according to its use, like "Missalschrift" or "Littera Psalterialis." Instead, he builds upon the threefold system of G. I. Lieftinck: Textualis (formal Gothic using two-compartment *a*), Cursiva (rapid looped Gothic), and Hybrida (rapid loopless Gothic). Derolez also accepts J. P. Gumbert's term *Semihybrida* for a manuscript that sometimes has loops and sometimes does not. To the Lieftinck-Gumbert system Derolez adds the term *Semitextualis* for a Textualis that uses single-compartment *a*. He divides Cursiva into Cursiva Antiqua and Cursiva Recentior, and he includes Gothico-Antiqua, a mixture of Gothic and Humanistic elements, a type already recognized by paleographers.

Derolez devotes a whole chapter or long section to each of the varieties of Gothic script. He also deals briefly with the structure, layout, decoration, and binding of medieval books, and he discusses Carolingian script and the "Pregothic" writing that foreshadows the fully developed Gothic script. At the beginning of the work stands a glossary of twenty-five terms, and at the end stand a bibliography, indexes, and numerous illustrations. Each of these plates is accompanied by a concise note that identifies the manuscript and script, gives a partial transcription, and points out special features of the handwriting.

Derolez's book can give rise to a few quibbles. Even though one may feel that substantial information about decoration is beyond the scope of the work, the reader misses a section about the representation of music and especially an extensive treatment about the writing in documents: the seriousness of this absence about documents is acknowledged by Derolez himself, who says that by not dealing with documentary scripts "[his book] will be unable to reveal the underlying backgrounds to the genesis and transformation of scripts" (6). Derolez also says nothing about watermarks in paper.

Medievalia et Humanistica, New Series, Number 31 (Paul Maurice Clogan, ed.), Rowman & Littlefield Publishers, Inc., 2005.

Open to doubt is his statement "book scripts ... must obey two rules, namely the demands of legibility and beauty" (6). There are not a few medieval texts that were strictly utilitarian and can hardly be described as beautiful. And though Derolez complains about subjective vocabulary in commentaries accompanying plates, words like "large," "small," "elegant," and "vigorous" (7), he cannot resist in his own commentary "solemn" (plate 87), "bold" (e.g., plates 95, 125, 139), "large" (e.g., plates 87, 115, 124), "small" (plates 20, 112), and "coarse" (plate 140).

One may also quibble about Derolez's term *Praegothica* for the preliminary stage of Gothic script: "Praegothica" can refer to a number of scripts preceding Gothic, like Insular and Merovingian. A better term, already adopted by some paleographers, would be Protogothica. Apart from the slip in English "a Uncial **d**" (189), there are a couple of other trivial matters: the *punctus* for punctuation appears not only on baselines or slightly above (185) but frequently also close to the top of words; and not just r, but rather *er*, must be designated by the superscript mark in *uen'atione* (plate 8).

The reader may harbor some uneasiness about the transcription of texts in the photographs, such as the change of capitals to lowercase and of lowercase letters to capitals, like *alipio* to *Alipio* (plate 7) or *Grammaticum* to *grammaticum* (plate 58). And since many modern editions favor lowercase letters for words of theological significance, it seems both inexact and unnecessary to change lowercase letters to capitals in such instances: for example, *domini* to *Domini* (plate 3), *deo* to *Deo* (plate 4), and *pater* to *Pater* (plate 6). Likewise, Derolez distinguishes the consonant v from the vowel u, even though many modern editions keep u for both consonant and vowel.

And he sometimes injects modern punctuation: for example, *nür, daz* (plate 28); *immolanda, quod* (plate 109); *causam, videlicet* (plate 127). Furthermore, Derolez reads *hoīm* as *hominem* instead of as, correctly, *hominum* (plate 34), which also accords with the text of Orosius's *Historia Aduersus Paganos* 6.22 (this passage unidentified by Derolez); he deciphers abbreviated *quia* as *quod* (plate 70, line 1 and again in line 2) and *dicunt* wrongly as *dicent* (plate 111). In his diagrams about ruling (46), he omits the style by which each column of text is bounded by single verticals while the horizontal rulings proceed between these verticals and go fully across the intercolumnal space.

In the comments on his photographs, it would have been a kindness if Derolez had identified by book and chapter or verse (and preferably with an edition) the passages that he exhibits. Sometimes even the titles are vague: which specific work of Augustine is meant by *Opuscula* (plate 122), which particular text of Cicero is meant by *Opuscula* (plate 96) and *Orationes et epistolae* (plate 134), which play of Terence is intended by *Comoediae* (plate 160)? And the title *Varia latina* (plates 78 and 80) is virtually meaningless. Finally, the General Index is too sparse, with numerous omissions.

The reader will look in vain for many entries, such as for Neil Ker, Michelle Brown, S. Harrison Thomson, ampersand, and tironian *et*. And an index of the plates by type of script would have been welcome.

But none of the above suggestions should demean the accomplishment of Albert Derolez. He describes the writing of many lands of Europe over six centuries. He explores texts letter by letter with extensive documentation and with astounding thoroughness: he devotes three pages and two lines (84–87) to the letter *a* in Northern Textualis. Derolez can acutely penetrate complex, nuanced writing and see, for example, the influence of Cursiva on Semitextualis (plate 67), the influence of Humanistica on Semitextualis (plate 69), a Semitextualis that is close to Hybrida (plate 71), and a Cursiva tending toward Semihybrida (plate 89). He does not hesitate to point out what he regards as weaknesses of such giants of paleography as Bernhard Bischoff (7–8), G. I. Lieftinck (20, 22), and S. H. Thomson (25–26). Derolez is sometimes reluctant to universalize, and so his work resorts wisely to cautionary expressions like "usually," "sometimes," and "generally."

Since no amount of verbal description is as effective as visual presentation, Derolez enhances his work with about 470 pen-and-ink drawings and with 160 photographs representing manuscripts that chiefly bear specific dates and evidence of the locale where they were written. These photographs are of superb quality, allowing the writing to be easily readable, even the minute "pearl" writing of a compact thirteenth-century Bible (plate 20).

Romantics who look at manuscripts primarily for their aesthetic appeal may be jarred by Derolez's book, with its cool scientific approach that dissects the anatomy of scripts. But the serious paleographer will find the work a valuable aid for research.

Marvin L. Colker
University of Virginia

Eamon Duffy. *The Voices of Morebath: Reformation and Rebellion in an English Village*. New Haven, CT, and London: Yale University Press, 2001 (paperback edition 2003). Pp. xvi + 232. 3 maps. 14 color illustrations.

One could hardly ask for a more learned, insightful, and engaging demonstration of the local impact of the English Reformation than this sympathetic account of continuity and change in the Devonshire parish of Morebath. Two men have combined to preserve the voices of Morebath and restore them to vigorous life. Christopher Trychay, Morebath's priest from his arrival there in 1520 until his death in 1574, kept the parish's accounts throughout that half-century of religious upheaval, registering in the hard currency of income and expenditures the local reverberations of Henry's ragged break with Rome, the sharp Edwardian swing toward a more Protestant theology and worship, the Marian restoration of Catholicism, and the Elizabethan settlement. Churchwardens' accounts have received considerable attention of late, and have provided essential documentary underpinning for the fine recent work on English parishes by scholars such as Clive Burgess, Katherine French, and Beat Kümin. Among the scores of parish accounts that survive from sixteenth century England, few are as continuous, consistent, and informative as those Christopher Trychay kept for Morebath, making them a marvelously revealing source for the ordinary practice of religion in those extraordinary times.

However, anyone who has worked with parish accounts will know how frustratingly reticent they can be, even when their keeper was someone as thorough and even, occasionally, garrulous as Christopher Trychay. Like the village community that produced them, they do not open themselves easily to strangers; and it is a tribute to Eamon Duffy's learning, persistence, and perspicacity that he has made Morebath's accounts speak so openly, and so eloquently, of life in a small world buffeted by the intemperate blasts of the larger one. As Duffy says, his book "deals with ordinary people in an unimportant place, whose claim to fame is that they lived through the most decisive revolution in English history, and had a priest who wrote everything down" (xiii). He aims first and foremost to give his ear and tongue to their voices and let them speak through him. In this, he succeeds admirably. But he is too modest in professing that he does not offer the story of Morebath in support of any thesis, for it is but one village among thousands and none of them could be held up as typical. Far from simply indulging an antiquarian fascination with the physical and mental relics of a vanished past, Duffy uses the scant currency of Morebath's accounts to make telling points about the dogged (if, in the end, futile) resistance of this rural community to changes it neither invited nor welcomed, and its grudging accommodation—when armed opposition failed—to the new order of things. His fundamental argument in this piece of close crewelwork, as on the broad canvas of his now classic *The Stripping of the Altars* (1992), is that traditional Catholicism did not wither naturally in England: this vigorous plant, deeply rooted in village life, was yanked from its soil by the brute force of reforming authorities; and as the plant died, the soil suffered lasting impoverishment. Village religion gave shape and structure and meaning to village life, and "as the progress of the Reformation inexorably dismantled the structures of Morebath's corporate life, and pillaged its assets," it threw this rural world into crisis (xiii). Duffy sees the hard realities of country living too clearly to romanticize life in this huddle of houses on the edge of Exmoor. But he also sees the bonds of fellowship and reciprocal support that made this hardscrabble life bearable and the religious values of charity and community that made it meaningful, and clearly laments the world that was lost with the Reformation.

Daniel Bornstein
Texas A&M University

Karl A. E. Enenkel and Arnoud S. Q. Visser, eds. *Mundus Emblematicus: Studies in Neo-Latin Emblem Books*. Imago Figurata Studies 4. Turnhout, Belgium: Brepols, 2003. Pp. ix + 383. 41 illustrations.

Modern emblem research was initiated and for long dominated by modern language scholars and art historians. Until recently Latinists participated only rarely, although most of the emblem books of the sixteenth century and many later ones were composed in Latin. The consequence has been that, with the exception of Alciato's *Emblemata*, these books have received comparatively little attention as far as their Latin text is concerned. This situation prompted two Latinists from the University of Leiden, Karl A. E. Enenkel and Arnoud S. Q. Visser, to edit a volume intended to present in their historical and literary context a selection of Latin emblem books postdating Alciato, analyze their structure and thematic composition, investigate their intertextual poetics and the relationship between their pictures and texts, and describe the distribution and influence of these books. The editors brought together seven Latinists, five modern language scholars, and three art historians from Austria, Belgium, the Czech Republic, France, Great Britain, Hungary, the Netherlands, and the United States as collaborators in this project: Alison Adams, G. Richard Dimler S.J., Chris L. Heesakkers, Elisabeth Klecker, Clara Klein, Lubomír Konečný, Ann Moss, Jaromír Olšvský, Jan Papy, Anne Rolet, Daniel Russell, Sonja Schreiner, Paul J. Smith, György Endre Szönyi, Toon Van Houdt, and Ilja M. Veldman. These scholars treat emblem books of the sixteenth and seventeenth centuries by Théodore de Bèze (Theodorus Beza), Achille Bocchi, Joachim Camerarius, Hieremias Drexel S.J., Arnold Freitag, Mathias Holtzwart, Hermann Hugo S.J., Hadrianus Junius, Krysztof and Andrzej Koryciński (Christophorus and Andreas Coricynius), Michael Maier, Nicolaus Reusner, and Gabriel Rollenhagen, as well as the *Loci communes* of Josephus Langius, in which emblems are listed, and the *Commentary on Alciato's Emblems* by Claude Mignault. The function of the emblem commentaries, the relationship of emblems to commonplace books, and a broad spectrum of greatly varying works, some of them very little known, including Aesopic and alchemical, Jesuit and

Protestant emblem books, are the topics of the volume they have produced.

The contributions, all in English, have a shared analogous scheme of composition in accordance with the programmatic guidelines and give careful analyses and informative presentations that introduce the reader to the character and peculiarities of the works treated and let the reader see their function in the cultural context of the time. Many new observations have been made in regard to the intertextuality of the emblem poems and the relationships between pictures and texts.

Factual errors and gaps are rare (p. 160: Nicolaus Reusner was born not in "Lvov [Lemberg]," but in Löwenberg in Silesia [now Lwówek Śląski]; pp. 71–99: only the 1580 edition of Beza's emblems is recognized, not their distribution in the somewhat modified editions of 1597 and 1599; p. 268: the title is "protonotarius," not "pronotarius"). Occasionally the source analysis jumps too quickly to the ancient models and does not register a mediating humanist source (p. 278, referring to an emblem of Rollenhagen: "In silentio et spe . . . a motto inspired by Isaiah 30:15"— Reusner intervened with Symbolum 152). Unfortunately, the original Latin texts are not given, as well as the translations, in some of the contributions, and one sometimes misses a more thorough philological and literary analysis, especially in view of the aims of this book.

Thus, one finds on page 83 with reference to Beza's emblem 38 (1597: 34), "The classical Danaides, who pour water into a barrel full of holes, are compared with a drunkard so befuddled that he drinks the water he passes." This is a grotesque misunderstanding of the Latin, which the interpreter does not quote. It reads, in the edition of the *Poemata varia* (1597) under the heading "Aqua in dolia pertusa infunditur" (Water is poured into perforated barrels), as follows:

> Belidas fingunt pertusa in dolia vates
>   mox effundendas fundere semper aquas.
> Nomine mutato narratur fabula de te,
>   ebrie, quae meias qui sine fine bibis.
> Quin etiam hoc in te quadrat, turba ebria, quod sint
>   corpora quae fuerant, dolia facta tibi.

[In their fictions the poets present the granddaughters of Belus always pouring into perforated barrels water that is soon to run out again. Under another name, the story is about you, drunkard: you are endlessly drinking what you are going to urinate. Yes, even this fits you drunkards, that your former bodies have become barrels.]

There is a difference between "bibis, quae meiis" and "bibis, quae meias." The subjunctive and the sense of the comparison make it evident that the drunkard does not endlessly drink his own urine, but that he endlessly drinks what he will pass again as urine. The illustration shows this, too. It presents a man whose body consists of a barrel. He has brought a goblet to his mouth with his right hand, while a jet of urine is pouring onto the ground through a tube in the lower part of the barrel. In the background is a perforated barrel into which three naked women, the Danaids, empty water jugs and from which seven jets of water are spouting onto the ground.

On page 88 Corrozet is considered as the possible source for this emblem, although he drew a quite different moral from the barrel of the Danaids and did not know the barrel man at all. Paradin and Aneau also used the myth of the Danaids for an emblem before Beza, but they too with a different function. There follows on page 89 the statement "it would be pointless to continue an analysis of the possible sources . . . it is rarely possible to establish more than a parallel." The contrary is correct. The "fons emblematis" was something that a contemporary reader was interested in, as the emblem commentaries demonstrate and as is rightly outlined in another contribution to this book. And it is in fact possible to name the exact source in this case. The figure of the drunkard whose body has become a perforated barrel derives from a statement of the ancient lexicographer Sextus Pomponius Festus (Lindsay, ed., 278ff.): "pertusum dolium cum dicitur, ventrem significat" (when "perforated barrel" is said, it signifies a belly). It seems that Festus is quoting a passage of an unnamed author in which the expression "pertusum dolium" was used in a metaphorical way for satiric purposes. Beza did not go directly to Festus, but he read Erasmus's Adagium 1.10.33 "Inexplebile dolium" (the unfillable barrel). Here Erasmus quotes the passage of Festus, connecting it with the barrel of the Danaids for the first time and taking it as referring to a drunkard:

Varius est huius adagionis usus. Quadrat enim primum . . ., congruentius autem in istos bibacitate inexplebili, qui, quo plus biberint, hoc plus sitiunt . . . Sic enim Festus sensisse videtur, qui citat nescio quem . . ., qui dolium pertusum dixerit, cum ventrem significaret. . . . Adagium natum est a notissima fabula puellarum Danaidum, quae . . . aquam hauriant atque in dolium item pertusum infundant.

[The uses of this adage are various. For it fits first . . ., but is even better suited to the insatiable drunkards, who are the more thirsty the more they drink. . . . For this seems to have been the feeling of Festus who quotes an unidentified author . . ., who spoke of a perforated barrel, when he wanted to signify a belly. . . . The adage originated from the well known story of the Danaids, who . . . draw water and pour it into a barrel which is likewise perforated.]

Beza got the comic visual idea for his invective against inebriation from the metaphor transmitted by Festus. Expressions in line 5 of the epigram and in the title echo expressions used by Erasmus in his commentary. A literary analysis would among other things have to evaluate the imitation of Horace in line 3 as well. The sentence introducing his allegory of Tantalus (sat. 1, 1, 69ff.: "Mutato nomine de te fabula narratur") had already been used by Alciato and Aneau in their emblematic epigrams about Tantalus.

There is still much to do in the philological and literary interpretation of the Latin emblem poems. The present book makes an important contribution. At the same time, it stimulates further study of the many Latin emblem books.

Walther Ludwig
Universität Hamburg

Mary C. Erler and Maryanne Kowaleski, eds. *Gendering the Master Narrative: Women and Power in the Middle Ages*. Ithaca, NY, and London: Cornell University Press, 2003. Pp. ix + 269.

The age of Hildegard of Bingen, or of St. Elizabeth of Hungary, who died young in 1231, was the time for growth of women's influence. The cultural background and mystical experiences of the abbesses of the thirteenth century equaled the educational upbringing of male abbots of the age. Princesses entered the monasteries to pursue a life spent in quiet contemplation in order to formulate and realize in themselves the Christian ideal. St. Elizabeth broke with this tradition. An innovator, she remained in the secular world in order to make popular the pastoral theological concept of the mendicant orders of her time. Elizabeth's secret and personality were rooted in active charity; she was unselfish and humble. She practiced self-control over her senses and acted self-assuredly with firm spiritual strength. She was a Christian social worker with an unchanging motto: one does not begin to diversify by raising up the poorer social strata, but by the upper strata's willingness to descend providing immediate help to those who live on the fringe of society.

The woman image being formulated during the second half of the twentieth century followed a different guideline. In fact, those who worked hard to shape this image also developed a different, rather *earthly*, view of the medieval woman ideal. A good example of this is this volume of learned essays by eleven contributors, thoroughly researched, written with dedication to particular detail, and edited with meticulous care by the two editors. The bulk of the articles outline the activities of medieval women of firm character and solid educational background projecting charitable love and sincere care for what they were doing, their private lives, or their appearance in public social life, while gaining strong influence in secular politics. The authors follow and depict in their essays the age and background of these medieval women—in essays based on original research drawn together in one volume devoted to such a theme.

The theme "women and power" is approached beautifully and yet professionally in Dyan Elliott's deep psychological analysis on how women relate to (auricular) confession (in this instance, sincere self-examination with oneself). The reasoning by Jocelyn Wogan-Browne on the roots and causes of the historical evolution of, and emerging parallels between, lives of the saints and women's history is a well researched and thoughtful contribution to this theme, while Wendy R. Larson's arguments concerning a mother's love and care for her offspring deal with the role played by St. Margaret of Antioch, patroness of parturient women, expectant mothers, and very young mothers recovering from the trauma of childbirth, in thoughtful humane terms.

Pamela Sheingorn prepared a beautifully drawn picture of St. Anne, the mother of the Virgin Mary, depicting her in her essay as the wise parent and the careful mother, a source of force that sprang from the well of inner love, while Katherine L. French prepared a serious sociological study of the lives and activities of women living in a late medieval parish. One may find the writing and trend of thought of Holly S. Hurlburt, who deals with the role married women of high society played in public life, refreshing and thought provoking. The essays by Nicholas Watson, Barbara Newman, Sarah Rees Jones, and Felicity Riddy, and, of course, Jo Ann McNamara's piece revisiting women and power through the family, all present cleverly conceived, thoroughly researched, and beautifully written contributions. This volume, a collection of learned essays, only enriches the growing academic literature on women who played so important a role in medieval society.

Z. J. Kosztolnyik
Texas A&M University

Jussi Hanska. *Strategies of Sanity and Survival: Religious Responses to Natural Disasters in the Middle Ages.* Studia Fennica Historica 2. Helsinki: Finnish Literature Society, 2002. Pp. 220. 8 black-and-white illustrations.

In this slender yet wide-ranging book, Jussi Hanska examines how medieval people used religious means to cope with natural disasters: to foresee and forestall disasters, to deal with disasters when they struck, and to pull themselves together in the wake of disasters. Wary of the tendency to focus on the Black Death to the exclusion of other natural disasters, he includes in his compass earthquakes, floods, droughts, famines, freezes, and tempests, as well as epidemics. He concentrates on the later Middle Ages, while glancing back to the influential early models provided by Gregory the Great and Mamertus of Vienne, and draws on a variety of sources, from chronicles and exempla to scriptural commentaries and liturgical texts, though with no pretense to being either systematic or exhaustive. On the contrary, Hanska is remarkably candid in declaring that he chose his sources largely because they were readily available. The one type of source that he treats systematically is the sermon literature. As a consequence, the most original portions of the book are those that detail preachers' explanations for natural disasters, and the most useful portions are the appendixes that catalog medieval catastrophe sermons and present editions of illustrative sermons by Eudes of Châteauroux.

Despite being concerned with sudden and catastrophic events, Hanska's book contains little that is dramatic or surprising. The examples he has culled from his sources confirm exactly what we would expect: people ascribed natural disasters to the hand of God, whether that hand was raised in wrath to chastise the wicked or in loving sternness to test the faithful; they used prayers, penitence, and processions to invoke divine protection before disaster struck and implore divine mercy once it was upon them; they took comfort in the conviction that even the greatest tribulations and most chaotic disturbances were all part of the divine plan; and they found relief from survivor's guilt by expiating the sins that had provoked God's wrath. Such attitudes, Hanska argues, endured well beyond the end of the Middle Ages, surviving the theological clashes and liturgical innovations of the sixteenth century and the philosophical currents of the Enlightenment, to finally fade only starting in the nineteenth century with the emergence of scientific explanations for natural disasters.

This pattern of religious thought and behavior is, in its broad outline, already familiar from earlier studies in a field that is rather better tilled than Hanska lets on. To cite just one classic study unmentioned here, decades ago Richard Trexler showed how Florentines deployed the Madonna of Impruneta for protection against flooding and drought. Other studies, however, have called into question some of its key components. In several important analyses of testamentary practice (all unmentioned here), Samuel Cohn has argued that the pattern of pious bequests changed decisively not with the Black Death of 1348, but with the recurrence of pestilence in 1362–63: that is, in contrast to Hanska's vision of a consistent and enduring pattern, the religious response to these two epidemics differed notably, with the second marking a sharp and lasting break with traditional habits of charity. Other studies have cast doubt on the idea that penitential processions were a standard response to catastrophes, natural or otherwise: depending on the circumstances, epidemics could either encourage such collective rituals or interfere with them, as public authorities enacted measures to slow the spread of disease. While one could certainly multiply examples that fit Hanska's pattern, it would be just as easy to point to any number of religious processions that were not provoked by any particular catastrophe and disasters that did not evoke any but the most rote religious responses.

The Finnish Literature Society is to be commended for publishing Hanska's book in English, thereby making it available to a far wider readership than if it had appeared in Finnish. An unfortunate byproduct of this decision, however, is the profusion of grammatical and typographical errors that mar nearly every page and distract the reader's attention from the substantive merits of this work. Such problems could be minimized if the publisher were to employ an expert copy editor who is a native speaker of English.

Daniel Bornstein
Texas A&M University

Yitzhak Hen and Rob Meens, eds. *The Bobbio Missal: Liturgy and Religious Culture in Merovingian Gaul.* Cambridge: Cambridge University Press, 2004. Pp. xii, 232; map.

This learned volume joins others in the series Cambridge Studies in Palaeography and Codicology, and as such is a valuable addition to the series. A one-day workshop on the Bobbio Missal, held at Utrecht in 2001, was the impetus for the book, which covers a wide range of aspects of this unique manuscript (Paris, BNF lat.13246). The last major study appeared eighty years ago: *The Bobbio Missal: Notes and Studies*, ed. A. Wilmart (London: E. A. Lowe and H. A. Wilson, 1924). Much has been added to the scholarly arsenal and methodology since then, and the present volume seeks to bring us up to speed on many fronts, specifically paleographical, linguistic, liturgical, theological, cultural, and historical. Perhaps the greatest shift in our outlook is reflected in getting beyond the *damnatio memoriae* perpetrated by the Carolingians upon the Merovingians, and thus being able to see the period of the sixth and seventh and early eighth centuries not as "Dark Ages" but as a period of dynamic creativity.

Yitzhak Hen presents the Bobbio Missal beginning with Mabillon's discovery of it at that North Italian monastery in 1686, and his account in Latin of it. The account is translated by Rob Meens. Rosamond McKitterick presents a thorough and illuminating discussion of the scripts of the Bobbio Missal, negotiating her way skillfully past Lowe's notion of its being cobbled together from bits and pieces by an old and obscure lowly cleric in an out-of-the-way place. Superb control of the scripts leads her to conclude that the Missal was compiled carefully, purposefully, and with codicological skill in the later seventh or early eighth century, conceivably in

Vienne itself. It was written for a priest's use, in monasteries and on the road, containing such items as liturgies for the profession of nuns, auricular confession, and the like.

David Ganz addresses the palimpsest leaves in the missal. These five leaves originally conveyed a section of Ambrose's Commentary on Luke, written in an elegant and accomplished script usually reserved for annotations, an example of the earliest true minuscule. Punctuation, word separation, and animated initials are studied by Marco Mostert. The grammar of legibility varies from hand to hand, the principal one following the conventions of late antique manuscripts that were largely unseparated letters or with interpuncts using minimal space, but sometimes spaces are introduced to facilitate reading. Consideration is carefully given to the role of the exemplars being copied.

Els Rose presents a nuanced overview of the large problem of the Latinity of the manuscript, particularly its liturgical Latin. After a detailed study of the Bobbio compiler, she concludes that contrary to what some others have held, the Bobbio compiler shortened certain prayers also found in the *Missale Gothicum*. This of course is the period in which intelligibility of liturgical Latin became a problem for lay congregants as the liturgical language of the church survives colloquial language, a phenomenon to be hastened later by the Carolingian reform as it trained clergy in "good Latin." What had been regarded as mangled and confused degradations of "correct" Latin texts are instead seen as valuable documents of the liturgical language still developing along with the vernaculars.

Two texts are seen to be additions to the missal itself: *De dies malus*, a sermon (viz. *De diebus malis*) attributed to Augustine, and the somewhat misnamed *Joca monachorum*, a kind of question-and-answer series constituting word games drawn from Biblical sources, a Bible quiz for monks. Charles D. Wright and Roger Wright provide a wealth of detailed observations on the context and function of these two works, their texts as represented in other manuscripts, their transmission, and an edition and translation of *De dies malus*, as well as of *Joca monachorum*. The language of both texts, including spelling, morphology (particularly verbs), and syntax, including the insight that the scribe remembered what the available endings were but could not remember when to use which, give us valuable details and comparanda with emerging and later vernaculars. It is possible that the writer of these two texts prepared them from dictation.

Yitzhak Hen presents a learned chapter on the liturgy of the missal, placing it against the background of the Gallican liturgy, here understood to be simply the liturgy of Merovingian Gaul, with its effusive and highly rhetorical prayers. Of the masses in honor of saints only one is specifically Burgundian, Sigismund. It is interesting to note that the first written versions of the so-called Roman canon of the mass were copied in Merovingian Gaul, and that its earliest complete version is the canon of the Bobbio

Missal. It is convincingly concluded that the missal is the vade mecum of a priest offering services to various communities and institutions: a unique and practical selection of diverse prayers, benedictions, a sample sermon, and the like.

Rob Meens discusses the missal as evidence for the reformation of contemporary clergy since its Penitential touches extensively on priestly purity. There are also masses for remission of sins. If the missal is as early as the end of the seventh century (McKitterick), then it is the earliest manuscript containing a penitential handbook, revealing a system of tariffed penances introduced into Gaul by Irish monks, part of a Burgundian reform movement coordinated by the episcopate and King Guntram at the end of the sixth century.

The prayers of the Bobbio Missal convey doctrinal and theological issues and themes that are the subject of the chapter by Louise P. M. Batstone, who assesses their principal doctrinal assertions. The missal uses instead of the *Gloria in excelsis* the *Aius* (viz. *Trisagion*), suggesting anti-Arian concerns, and a Mariology perhaps derived from sermons of Leo the Great.

One mass in the missal is of special interest: *the Missa pro principe*, to use Mabillon's title for it. No other early medieval liturgical manuscript offers parallels. Its Old Testament exempla evoke an idea of kingship straight out of a warlike society. A translation of this text is provided, as well as an extensive comparative table offering parallels from somewhat similar texts. Ian N. Wood studies liturgy broadly considered within the context of the Rhone valley, that scene of interesting liturgical innovation in the fifth and sixth centuries, specifically rogations, the peculiar *laus perennis* at Agaune, that King Sigismund invoked for healing, reasonably assessed in light of the evidence to be specifically relief from malaria, brought from northern Italy over the Alps frequently enough. Traces from the liturgical world of Avitus of Vienne are also detected in this study.

The conclusion by Hen and Meens recapitulates the excellent presentations contained in this volume. There is a comprehensive index of manuscripts cited, and a useful general index. A bibliography would have been a valuable addition. It is regrettable that the English translation provided for the Latin text of Mabillon (would readers of so learned a volume need it?) is marred by inaccuracies, for example, "a certain St Benedict is commemorated" for "Fit quidem sancti Benedicti commemoratio"; "The faithful will stay, they should come to the place of Prayer" for "manebunt Fideles; venietur ad locum Orationis" where *venietur* represents Mabillon moving on to discuss the Lord's prayer, not the faithful going someplace; there is confusion again between the future and the subjunctive in Mabillon's saying what edition of Augustine he will use (*utemur*), not what "we should be using."

All in all, *The Bobbio Missal: Liturgy and Religious Culture in Merovingian*

Gaul is a definitive study not only of this fascinating manuscript but of a wealth of other related matters of the highest importance.

Charles Witke
University of Michigan

Isaac Ibn Sahula. *Meshal Haqadmoni: Fables of the Distant Past*, 2 vols., ed. and trans. Raphael Loewe. Portland, OR: The Littman Library of Jewish Civilization, 2004. Pp. cxxxi, 816. 156 illustrations.

Isaac Ibn Sahula, the Spanish Hebrew writer (born in 1244), is an enigmatic figure. Although he has autobiographical passages in his *Fables of the Distant Past,* he does not mention in them his parentage and birthplace, his education, or the city of his main residence. We do learn from Ibn Sahula's introduction that at the age of thirty-seven he was in Egypt and that he was interested in medicine. But why did he go to Egypt and why does he describe himself as an isolated wanderer who has failed to find love and friendship? To what does he specifically refer when he laments, "The lover dies and the love remains"?

Ibn Sahula does disclose the motivation for composing his *Tales of the Distant Past*: to demonstrate the effectiveness of Hebrew expression as a counterattraction to Homer (i.e., pagan classical writers), heretics, and free-thinkers. And he claims to be independent of Arabic and Christian literature, though in reality his technique of rhyming prose is of Arabic background (the *maquama* used for moralizing anecdotes).

Ibn Sahula's work presents five groups (called "Gates" in Hebrew) of tales: on wisdom, on penance, on sound advice, on humility, and on reverence. Each group opens with the statement of a cynic, who tries to prove his position with narrative material, and he is later challenged by a moralist, who advocates traditional values with his own narrative material. So, excellent tales about humans and beasts are reported. In part 1, the cynic regards wisdom as foolish and supports his view by a story about a philosopher in Egypt who lost his reasoning and became an amusing fool much favored at the palace, but after he regained his mind and insulted the royal council, he was removed from court and fell into poverty. The moralist counters with a story about a dog that persuades a stupid cow to swim a river, and she drowns. In part 2, the cynic tells a story about a pious man's wife running away with her lover. The moralist replies with a tale about how a religious man helped a robber to become a religious scholar. Within part 2 there is a memorable picture (222–26) of the procedure and etiquette of a medieval classroom. In part 3, a man disregards the advice of a bookish person yet prospers, as the cynic relates; the moralist retorts with a story about a rat that rejected advice and was caught in a trap. In part 4, a haughty youth refuses to learn magic from an old magician. To prove his power the magician gives him a drugged drink, and the youth has a realistic dream about his marrying a princess and becoming a ruler. Part 5 includes a story about the power of astrology, as told by the cynic: astrologers predict the death of a king's son at the age of twenty-five. The moralist's antidote to this story concerns astrologers predicting a rebellion. When they turn out to be wrong, they are executed.

The stories are interspersed with learned excursuses about a wide variety of subjects, such as time, geography, the trivium and quadrivium (except rhetoric and music), science and philosophy, the basics of medical practice, and astrology (astrologers are regarded as quacks). There are even didactic discussions on the kinds of love, the qualities of a good wife, the three kinds of villains, and the ways that people predict the future, which include hitting the air with a stick.

Readers may be surprised by certain ideas in Ibn Sahula. Thus polygamy is still tolerated: a king may have eighteen wives, while an ordinary man may have as many wives as his strength permits (263), and a Ram is represented as virtuous though he has ten concubines (157). Also, there are strange remedies: a dog's earlobe cures fevers (125), and balm from Gilead can treat every illness (375).

Raphael Loewe, formerly Goldsmid Professor of Hebrew at University College, London, provides a well-equipped edition and translation of *Fables of the Distant Past*. Loewe's introduction of 131 pages discusses the scholarly atmosphere encouraged by King Alphonso X, el Sabio; parables in Hebrew literature; the structure, themes, and style of Ibn Sahula's book; the sources of his excursuses (e.g., Aristotle, Ptolemy, Averroes, Maimonides, and Ibn Gabirol).

In the introduction Loewe writes about the seven manuscripts, none of which were written before the fifteenth century, and the printed editions of his predecessors (the *editio princeps* is from Brescia c. 1491). Loewe declares that he is offering the first critical edition based on the manuscripts and early editions but admits that he did not collate all the manuscripts word for word throughout (cxxii). He states that for his text he is following basically the edition of I. Zamora (Tel Aviv, 1953) and that for his translation he employs rhyming couplets or triplets of ten or twelve syllables. After the introduction, a page of Hebrew accompanies a page of translation. The text and translation are enhanced by critical apparatus, explanatory footnotes, and side-notes indicating sources. Lastly appear bibliography and indexes. Loewe's work is liberally sprinkled with illustrations reproduced from a manuscript of c. 1480 and from a printed text of c. 1547.

It seems a desecration to uncover any faults in Loewe's handsome volumes. But some readers may object to liberties taken with the original Hebrew. For example, Loewe has:

> (p. 14) "I brought a case for judgment to the royal court" for "I relate my actions to the king"
> (p. 18) "a whirling heart" for "and my heart burned"
> (p. 26) "urged him on and on again" for "and his heart travels from wandering to wandering"
> (p. 30) "to pour my very being forth" for "to pour out my blood and my milk"
> (p. 222) "The pupils ranged around their desks inside" for "And all the pupils sat in their circle"
> (p. 492) "trained to apply their minds to philosophic thought" for "would think correct thoughts"

No doubt many liberties in translation were impelled by the constraints of rhyme and rhythm.

Sometimes the translation is less instantly clear than the Hebrew itself: for example, "naught His strength can sap with weariness" (20) for "He toils and does not weary" and "whether remote or such that man can see" (20) for "far or near." Sometimes the translator assumes the role of commentator or glossator as he pursues meaning or application instead of direct interpretation: for example, "there was no shred of moral leprosy in all he said" (24) for "his hair did not turn white" and "Whence sloth allows death-watch [sc. beetle] to eat his beam" (386) for "where laziness will sink the ceiling" (cf. Ecclesiastes 10:18). Many readers may prefer that the translator adhere to the bald words of the original text and then explain the thought in a note. A few translations are awkward and convoluted: for example, "care thy master news to give" (72); "Where dragged he him he slew?" (302); and "But mercy him that trusts in God surrounds" (626).

Also, the translation gives the impression that Ibn Sahula used pagan classical references. But the exact rendering of the Hebrew eliminates the classical references. Loewe writes:

> (p. 30) "lend strength, O Muse" for "strengthen my song"
> (p. 36) "portals of the Muse" for "doors of fancy language"
> (p. 150) "to Lethe's land" for "to the land of forgetfulness"
> (p. 174) "Argus-eyed" for "full of eyes"
> (p. 178) "cupid's glow" for "pleasure"
> (p. 256) "Lethe" for "forgetfulness"
> (p. 578) "Hades" for "Sheol"
> (p. 588) "bed of Procrustes" for "shorter the mattress than (the means for) stretching oneself out"

There are still other expressions that can mislead: for example, "ermine" (46) for "clothes," "Reynard" (72) for "fox," "keeping Lent" (196) for "fasting," "A message writ in runes" (500) for "a copy of a letter," and "crying tally-ho" (623) for "a shout."

Furthermore, "Let us gather rosebuds while we may" (116) might seem to echo the Pseudo-Vergilian *De Rosis* 49 and to anticipate Robert Herrick, but the Hebrew only says "And let us collect roses"; "To see and to be seen" (182) might seem to show the influence of Ovid's *Ars Amatoria* 1.99, but the strict Hebrew translation says "to go up and to see" (cf. Exodus 34:24); "where thou goest, I shall go" (186) might seem to be from Ruth 1:16, but the Hebrew really says "I shall surely go with you."

Some readers may feel uncomfortable with the archaic language in the translation. Besides the frequent use of *thou* and *thee*, there are these expressions: *quoth* (yet Loewe can write "Said he" [494]), *perchance, haply, nathless, dost, prithee, peradventure, whilom, hap, eld, howbeit, for aye, forsooth,* and *In sooth*. One finds "Wouldst thou, forsooth" (44), "His deeds bespake" (404), and "'Sirrah' quoth he" (404). Such archaisms raise the question whether Shakespearean language is suitable nowadays for translating even a classical or medieval text. Also, Loewe's translation may make readers scurry to their dictionaries for words like "gentles" (= "noblemen" [6]), "tailory" (238), "mollities" (256), "Endenizened" (634), and "astronomise" (640).

Along with archaisms and elite words, the translation can resort to informal English and thus produce a jolting contrast. One sees, for example, "upper crust" (58), "squaw" (= "wife" [144]), "high brow" (146, here for Hebrew *maskil*, i.e., "enlightened"), and "noodles" (= "fools" [514]).

A few more points should be raised. According to the index (814), Loewe must have meant to include Samuel Hanagid in 4.509, note 34, but while this note examines a couple of Hebrew words, it omits mention of Samuel Hanagid, who rose to the court of Granada because of his skill in writing, a motif of the story on the page (466). Loewe might also have mentioned that the tale about the robber who repented is very similar to a tradition about Resh Lakish. And there are overlooked possible verbal echoes, for example, Prologue, line 1 recalls Song of Songs 2:13; Preface to part 1, line 12 echoes Ecclesiastes 9:11; and Preface to part 1, lines 44–45 of part 1 carry a reminiscence of Mishnah, Abot 1:4. Finally, though the extensive bibliography of twenty-one pages (769–90) records many items relating to medieval science, folklore, and folktales, including Greek and Latin dictionaries, there are nonetheless striking omissions, for example: Lynn Thorndike, *History of Magic and Experimental Science*, 8 vols. (1923–58); H. Bächtold-Stäubli, *Handwörterbuch des deutschen Aberglaubens*, 10 vols. (1927–42); and F. C. Tubach, *Index Exemplorum* (1969).

But overall, Loewe's work displays many admirable features. The structural diagram, together with the synopsis, provides an essential map to guide the literary traveler, since many of the stories melt into each other like Chinese boxes or classic Russian dolls. The explanatory notes are helpful, too, especially the notes on astronomy-astrology, a topic obscure to many. The same footnote numbering and the same side-note lettering for both the Hebrew and the English enable the reader to coordinate the translation with the Hebrew text. The translation itself, sprightly and sparkling, captures the vigorous flavor of the Hebrew. And so, as the first English translation of the tales of Ibn Sahula, Loewe's work will present to many readers attractive medieval stories, of which they might not otherwise be aware.

Marvin L. Colker
University of Virginia

Walter E. Kaegi. *Heraclius: Emperor of Byzantium*. Cambridge: Cambridge University Press, 2003. Pp. xii, 359.

"No Byzantine emperor experienced such a great spread between success and failure in the same reign" (321); "He and his reign represent both an end and a beginning" (18). Such is the assessment of Walter Kaegi in his splendid historical biography of Heraclius (r. 610–41), the first of its kind in English and the single most important monograph devoted to this emperor's reign in any language. Drawing and expanding upon his earlier research, including *Byzantium and the Early Islamic Conquests* (rev. ed., Cambridge: Cambridge University Press, 1995), Kaegi reminds us that the first half of the seventh century was a pivotal time for Byzantium and its neighbors.

As Kaegi repeatedly demonstrates, the Byzantine Empire was intimately connected with the Afro-Eurasian world around it. It is unfortunate that this monograph's Library of Congress subject description connects it only with Byzantium (i.e., "Heraclius, Emperor of the East"; "Byzantine Empire—History"; "Emperors—Byzantine Empire"), for this is a book as much about the interconnected histories of the Mediterranean, Near Eastern, and Middle Eastern worlds as seen through the experiences and policies of Heraclius as it is about Byzantium proper. The wide range of contemporary sources brought to bear is a clear indication of this: Greek Byzantine texts are employed alongside those in several other languages, including Armenian, Arabic, Syriac, Georgian, and Latin.

The most prominent theme in this book is one that resonated long after the death of Heraclius: the successive wars of the Byzantines against the Sasanid Persians and the Muslim Arabs. Having carefully sifted the relevant surviving literary and nonliterary sources, Kaegi has constructed a critical narrative, organized chronologically, of the Persian gains in the Near East and Anatolia, Heraclius's successful counteroffensive, and the eventual Byzantine victory and its aftermath. The author proposes four phases of the conflict from the Byzantine perspective: defeat and stabilization (610–20); testing techniques of offensive warfare against the Persians (622); large-scale offensive expeditionary warfare (624–27); and the invasion of Mesopotamia and the defeat of Persia (627–29). Following this discussion is an examination of the initial Arab advances into Byzantine territory during the course of which Kaegi offers an explanation of Arab success which is far more nuanced than the persistent thesis that Byzantium and Sasanid Persia were simply too exhausted to organize any meaningful resistance (258ff.).

Although the primary focus is on the military, Kaegi frequently demonstrates how military concerns, policies, and outcomes were linked to a broad spectrum of other issues, including the economy and taxation, the imperial image, building projects sponsored by the Byzantine government (especially after the conclusion of the Persian war), the problem of refugees, the many divisions among Christians (within and beyond the borders of Byzantium) and Heraclius's failed attempt at compromise, the multicultural condition of Byzantium and especially the role of Armenians at Heraclius's court, the colonization of the Balkans by the Slavs and Avars, and the strategic importance of Caucasia for the great empires of western Eurasia.

This book, then, is as much about the history of Byzantium as it is about Byzantium's long-standing and evolving connections with the world around it. Particularly significant is Kaegi's astute observation that

[i]n the first twenty-five years of his reign Heraclius unwittingly tilted the empire towards becoming more Middle Eastern through his continued presence in western Asia, during and after his campaigns against the Sasanians. External pressures, not his own volition, were the cause. . . . The empire that he had wrested from Phokas was not an innately near Eastern one. . . . But by the end of [Heraclius's] reign the western and central Mediterranean elements, however important, had become more tenuous and exposed and were slipping away, leaving a torso that was more Middle Eastern, although never completely so, given its Romano-Hellenic heritages. (259; cf. 316)

Though the pendulum had wildly swung against him at the end of his long life, Heraclius could not have imagined that Byzantium's torso would soon be considerably shortened and pushed back to a mere corner of southeastern Europe and far western Asia.

Stephen H. Rapp, Jr.
Georgia State University, Atlanta

Shannon McSheffrey and Norman Tanner, eds. *Lollards of Coventry, 1486–1522.* Camden Fifth Series 23. Cambridge: Cambridge University Press, 2003. Pp. x, 361.

In October 1511, a cutler from Birmingham called John Jonson appeared in court suspected of heresy. At first he said nothing, but on two later occasions he spoke at some length about his career as a cutler and the heretical contacts he had maintained over many years. His questioners seem to have been particularly interested in where he had lived and for how long, and hardly interested at all in the substance of his religious beliefs. Jonson had been born in Yorkshire and had become an apprentice in London, after which his work had taken him to Maidstone, Coventry, and Gloucester, back to Coventry, then to Bristol, Taunton, Brittany, Bordeaux, London again, and Coventry for a third time before he settled in Birmingham. In his interrogation he was asked about his contacts with a total of thirty-three persons, many of whom were also questioned in court. The investigators, working for the bishop of Coventry and Lichfield Geoffrey Blythe, were trying to halt the spread of heresy by cracking down on its most mobile adherents. They recognized the danger of highly mobile and well-connected individuals creating what one recent historian, working with an economist, has called "scale-free networks": it was impossible to follow up all the contacts, but the connectors could be neutralized.[1]

The tactics and capabilities of English inquisitors are amply demonstrated in this new edition and translation of heresy trials and related commentaries drawn from six separate sources: the registers of bishops Blythe and John Hale, the "Lichfield Court Book," an episcopal visitation book, John Foxe's *Rerum in ecclesia gestarum*, and the civic annals of Coventry. McSheffrey and Tanner have done students of heresy and inquisition a great service in publishing these texts, and the provision of a facing-page English translation of the largely Latin records will ensure that the myriad courses on Wycliffe and Lollardy in British and North American universities are able to focus on the judicial records of heresy to a much greater extent than they have to date.

The texts are supported by an introduction and lists of defendants, judges, and lawyers, which are a welcome study aid. The introduction consists mainly in a discussion of the defendants' practices and beliefs, which will be familiar to most readers. The major omission is any discussion of, or reference to, the law that was being applied, apart from a short comment on punishment and narrative descriptions of the proceedings themselves. These are legal records, but there is little sense of a legal context here. The curious reader receives no hint of where further information on canon law and English ecclesiastical statutes could be obtained, and the tone of surprise on page 20, note 71, that the trials bear a close resemblance to "inquisitorial discourse" only highlights this lack. The reason for the omission may be that the texts are not intended as sources for legal history or the history of inquisition, but such editorial decisions tend to become quickly apparent as the academic spotlight shifts. The editors invite research into a prepackaged "Lollard community," a notion that skeptical readers may wish to question, but the wherewithal to do this, some insight into the mental world and learning of the prosecutors, is missing.

Nonetheless, McSheffrey and Tanner's edition will deservedly fly off the shelves.

Ian Forrest
All Souls College, Oxford

Notes

1. Paul Ormerod and Andrew Roach, "The Medieval Inquisition: Scale-Free Networks and the Suppression of Heresy," *Physica A* 339 (2004): 645–52.

Miri Rubin. *Gentile Tales: The Narrative Assault on Late Medieval Jews.* 2nd edition. Philadelphia: University of Pennsylvania Press, 2004. Pp. 266. 4 maps and 25 illustrations.

Gentile Tales first appeared, to much acclaim, in 1999. The first edition (published by Yale University Press) was described by reviewers as a major contribution to the history of anti-Semitism, and indeed *Gentile Tales* has established itself as a key reference work for students and scholars interested in the discourses of blood and violence that were so central to late medieval Latin Christian culture. This new edition, in paperback, of *Gentile Tales* is very welcome, for it is hoped that such an important and sensitive book should reach as wide an audience as possible.

Rubin's topic is the host desecration narrative; Rubin locates the birth of the narrative in Paris in 1290, developing out of images drawn from European *exempla* collections. Rubin divides her enquiry into "patterns of accusation," "persons and places," the ways in which the narrative was made to "work," and the role of memory; as an interjection, Rubin asks, "What Did Jews Think of the Eucharist?" providing a fascinating counterweight to the book's otherwise largely Christian sources. *Gentile Tales* closes with a Hebrew translation into English of a lamentation by Rabbi Avigdor Kara. Thus the sweep of *Gentile Tales* is large; trans-European, polyglot, multimedia, from the tenth century to the sixteenth, the narrative of host desecration mediated anxieties about the status and efficacy of the Eucharist via the Jews (both real and imagined). However, Rubin is not interested in overarching or heuristic paradigms; she brings to this slippery topic both attention to detail and an insistence on the importance of context. Rubin usefully shows how even while an allegation can appear to be the same as one made earlier or elsewhere, context can give it radical new valence.

Rubin writes in a humane, unpretentious, and engaging tone, at once sensitive to her emotive and controversial subject matter but never mawkish. Informed by her earlier book *Corpus Christi: The Eucharist in Late Medieval Culture* (Cambridge: Cambridge University Press, 1991), Rubin adeptly locates anti-Semitism within the precise cultures that engendered it, rather than settling for a transhistorical narrative that sees anti-Semitism as somehow inevitable. In this way *Gentile Tales* chimes with other recent key works in the study of medieval anti-Semitism, not least David Nirenberg's *Communities of Violence: Persecution of Minorities in the Middle Ages* (Princeton, NJ: Princeton University Press, 1996) and Sara Lipton's *Images of Intolerance: The Representation of Jews and Judaism in the Bible Moralisée* (Berkeley: University of California Press, 1999). Rubin is focused always on agency: the idea that Jews might wish to attack the Eucharist did not appear by itself, but required authors, audiences, translators. *Gentile Tales* is thus a major resource in helping us to understand who favored anti-Semitic expression and for what reasons. The answers Rubin provides are diverse, but they usually include both self-regard and doubt on the part of those Christians who found the allegation meaningful.

The new edition of *Gentile Tales* is largely a reprint of the first edition. My only cavil is that a slightly unwieldy referencing system has been retained, for the book has no cumulative bibliography; this is a shame, for such a bibliography would have been a first-class asset. This edition does retain the glossy, stimulating, and relevant illustrations and useful maps. *Gentile Tales* remains an incisive and defining book that should be read by all those interested in the cultural history of religion, the media of violence, and the pedigree of religious self-doubt.

Anthony Bale
University of London, Birkbeck

Emily Steiner. *Documentary Culture and the Making of Middle English Literature*. Cambridge: Cambridge University Press, 2003. Pp. xvi, 266. 11 illustrations.

Emily Steiner investigates here the relationship between legal documents and forms of literary writing in the period c. 1350 to 1420, arguing that reflection on literary practice during a period crucial for the development of English as both an administrative and a literary language was fostered by creative appropriation of the textual apparatus of the law. She signals the often curious dimensions of textuality in this period (charters that announce themselves to be written on Christ's skin, "books" and other forms of material document compiled from the oral testimony of illiterate subjects, for example) and explores the pervasiveness of legal forms like the testament or the letter of commission in written discourses of many kinds. Her work adds much of interest to a steadily growing body of publications on medieval literate, legal, and bureaucratic practice, and it opens rewarding possibilities for the understanding of a number of texts.

At the heart of the book are discussions of *Piers Plowman*, the "Short" and "Long" *Charters of Christ*, selected Lollard writings, and *The Book of Margery Kempe*. These are prefaced by a chapter that explores documentary culture as characterized in Bracton's thirteenth-century compendium *De legibus et consuetudinibus Angliae* and compares with it the workings of quasi-legal instruments in Deguileville's three *Pèlerinage* poems. Bracton's insistence that documents transform will into act, it is argued, gives such instruments special power in the context of personification allegory, where readers have the opportunity to appropriate for their own benefit what is proffered in documentary form. This point leads into a wide-ranging survey of the shapes and workings of the many surviving versions of the *Charter of Christ* and prepares the ground for consideration of the "archive of redeeming texts" that is constituted by *Piers Plowman*. Some of the best writing in the book is located in these sections, which illuminate much about Langland's milieu and grapple productively with aspects of his creative practice as a "public" poet.

Discussion of the vitality of documents in post-Langlandian forms of public writing takes in *Mum and the Sothsegger* and John Ball's letters before moving on to texts associated with the Lollard community. En route, some versions of the *Charter of Christ* are briefly revisited as examples of revision undertaken in response to heterodox views, and a case is made that while "medieval documentary culture served as an easy target for criticism of bureaucratic corruption and institutional oppression . . . it also provided its critics . . . with rhetorical alternatives with which that criticism might be effectively deployed" (229). The book concludes with an epilogue on the range of documents so essential to Margery Kempe's self-construction, and some suggestive remarks about the role of documentary culture in medieval forms of writing the subject.

As this summary makes clear, Steiner's coverage—with its emphases on 1381, on Lollardy, and on Margery Kempe—matches the focus of much other recent writing on the centrality of social relationships to Middle English textual forms. The late fourteenth and early fifteenth centuries are clearly rich in suggestion for those exploring these issues, and Steiner gives her study a new edge (and an elegant structure) by beginning and ending it with the *Charters*; but her case for singling out the years between 1350 and 1420 for special consideration, as indeed for singling out the documentary culture of this period as a specifically English phenomenon, does not seem to me compelling without further elaboration. There seems room, too, for more extensive analysis of the range of documents likely to inform creative practice: Bracton's compendium is used in a representative way without much acknowledgment that it is surely only the tip of a documentary iceberg. To answer these criticisms would clearly be to write several more books, and I advance them not to lessen Steiner's achievement in this one, but to point to the fact that she broaches very large questions whose implications extend beyond the boundaries imposed by parts of her argument. In its provision of local detail, in the clarity of its analysis of specific texts, and in the issues it raises and probes, this is a consistently readable and stimulating book.

Julia Boffey
Queen Mary, University of London

Benjamin C. Withers and Jonathan Wilcox, eds. *Naked Before God: Uncovering the Body in Anglo-Saxon England*. Morgantown: West Virginia University Press, 2003. Pp. xii, 315. 45 illustrations.

Naked Before God is an anthology of eleven scholarly articles about the body in Anglo-Saxon England. Scholarly investigation of the body has come to prominence during the past decade in the broader field of literary studies. The volume Withers and Wilcox have assembled brings the disparate methods of such work to Anglo-Saxon studies.

After a brief treatment of two previous studies of the body in Anglo-Saxon culture (those of O'Keeffe and Lees/Overing), Withers, as is customary in essay collections, summarizes the book's offerings. Suzanne Lewis follows with a general introduction ("Medieval Bodies Then and Now: Negotiating Problems of Ambivalence and Paradox") in which she situates the volume in previous discussions of the body in the Middle Ages (Bynum) and in postmodern theory (Foucault).

Lewis's abstractions give way to Sarah L. Higley's philology in "The Wanton Hand: Reading and Reaching into Grammars and Bodies in Old English Riddle 12." The riddle in question, whose "innocent" meaning depicts a servant girl doing kitchen chores, has attracted various "obscene" interpretations. Higley surveys them, suggesting that the word *swife* in line 13a could possibly bear the sexual meaning it later accrues in Chaucer's time, when *swiven* obviously suggests the motion attending sexual intercourse. Noting the poem's complexities in grammar, Higley backs off from asserting this meaning for Riddle 12, preferring to remain suggestive about the poem's suggestiveness.

Mercedes Salvador is also interested in the Exeter Riddles in her "The Key to the Body: Unlocking Riddles 42–46." She analyzes the famous cluster of obscene riddles (42, 44, 45, and 46), suggesting that the interloper, 43, whose solution is "the soul and the body," is an integral part of that group, which presents various ways of looking at the body. Salvador cites analogues from theologians and exegetes to support her suggestion that this group of riddles be read as religious allegories.

In "The Body as Text in Early Anglo-Saxon Law," Mary P. Richards seeks to adjust the findings of Katherine O'Brien O'Keeffe, who in an influential article looks at the mutilation of convicted criminals as a means of inscribing crime and consequent punishment on the malefactor's body, which thus becomes a text others may read. O'Keeffe focuses on law codes of the Benedictine Revival and later but suggests that the origins of the criminal body as text can be found among earlier Anglo-Saxon law codes. Richardson looks at the codes of Æthelbert and Alfred and sees there not so much attention to the bodies of the perpetrators as text but to those of the victims.

John M. Hill concentrates on body parts in his "The Sacrificial Synecdoche of Hands, Heads, and Arms in Anglo-Saxon Heroic Story." Focusing on texts like Aelfric's *Life of St. Oswald*, *Beowulf*, *The Battle of Brunanburh*, and *The Battle of Maldon*, Hill demonstrates how the body parts mentioned in his title—severed or otherwise—partake of the ancient Germanic myths of Odin and Tyr, gods who respectively lost eye and hand as sacrificial gestures. The body parts of the saints and heroes Hill treats function as emblems of the sacrificial heroic action that preserves community in the face of hostile antagonists.

We return to the obscene with Karen Ross Mathews's "Nudity on the Margins: The Bayeux Tapestry and Its Relationship to Marginal Architectural Sculpture." Although focusing primarily on early Anglo-Norman culture rather than on the strictly Anglo-Saxon, the article is justified in the book because of the Anglo-Saxon content of the Bayeux Tapestry. The tapestry's upper and lower zones (or margins) depict a variety of people, animals, and mythic creatures, including five scenes in which naked men and women appear in sexually explicit attitudes. Mathews finds analogs to these scenes in relief sculptures in churches and cathedrals in Ireland and the continent. These sculptures, like the scenes from the Bayeux Tapestry, are "marginal"—found on capitals, metopes, or corbels. As marginal art, the tapestry nudes and relief sculptures undercut the officially sanctioned art they attend.

In her "The Donestre and the Person of Both Sexes," Susan M. Kim looks at the illustrations to *The Wonders of the East* and the *Liber Monstrorum* to explore the relationship between the naked body and the monstrous. The androgene and the Donestre (the latter a monster having a lion's upper body and a human's lower), in their disturbing sameness to us, rather than alterity, reveal "the limitation of our systems of representation" (180).

Catherine E. Karkov's "Exiles from the Kingdom: The Naked and the Damned in Anglo-Saxon Art" notices the reluctance of Anglo-Saxon illuminators to depict the naked female body but posits an association between the naked male body and the "tenth" order of angels—those that have fallen. Karkov includes some pertinent information from Anglo-Saxon law and archaeology to show that the artists' attitudes toward both the naked female and the naked male are discernible in Anglo-Saxon culture as a whole.

In her "Breasts and Babies: The Maternal Body of Eve in the Junius 11 *Genesis*," Mary Dockray-Miller turns her attention to one of the exceptions to Karkov's rule—the depiction of the naked Eve in the Junius MS. For her, the illustrations to the Adam/Eve section of the Old English *Genesis* undercut the male-dominant ideology of the text. Eve is portrayed as active, especially maternally—not as the lower element of a binary hierarchy.

Janet S. Ericksen continues the book's prolonged gaze at the naked people in the Old English *Genesis* in her article, "Penitential Nakedness and the Junius 11 *Genesis*." Concentrating mainly on the text itself, she demonstrates a metaphorical connection between nakedness and sin and between the need for clothing and the need for confession and penance—connections Anglo-Saxon homiletic literature make explicit.

Jonathan Wilcox's "Naked in Old English: The Embarrassed and the Shamed" takes issue with the theory proposed by Cristopher Ricks in his *Keats and Embarrassment* that the concept of embarrassment is a construction of the eighteenth century. Wilcox surveys a wide variety of Old English texts, mostly religious, to show that the naked body was associated in Anglo-Saxon England not only with the concept of shame, which is deep and lasting, but also with embarrassment, which is momentary and "skin deep."

These summaries should make clear one of this book's strengths. There is a focused thematic connection among all the individual articles, yet they range far and wide, investigating many aspects of Anglo-Saxon culture—texts, visual art, and law. The articles, moreover, dialogue with one another and support one another. Some articles concentrate on the abstract, while others narrow in on concrete instances of the naked body in Anglo-Saxon England. As with any multiauthored volume, there is some inconsistency in tone; a few of the authors invest too heavily in postmodern jargon, and there are some passages of muddy prose. But most of the book avoids this. There is much of real interest and many intelligent, insightful conclusions.

Robert Boenig
Texas A&M University

Books Received

Andersen, Peter, ed. *Medieval Translation Practices: Papers from the Symposium at the University of Copenhagen 25th and 26th October 2002*. Copenhagen: Museum Tusculanum Press, 2004. Pp. 234.

Beach, Alison I. *Women as Scribes: Book Production and Monastic Reform in Twelfth-Century Bavaria*. New York: Cambridge University Press, 2004. Pp. 198. $70.00.

Beckett, Katharine Scarfe. *Anglo-Saxon Perceptions of the Islamic World*. Cambridge Studies in Anglo-Saxon England 33. New York: Cambridge University Press, 2003. Pp. 276. $65.00.

Bjork, Robert. *The Cynewulf Reader*. 1996. New York: Routledge, 2001. Pp. 367. $40.00 (paper).

Birmingham, David. *A Concise History of Portugal*. 2nd edition. New York: Cambridge University Press, 2003. Pp. 225. $22.00 (paper).

Bisaha, Nancy. *Creating East and West: Renaissance Humanists and the Ottoman Turks*. Philadelphia: University of Pennsylvania Press, 2004. Pp. 320. $59.95.

Boitani, Piero, and Jill Mann, eds. *The Cambridge Companion to Chaucer*. 2nd edition. New York: Cambridge University Press, 2004. Pp. 317. $60.00.

Bourdua, Louise. *The Franciscans and Art Patronage in Late Medieval Italy*. New York: Cambridge University Press, 2004. Pp. 242. $75.00.

Bouza, Fernando. *Communication, Knowledge, and Memory in Early Modern Spain*. Translated by Sonia López and Michael Agnew. Phildelphia: University of Pennsylvania Press, 2004. Pp. 128. $32.50.

Brann, Ross, and Adam Sutcliffe, eds. *Renewing the Past, Reconfiguring Jewish Culture: From al-Andalus to the Haskalah*. Philadelphia: University of Pennsylvania Press, 2004. Pp. 237.

Bull, Marcus, and Norman Housley, eds. *The Experience of Crusading*. Vol. 1: *Western Approaches*. New York: Cambridge University Press, 2003. Pp. 307. $60.00.

Campbell, Stephen J., and Stephen J. Milner, eds. *Artistic Exchange and Cultural Translation in the Italian Renaissance City*. New York: Cambridge University Press, 2004. Pp. 371. $95.00.

Chance, Jane, ed. *Tolkien and the Invention of Myth: A Reader*. Lexington: University Press of Kentucky, 2004. Pp. 360. $35.00.

Chapman, Hugo, Tom Henry, and Carol Plazzotta. *Raphael: From Urbino to Rome*. New Haven, CT: Yale University Press, 2004. Pp. 320; 70 b/w + 170 color illustrations. $65.00.

Chazan, Robert. *Fashioning Jewish Identity in Medieval Western Christendom*. New York: Cambridge University Press, 2003. Pp. 379. $75.00.

Connor, Carolyn L. *Women of Byzantium*. New Haven, CT: Yale University Press, 2004. Pp. 416. $45.00.

Constable, Olivia Remie. *Housing the Stranger in the Mediterranean World: Lodging, Trade, and Travel in Late Antiquity and the Middle Ages*. Cambridge: Cambridge University Press, 2003. Pp. 427. $65.00.

Coudert, Allison, and Jeffrey S. Shoulson, eds. *Hebraica Veritas? Christian Hebraists and the Study of Judaism in Early Modern Europe*. Philadelphia: University of Pennsylvania Press, 2004. Pp. 328. $49.95.

Dagron, Gilbert. *Emperor and Priest: The Imperial Office in Byzantium*. Past and Present Publications. New York: Cambridge University Press, 2004. Pp. 337. $75.00.

Delany, Sheila, ed. *Chaucer and the Jews: Sources, Contexts, Meanings*. New York: Routledge, 2002. Pp. 258. $90.00.

Derbes, Anne, and Mark Sandona, eds. *The Cambridge Companion to Giotto*. New York: Cambridge University Press, 2003. Pp. 313. $95.00.

Edbury, Peter, and Jonathan Phillips, eds. *The Experience of Crusading*. Vol. 2: *Defining the Crusader Kingdom*. New York: Cambridge University Press, 2003. Pp. 311. $65.00.

Ekrem, Inger, and Lars Boje Mortensen, eds. *Historia Norwegie*. Translated by Peter Fisher. Copenhagen: Museum Tusculanum Press, 2003. Pp. 245. $31.00.

Enenkel, Karl A. E., and Arnoud S. Q. Visser, eds. *Mundus Emblematicus: Studies in Neo-Latin Emblem Books*. Imago Figurata Studies 4. Turnhout, Belgium: Brepols, 2003. Pp. 383. EUR 75.00.

Finke, Laurie A., and Martin B. Shichtman. *King Arthur and the Myth of History*. Gainesville: University Press of Florida, 2004. Pp. 272. $59.95.

Folchini de Borfonibus. *Cremonina (Grammatica, orthographia et prosodia)*. Edited by Carla DeSantis. Corpus Christianorum Continuatio Mediaevalis 201. Turnhout, Belgium: Brepols, 2003. Pp. clxxix + 336. EUR 215.

Franklin, David. *The Art of Parmigianino*. New Haven, CT: Yale University Press, 2003. Pp. 312. $60.00.

Freely, John, and Ahmet S. Cakmak. *Byzantine Monuments of Istanbul*. New York: Cambridge University Press, 2004. Pp. 322. $80.00.

Gaimster, David, and Roberta Gilchrist, eds. *The Archaeology of Reformation 1480–1580: Papers Given at the Archaeology of Reformation Conference, February 2001*. Leeds: Maney, 2003. Pp. 486. $120.00.

Goffen, Rona. *Renaissance Rivals: Michelangelo, Leonardo, Raphael, Titian*. New Haven, CT: Yale University Press, 2002. Pp. 304; 120 b/w + 80 color illustrations. $29.95 (paper).

Graizbord, David L. *Souls in Dispute: Converso Identities in Iberia and Jewish Diaspora*. Philadelphia: University of Pennsylvania Press, 2004. Pp. 272. $45.00.

Harris, Jonathan Gil. *Sick Economics: Drama, Mercantilism, and Disease in Shakespeare's England*. Philadelphia: University of Pennsylvania Press, 2004. Pp. 272. $49.95.

Havely, Nick. *Dante and the Franciscans: Poverty and the Papacy in the Commedia.* New York: Cambridge University Press, 2004. Pp. 212. $75.00.
Heckett, Elizabeth Wincott. *Viking Age Headcoverings from Dublin.* Dublin: Royal Irish Academy, 2003. Pp. 152. $32.50.
Hen, Yitzhak, and Rob Meens, eds. *The Bobbio Missal: Liturgy and Religious Culture in Merovingian Gaul.* New York: Cambridge University Press, 2004. Pp. 232. $90.00.
Hines, John, Alan Lane, and Mark Redknap, eds. *Land, Sea and Home.* (Proceedings of a Conference on Viking-period Settlement, at Cardiff, July 2001.) Leeds: Maney, 2004. Pp. 482. $99.00.
Hope, Charles, et al. *Titian.* New Haven, CT: Yale University Press, 2004. Pp. 192, 150 color illustrations. $25.00 (paper).
Howard, Deborah. *The Architectural History of Venice.* 1980. Revised and enlarged edition. New Haven, CT: Yale University Press, 2004. Pp. 346. $20.00 (paper).
Humfrey, Peter, ed. *The Cambridge Companion to Giovanni Bellini.* New York: Cambridge University Press, 2003. Pp. 355. $95.00.
Ibn Sahula, Isaac. *Meshal Haqadmoni: Fables from the Distant Past.* Edited and translated by Raphael Loewe. Portland, OR: The Littman Library of Jewish Civilization, 2004. Pp. cxxxi + 816. $125.
Kaspersen, Søren, ed. *Images of Cult and Devotion: Function and Reception of Christian Images in Medieval and Post-Medieval Europe.* Copenhagen: Museum Tusculanum Press, 2004. Pp. 312; 22 color plates. $28.00.
Lampert, Lisa. *Gender and Jewish Difference from Paul to Shakespeare.* Philadelphia: University of Pennsylvania Press, 2004. Pp. 288. $55.00.
Lee, Peter H., ed. *A History of Korean Literature.* New York: Cambridge University Press, 2004. Pp. 580. $95.00.
Levack, Brian P., ed. *The Witchcraft Sourcebook.* New York: Routledge, 2004. Pp. 348. $27.95 (paper).
Lightbown, Ronald. *Carlo Crivelli.* New Haven, CT: Yale University Press, 2004. Pp. 384; 200 b/w + 100 color illustrations. $75.00.
Linden, Stanton, ed. *The Alchemy Reader: From Hermes Trismegistus to Isaac Newton.* New York: Cambridge University Press, 2003. $24.00 (paper).
Lionarons, Joyce Tally, ed. *Old English Literature in Its Manuscript Context.* Morgantown: West Virginia University Press, 2004. Pp. 376.
Marsden, Richard, ed. *The Cambridge Old English Reader.* New York: Cambridge University Press, 2004. Pp. 532. $85.00.
McCarthy, Mike, and David Weston, eds. *Carlisle and Cumbria: Roman and Medieval Architecture, Art and Archaeology.* The British Archaeological Association. Leeds: Maney, 2004. Pp. 290. $87.00.
McCracken, Peggy. *The Curse of Eve, The Wound of the Hero: Blood, Gender, and Medieval Literature.* Philadelphia: University of Pennsylvania Press, 2003. Pp. 200. $38.95.
McSheffrey, Shannon, and Norman Tanner, eds. *Lollards of Coventry,*

1486–1522. Camden Fifth Series 23. Cambridge: Cambridge University Press, 2003. Pp. 361. $70.00.

Meilman, Patricia, ed. *The Cambridge Companion to Titian*. New York: Cambridge University Press, 2003. Pp. 372. $95.00.

Murasaki Shikibu. *The Tale of Genji*. Edited by Richard Bowring. 1998. 2nd edition. New York: Cambridge University Press, 2004. Pp. 106. $15.00 (paper).

Neville, Leonora. *Authority in Byzantine Provincial Society, 950–1100*. New York: Cambridge University Press, 2004. Pp. 210. $75.00.

Nijsten, Gerard. *In the Shadows of Burgundy: The Court of Guelders in the Late Middle Ages*. New York: Cambridge University Press, 2004. Pp. 470. $95.00.

O'Callaghan, Joseph F. *Reconquest and Crusade in Medieval Spain*. Philadelphia: University of Pennsylvania Press, 2002. Pp. 336. $39.95.

Oggins, Robin S. *The Kings and Their Hawks: Falconry in Medieval England*. New Haven, CT: Yale University Press, 2004. Pp. 296; 5 b/w + 12 color illustrations. $40.00.

Pollard, A. J. *Imagining Robin Hood*. New York: Routledge, 2005. Pp. 272. $27.95.

Purdon, Liam. *The Wakefield Master's Dramatic Art: A Drama of Spiritual Understanding*. Gainesville: University Press of Florida, 2003. Pp. 368. $55.00.

Quiney, Anthony. *Town Houses of Medieval Britain*. New Haven, CT: Yale University Press, 2004. Pp. 320. $60.00.

Rosenthal, Joel T. *Telling Tales: Sources and Narration in Late Medieval England*. University Park: Pennsylvania State University Press, 2003. Pp. 217.

Rubin, Miri. *Gentile Tales: The Narrative Assault on Late Medieval Jews*. Philadelphia: University of Pennsylvania Press, 2004. Pp. 280. $26.50 (paper).

Ruvoldt, Maria. *Italian Renaissance Imagery of Inspiration: Metaphors of Sex, Sleep, and Dreams*. New York: Cambridge University Press, 2004. Pp. 244. $85.00.

Scheepsma, Wybren. *Medieval Religious Women in the Low Countries: The "Modern Devotion," the Canonesses of Windesheim and Their Writings*. Translated by David F. Johnson. Woodbridge: Boydell, 2004. Pp. 280. $99.00.

Shepard, Alan, and Stephen D. Powell, eds. *Fantasies of Troy: Classical Tales and Social Imaginary in Medieval and Early Modern Europe*. Toronto: Centre for Reformation and Renaissance Studies, 2004. Pp. 306.

Somerset, Fiona, and Nicholas Watson, eds. *The Vulgar Tongue: Medieval and Postmedieval Vernacularity*. University Park: Pennsylvania State University Press, 2003. Pp. 277. $55.00.

Steiner, Emily. *Documentary Culture and the Making of Medieval English Literature*. New York: Cambridge University Press, 2003. Pp. 266. $60.00.

Verkerk, Dorothy. *Early Medieval Bible Illumination and the Ashburnham Pentateuch*. New York: Cambridge University Press, 2004. Pp. 262. $75.00.

Waters, Claire M. *Angels and Earthly Creatures: Preaching, Performance, and Gender in Later Middle Ages*. Philadelphia: University of Pennsylvania Press, 2004. Pp. 296. $55.00.

Wetherbee, Winthrop. *Chaucer: The Canterbury Tales*. 2nd edition. New York: Cambridge University Press, 2004. Pp. 125. $15.00 (paper).

Wolper, Ethel Sara. *Cities and Saints: Sufism and the Transformation of Urban Space in Medieval Anatolia*. University Park: Pennsylvania State University Press, 2004. Pp. 134. $60.00.